The Cape House
A Memoir

Rea Bochner

ISBN-13:978-1520616308

Chapter One

When I was a kid, I invented a game called "Kidnapped." The gist was simple: I would hide in some dark corner of the house and pretend a good-looking psychopath was holding me hostage. Any funny business, he warned, and they'd find pieces of me in the dumpster behind Linda's Rotisserie. Ignoring the inevitable urge to pee, I'd have breathless exchanges with my captor that made my arms tingle with goosebumps. Through wit and pluck, I'd loosen his guard enough to uncover a tragic backstory: the loss of someone with, say, blue eyes like mine. Eventually, he would agree to let me go, in exchange for a kiss, so I'd make out with the sleeve of my mother's down jacket, then jet for the bathroom.

It was good, wholesome fun.

One afternoon, deep in my mother's closet with Ralph Maccio from "The Karate Kid," a ripple of tiny somethings, like a sheet of ants, brushed up against my skin. I heard an airy crinkle, the kind my tutu made when I bent into a plié, and my ears perked up. Crawling out from beneath Mom's rack of blazers, I reached deep into the back, feeling around blindly until I found the ants again. Then I grabbed on and pulled.

They weren't ants, I discovered. They were *beads*, shimmering like a million iridescent stars on a gown of apricot chiffon.

I caressed them, dazzled. Could this have been here for years and I'd never known?

The gown was heavy; I had to yank hard to get it off the hanger. As it billowed to the floor, I noticed something else, something black and pouffy, behind it. And behind that, a flash of purple velvet. Like a conquistadora, I unearthed a feast of evening wear: taffeta, satin, lace, and real fur, all rich, luxurious and breathing the scent of Mom's Chanel Number 5.

I was so excited, I almost passed out.

I quickly set to work trying on everything. Being four feet tall, the sleeves on every dress stretched far past my fingers, the necklines drooped down to my belly and the trains pooled around my feet. But I slipped on a pair of Mom's size-10 Stuart Weitzmans and strutted around her bedroom like Naomi Campbell. When my mother found me, she smiled as if it was perfectly normal to see her kindergartener swimming in apricot shimmer, waving to no one atop a mountain of evening gowns.

"Don't you look hotsy-totsy!" she exclaimed.

I preened like a peacock. "Can I have this when you die?"

"Sure, Honey," she said, not missing a beat. "You can even borrow it before I go."

My mother told this story for the next twenty years, and it's the one I think of as I pick through her closet for a fleece sweatshirt. This time I have her permission.

Even though Dad has the heat pumping constantly through this house, the New England cold right off the ocean sneaks in through the windows and burrows into my bones. I shiver my way through a good nine months of the year here, sipping desperately at mugs of Bengal Spice tea like a hamster from a water bowl. Thankfully, Mom lets me help myself to extra layers when I'm too lazy to climb the stairs to my room.

As I grab a baby pink sweatshirt, the telephone trills. The noise is jarring against the silence of the house, which has become a companion of sorts during this long, sleepy winter. Mom's cell is on the caller ID.

"Heleh-o?" I say, exactly the way she does.

"What are you up to?"

"Stealing one of your sweaters."

"Which one? The pink?"

"How did you know?"

"I'm your mother," she says. "I know everything."

Tucking the receiver under my chin, I absently wander into the little shul, the mini-synagogue my father built in what was supposed to be the dining room. When they first moved into this house, a gray, beachside McMansion, Mom took one look at the ashtray-sized room and dismissed it as a proper entertaining space. Dad, the owner of a summer home out of walking distance to a synagogue, claimed it for himself. He went into the garage, and, like Noah with his ark, grabbed some wood and his trusty electric saw and made a tall cupboard to house his Torah scroll. He mounted it on the wall and filled the bookshelves with classic titles of Jewish history, philosophy and folklore, along with the Talmud, the multi-volume code of Jewish Law. He also bought a hefty supply of prayer books for those who might come to spend the holidays. Mom was surprisingly game for this, and hung lace curtains embroidered with seashells on the windows that set a mosaic of shadows on the wood floor when the sun shone through them. (If she had to have a synagogue in her house, it should at least be a *pretty* one.) My parents' collective effort resulted in the house's coziest room, warm in the winter, cool in the summer, and miraculously, always quiet despite being right off the kitchen. By design, it's a sacred space, a retreat for anyone who wants privacy.

"So any news?" I ask, perching on the arm of a wide, white leather chair.

"Nope," she replies. "Still in quarantine."

When my mother first told me a week ago that she was being quarantined in an Infectious Disease Unit, my first reaction was shock: "They still do that?" Quarantine struck me as one of those antiquated practices, like leeching, that the medical establishment abandoned when they realized the patient might as well drink Windex. But apparently, quarantine is still very much in vogue. Mom is on an entire floor of patients who have been shut away to protect the rest of humanity from their nuclear germs. From what Dad tells me, anyone who wishes to see her (except he) is required to wear full scrubs and a surgical mask.

"Is it weird to have everyone treating you like the boy in the plastic bubble?"

"Are you kidding?" she says. "I *love* quarantine! It's like a hotel suite all to myself!"

Like the Four Seasons, I think, *with blood transfusions.*

She goes on, "Plus I have this nurse, Uri. He's just out of the Israeli army and *gorgeous.* Curly hair, brown eyes, dark skin. Pure Sabra. He reminds me of your brother a little, at the end of the summer when he's all tan…"

The woman is practically giggling. I can understand why, recalling the lean, swarthy soldiers I saw strutting around Jerusalem with M-16s hanging off their belts. There were always one or two of them on the busses I rode across the city, quick to flash their bright white teeth and flirt in perfect English. But if I was in Mom's position, not even a young, rugged Israeli with a gun would have been able to keep me distracted from the facts: after a year of cancer treatment, the doctors have discovered a nodule in my mother's lung. They don't know if it's a bacterial infection (hence the quarantine) or the cancer, spreading. While they run test after inconclusive test, she has to wait out the results in her antiseptic getaway.

"Do the doctors know anything yet?"

She sighs, long and deep. "Well, my oncologist came in about an hour ago. He sat down on the bed next to me and said, 'You know, if this is more cancer, it's terminal. We won't be able to catch up with it. You're looking at maybe six weeks.' Then he gave me this little pat on the knee and left."

The room seems to tilt a few degrees to the right, and I grab the armrest to steady myself. "Was that supposed to be a joke?"

"I don't think so."

"What did Dad say?"

"He was at *minyan.*" Every morning, my father leaves the house at 6 am to study Talmud and pray with a *minyan,* the required quorum of ten men.

"Wait a minute. You mean Dad wasn't even *there*?" I'm yelling, though I'm not sure at whom.

"Yup. I got the good news all by myself." She's being flippant, which means she's angry. I suppose I would be, too, if someone gave me a death sentence and then practically skipped away.

I'm quiet for a moment, staring at the pastel-colored spines of "The Little Midrash Says," a children's bible series I hated as a kid. "So he thinks it's more cancer?"

"I don't know what he thinks. We know there are cancer cells in my lungs. The nodule could be something else, but..." She trails off, an engine losing steam.

"But...?"

"If it is more Cancer, you're probably going to be getting some company."

"What do you mean?" I ask, but I know exactly what she means. She's saying that if she's terminal, she wants to come up here, to the Cape House, to die.

She knows that I know, so she doesn't answer.

"You know, Ma, people live this way for years."

"Well," she says, "maybe I don't want to live this way."

Cancer is a shifty little word. At first, it charges at you with that harsh "kan" sound, like your slap-happy cousin after too many beers at the barbecue. Then the C downshifts to its gentler counterpart, the "sssss," slithering past the teeth and into a purr as the tongue curls up for the final R. *Cancer*. It comes from the Greek word for crab, *karkinos*, courtesy of Hippocrates, who in ancient times thought that tumors resembled little clawed crustaceans. The word is as unsettling as the creature that inspired it, appearing from nowhere and scuttling madly around as you stand, petrified, on your beach chair.

But cancer's many guises, Sarcoma, Lymphoma, Leukemia, Melanoma, all sound like Russian princesses. Even the word "surgery," a frequent follow-up to "Cancer," has a lilting romance to it. It's all advertising, I think, glossing over the nasty particulars with pretty jargon. It's much easier to tell someone, "You have Hemangiosarcoma" than, "You have a clump of cannibal cells devouring your spleen."

On a flight home from Florida last March, the nagging pain in Mom's back became unbearable. A visit to the doctor and a few scans later, my parents learned that Mom had bladder cancer which had traveled up into her kidney. They called it Transitional Cell Carcinoma, a very rare type of cancer and also the sneakiest. Carcinoma cells are shape-shifters, like The Agents in "The Matrix," changing their properties at random. This means that treatment could be effective, but only until the cells decide to bait-and-switch and send everyone scrambling back to square one. Mom's Cancer also happened to be one of the fastest-spreading types, which is why, almost overnight, she grew a tumor on her kidney the size of a baseball.

"Leave it to me to get crazy cancer," she said. "Why couldn't I get normal breast cancer like everyone else?"

From the moment I found out my mother was sick, it never once occurred to me that she wouldn't get better. She's a click or two more alive than anyone I know, the one whose laugh rings out across a crowded room. She can do anything, do it well, and make it look easy. Every year, she takes a crew of inner city preschoolers, kids who can load a Glock before they start walking, and drills them into a crop of *mensches* so refined you'd think they were in finishing school. Before that, she used to teach corporate executives across the country how to act like human beings instead of bosses. She's made gourmet dinners in under an hour and thrown parties that people talked about for years afterwards. She can design an entire house with a number two pencil and a sheet of graph paper. And she's raised four children, born in less than five years, without killing herself or any of us. A pesky little thing like cancer had nothing on her; I just assumed this whole thing was a bad hand we would have to play for a while until she got her clean bill of health. Later, the "When Mom Had Cancer" stories would join the annals of our family folklore, and we'd tell them with belly laughs and sighs of relief.

But for all of my mind's conviction, my body metabolized the news much differently. Like when my husband, Ben, and I drove to my parents' place in Manhattan for Shabbos, the Jewish Sabbath that runs from Friday evening to Saturday night, just a few days after Mom's diagnosis. My three siblings had traveled in for the occasion, reprising our childhood tradition of gathering around the table every Friday night for Shabbos dinner.

Mom answered the bell in an apron, wielding a ladle. "They're here!" she exclaimed, cheeks pink and eyes starry, as if she hadn't seen us just a week before. She pulled me in for a good hug, then put her hands on my belly, where my baby was growing.

"Everything's basically done," she reported, answering a question I hadn't yet asked. "I just need to get the food in the oven and light candles. I made you extra veggies!" Then she flitted back into the kitchen.

My family filled the apartment's small living room. Despite the news that had brought us all home that night, there was a mood of celebration in being together after way too long. Mom was determined to make the evening a festive one, and had laid a rich purple runner down the length of the dining room table. She'd even put out the good china and silver, and a mahogany wicker basket of fake pears and apples as a centerpiece. The apartment had a warm, rosy glow, like after a glass of red wine, and the smell of chicken soup sweetened the air. I closed my eyes and breathed deeply, drinking in the feeling of home.

As my siblings and I exchanged hugs and kisses, I kept an eye on my mother as she buzzed happily in her element. She chatted with Samantha, my brother Noah's wife, sliding pans into the oven to warm and offering her daughter-in-law a spoonful of soup to taste. Sammy opened her mouth like a baby bird, one hand cupped under her chin to protect her sweater set from spills, and nodded her approval. Noah, all 6'3" of him, lumbered over, laptop angled against his belly to flash the Fantasy Hockey homepage up to his face. Sammy, at 5'2, barely reached the chest of her husband's sweatshirt, which bore the logo of the law school they both attended. Noah jokingly placed his computer on top of Sammy's head, then accepted his own taste of soup. As Mom gabbed away with them, her hands flew around her like sparrows.

"What do you think?" asked Dena, sidling up next to me. My sister's chestnut curls, still wet from the shower, held the scent of apples. She stood a head taller than me, like everyone else in my family.

"She looks good. You wouldn't even know."

"It's stage four," she said. "That's like maybe five percent survival rate. Maybe."

"How do you know that?"

"I was up doing research until four in the morning. Then I ate a lot of peanut butter."

The image of my sister's face illuminated by her computer screen, with a spoon of Jif hanging from her mouth, made an excellent argument for why physicians never treat family. Dena, a doctoral candidate in physical therapy, was born with a talent for healing which she used to assist children with major neurological issues, accident victims, and the injured. I'd seen her in action, and the only word to describe it was magic. Dena subtly morphed into some kind of medium, calming a deeply agitated spirit with her voice and touch alone. She could tell you anything you'd like to know about the body's structure, function, and pathology, clearly an asset in her profession. But her knowledge turned around and bit her when the patient was her own mother.

"Look at her," I said, gesturing toward Mom, who picked up a piece of brownie, took a furtive look around and popped it into her mouth. "She's totally fine."

"Right now, maybe," my sister replied. "But wait until the chemo starts."

I joined Mom at the window to light Shabbat candles. On the Hudson, I watched two tugboats glide silently past each other as a Georgia-peach sun dipped into New Jersey. I lit my candles then watched Mom light hers, waving her hands three times over the flames as if to beckon the warmth toward her. Then she covered her eyes, lingering in silence for longer than usual before singing the blessing softly in Hebrew: *Blessed are you, Oh God, King of the Universe, Who Sanctified Us with the commandment He commanded us to light Sabbath Candles.*

When Mom took her hands away from her eyes, I saw tears glinting in the candlelight.

We took our seats around the table and slipped comfortably into the old routine, singing "*Shalom Aleichem*" to welcome the Sabbath. As Mom looked on contentedly, Dad recited "*Eishet Chayil,*" The Woman of Valor, a passage of praise to the Jewish Wife:

"An accomplished woman, who can find? Far beyond pearls is her value...

She opens her mouth in wisdom and the lesson of kindness is on her tongue...

Her children rise and praise her, her husband lauds her…
Charm is deceptive and beauty is vain, but a God-fearing woman,
she should be praised..."

As Dad spoke, I looked across the table at my brother, Gabe, who had shaved off his dark, wiry curls since I'd seen him last. His skin, already dark, was tanned to a deep gold after a kiteboarding trip in Mexico, the latest of his long string of adventures. A combination of free spirit and enterprising entrepreneur, Gabe worked diligently in software sales to support his love of music festivals, travel, good food and craft beer, building a life for himself in California that I secretly envied. He caught me staring at him, self-consciously adjusted his suede yarmulke (from his bar-mitzvah, over a decade ago), and stuck his tongue out at me.

"Where's Erin?" I mouthed, asking after his longtime girlfriend.

"Had to work," he mouthed back. "Next time."

Dad blessed a cup of Manischewitz, then passed it around for each of us to sip. My mouth watered at the wine's syrupy sweetness, as familiar to me as my father's voice. Then we filed into the kitchen for the ritual washing of hands, anticipating the highlight of the evening: my mother's challah.

Baking challah, our modern throwback to the biblical manna, is an art of which my mother is a master. Her challah can fill the empty pockets in your soul. Over the years she has perfected the combination of firm crust and sweet, dense crumb, undercooking it just a touch to keep the give of dough. Its aroma, a fusion of hot cinnamon and yeast, is, to me, what love smells like. Years ago, Mom taught challah baking classes in our house, setting out fruit and warm brownies on the fancy dishes while the coffeemaker burbled on the countertop. I would creep down the steps and peek over the balustrade to watch two dozen women, women who hired other people to do their cooking, laugh as their manicured hands grew sticky with dough.

After making the blessing, Dad tore one of the loaves open, releasing spindly curls of steam into the air. Within seconds, everyone (save me, who stuck with spelt matzah) had pounced.

"Ma," Ben said with his mouth full, "You've outdone yourself."

As if on cue, I walked over to my parents, ready for their blessing. As the oldest, I have always gone first. Mom and Dad placed their cupped hands on my head and recited the familiar words: *May God make you like Sophie, Rebecca, Rachel and Leah. May God bless you and protect you. May God illuminate his countenance for you and be gracious to you. May God turn his countenance to you and give you peace.* Then, together, they kissed my cheeks.

After they had repeated the blessing for everyone else at the table, my parents turned to one another and put their hands on each other's heads.

I caught Noah's gaze and tipped my head in question. *When did they start doing this?*

My brother turned his palms upward. *No idea.*

Mom and Dad pressed their foreheads together and whispered the prayer again. As they spoke, my father curved his fingers into Mom's rich auburn hair and shut his eyes tightly, as if by force of concentration he could keep her tethered to the earth. My mother's eyes stayed open, her gaze steady on him. For a moment, they looked like two frightened children, clinging to each other in the dark. It was so intimate, I had to look away.

When they finished, Mom turned to us. "Who wants soup?"

"Sit, Ma. I'll do it," I said, retreating from the table.

In the kitchen, the ladle and bowls I tried to line up were slippery in my hands. I couldn't shake that image of my parents, the naked desperation I'd seen in their faces. It knocked my center of gravity out of place. As I pulled the lid off the soup pot, a cloud of steam rushed up to my face. There was a sudden flash of heat, and my knees gave out.

One minute later, I sat on the white-tiled floor, my back pressed against a cabinet. Ben held a bottle of seltzer to my lips. Dena, brow furrowed, studied my face.

"I don't know what happened," I told them.

"Just drink," ordered Dena. "It's hot in here."

It was true, but we both knew that wasn't why I fainted.

The following week, my mother started chemotherapy, a one-two punch of Cisplatin and Gemcitabine. Soon enough, the woman who got a hangover from a Tylenol became unrecognizable. The nausea was overpowering; she would barely touch the child-sized portions of grilled cheese and pierogies I made for her. Her skin turned the color of ash. Her fevers spiked and her blood pressure plummeted, sending my parents on late-night dashes to the hospital across town for blood transfusions. While Mom slept in waiting room chairs, Dad would hassle the staff to speed up the molasses-slow admitting process, and once she was stabilized, spend the rest of the night catching up on work. Over the next year, they made countless rounds to specialists and cancer teams, while Mom's treatment expanded to include more chemo, radiation, and surgery. Dad spent his days running for prescriptions, working with the pain management crew to keep Mom comfortable, haggling with insurance companies, schlepping his wife to acupuncture and physical therapy, and sleeping on too many crappy hospital couches to count. Meanwhile, Mom deteriorated. There were days when the woman whose energy at 55 had well eclipsed mine couldn't get herself out of bed. She would lay there for hours, looking up at the ceiling, and cry.

I, meanwhile, lost control of my body. I dropped things constantly, walked into doorways and chairs, tripped over my own feet, and burned myself on the stovetop. I told myself it was the pregnancy that had thrown me so off balance, until the morning Mom was scheduled to have the tumor on her kidney removed. As I lifted my breakfast from the counter, a thought passed through my mental news ticker: *Mom is having surgery today.* Suddenly, the bowl dropped out of my hands like they had evaporated, and splattered my leg with hot oatmeal and shards of ceramic. As I wiped the mess away, a thick strip of skin peeled off, and I began to realize that my body knew something my mind didn't.

I was never naive; I knew very well that Cancer kills people. I'd lost two friends to the disease by the time I was 14. But *Mom*? Never. Even when I would drive across the bridge after work and find her throwing up into a garbage can, even when I picked her up from a hospital floor where all the patients looked like waxy blue corpses, even when I heard her weeping in pain, and even when she told me her oncologist's grim prognosis, I never, ever thought that she would die.

Until right now. The moment Mom said, "Maybe I don't want to live this way," it was as if the back curtain had dropped in the middle of our family play, in which she was supposed to star forever. Revealed are the disorder of old scenery backstage, the trap doors and pulleys, and the openmouthed extras, halfway through their costume changes, staring at the audience in shock. The illusion is ruined forever.

So now I have a new word to fondle: *terminal,* which is about as elegant as a cardboard box. It's the end of the line, the last stop before the drop-off, the funnel to your final destination.

And it's a sucker punch, with the gloves off.

Chapter Two

I'm thinking of selling my son on Craigslist.

From the moment Ezra was born, he was the poster child for procreation. Alert and placid, he was too busy being delicious to complain. His little *punim* left a stream of rubberneckers at the supermarket, and he was smart enough to love me more than anyone.

Then he cracked a tooth.

After twenty-four hours of marathon crying, my baby's face is glistening with rivulets of snot. He won't let me hold him and he won't let me put him down. He screams in my ear and gums my face for relief. I've never met anyone with such a bad attitude, and I used to work in Hollywood.

Ben has a meeting in Boston today and there is no way I am hanging around here alone with Baby Stalin. I call my friend Iris, a recent college grad with six months of sobriety, and beg her for two hours of her time.

"Don't worry," I tell her. "The hardest thing we have around here is Similac."

When she arrives, I practically throw my wailing child at her. Of course, he settles as soon as he catches a glimpse of her medieval-maiden hair, and by the time I walk out the door, Ezra's eyelids are drooping closed.

No one tells you what you're in for with babies. A few did mention that I might be tired (tantamount to saying that napalm might sting a little), but not once did anyone say that having a child overturns your life like a house in a hurricane. My vision of motherhood, pre-Ezra, was of me in a sundress, pushing a stroller through Brookline. I'd meet a few girlfriends outside of Peet's, where we'd sip iced coffee and laugh. Every few minutes, the T would unload its cheerful passengers onto Beacon Street, many of whom would smile at my dozing infant as they passed by. Basically, my baby would be an accessory to the life I was already living. Like a purse dog. Of course, I knew reality would look somewhat different. But after a 26-year career of pathological selfishness, I couldn't envision a world that didn't have me at the center.

"I think I'm unqualified for parenthood," I said to Mom one afternoon as we lay side by side in her bed. She was weak and nauseous from the chemo, and I was weak and nauseous from the fetus. "What if I just end up resenting him?"

Mom shook her head. "You'll see. The minute you see that face, your whole life will change."

I think I might have been more confident if Mom had been well. But only a few weeks after I told my parents I was pregnant (by throwing up all over the backseat of their Jeep), Mom was diagnosed. I was barely in my second trimester when the chemo started.

A first pregnancy is like skydiving; it's easier to jump with someone who's done the drop before. You can do it alone, but it's a hell of a lot scarier. I had always assumed that when I got pregnant, Mom would steer me through it. She'd take me shopping for everything, help me decorate the nursery, and reassure me that I could indeed handle motherhood. And, of course, she would throw me a fabulous shower. But Mom got sick instead. So I turned to the next best thing: Google. I spent weeks scavenging the internet for everything pregnancy and baby, where I discovered that there is enough information out there, both true and false, to scare any expectant mother into early labor. And even if you manage to sleep after reading about things like placental abruption and sepsis, you'll probably go broke on all the merchandise they insist you absolutely must have if you don't want your baby selling crack on the playground by third grade.

Thus came the trip to Babies R' Us, which I was foolish enough to tackle alone. I wandered the aisles of diapers, strollers, layettes, car seats, diaper bags and wipe warmers (Seriously?), staring at everything with the dazed expression one wears in the split second after they're slapped. Eventually, I found my way to the baby furniture, where I sank into a glider and rocked for half an hour. Then I went home.

But there was a window of time, just around my due date, when Mom had finished chemo and was waiting for surgery. With all those poisons out of her system, she sprung from her bed with an energy she hadn't had in months. Naturally, we went shopping. Within a few hours, we had an entire nursery stuffed into in her trunk. After she and Ben put everything together, Mom regarded the room with pride.

"Now you're ready to have a baby," she said.

That night, I went into labor.

After nineteen hours, there he was: my Ezra. I spent the first two days of his life staring at him, his rosebud lips, his tiny toes and feet, the thousand expressions that flickered across his face as he slept. And I knew that, forevermore, I had been unseated as the Center of the Universe.

From the hospital, we headed to my parents' for Shabbos. In honor of their grandson, my parents threw a *Shalom Zachor*, a party held on the first Friday night after the birth of a boy. Ezra slept contentedly as he was passed around the room and waves of talk swelled around him. Mom held court as hostess, thrilled to have the energy to entertain. By ten, the guests were gone, and Mom shooed Ben and I off to bed, where we fell asleep with the baby between us.

An hour later, Ezra woke up with a sweet little whimper. I scooped him up and fed him, whispering sweet nothings until he fell back asleep. But just as I laid down, he was up again, this time with a furrow-browed bellow that made him look like a disgruntled bus driver. He jerked his head away when I tried to get him to nurse. I checked the diaper: dry. What was wrong? I rocked him, singing "Raindrops Keep Falling on my Head," until he finally passed out. *Thank God that's over,* I thought, as my body sank into sleep. Within seconds, Ezra's wailing wrenched me awake again. This time, he was *pissed*.

And so it went for the entire night.

At around four in the morning, drunk with exhaustion, I looked down at my wailing son and thought of that scene in "Happy Gilmore" when the peaches-and-cream orderly, played by Ben Stiller, turns on Adam Sandler's hapless grandmother as soon he gets her alone: "You're in my world now, Grandma."

No more would I sleep past dawn or know the pleasure of going grocery shopping alone. No longer could I plan anything, from a coffee date to a career, without considering the needs of this tiny person. My brain would regularly short-circuit, and my feet would ache from stepping on renegade toys. Raffi would commandeer my car stereo, and the strains of "Willaby Wallaby Woo" would taunt me in my sleep. I'd be thrust into the crucible of fevers, ear infections and colds, weeping on the phone with the pediatrician's answering service in the middle of the night. "Please," I'd beg them, "just tell me he's not going to die!"

But I would also get to watch the sunrise every morning with my son. He'd smile at me for the first time, and the moment would be so sweet it hurt. I'd feel a primal rush from the smell of his hair after a bath, or his laughter when I buried my nose in his belly. Once in awhile, my baby would reach for me with an expression of unfiltered love, and I'd think, *Right. This is what I'm here for.*

Today, though, I can't get away from my psychotic baby fast enough.

I drive past the naked trees and saltbox homes that line 6A, the ambling route that runs a good length of the Cape. My body leans into the road's familiar curves, and my eyes seek out my favorite houses just before they come into view. Dennis, our antique town, is tucked high in the bicep of Cape Cod's flexed arm, right on the lap of the bay. Here, you'll find colonial-era meeting houses, church lawns peppered with crooked tombstones, and rustic bed and breakfasts. The air is clean as glass and smells faintly of salt. Whenever I return from off-Cape, the first thing I do is open the window, inhale deeply, and remember that I'm alive. I straddle the line between tourist and full-timer, living in my parents' vacation home while Ben works on his startup and we plan our move to Boston. But, after almost three decades of summers and stolen weekends on this quiet island, there is nowhere in the world that feels more like home.

I turn into the parking lot of The Optimist Cafe, a gingerbread house of mauve and green. Out front, a round wooden butler holds his post. The cafe is empty, as are most places on the Cape in the winter, and the floor of the dining room creaks under my feet. The owner and I exchange brief hellos, and within minutes, I have a teapot of Mint Melange and my open laptop in front of me.

A painting of a sailboat on a pink sea hangs next to my table, and the sun's reflection on the glass makes the water look like it's waving. As I polish a press release, I keep looking up, thinking I've seen something move. My assignment wraps up quickly, leaving me a good hour before I have to go home. For a quarter of that hour, I peck halfheartedly at my keyboard, composing, erasing, rewriting, fiddling, going through the motions of being a writer without actually writing anything. It's been this way for years, writing and editing other people's work and choking on my own. Part of it is fear of finishing something that other people could read and (gasp!) reject. But there's also the feeling that, despite 27 years on this planet, my story hasn't started yet.

Eventually, I give up and go online.

There's a new post on Mom's blog, which my parents started the day after the diagnosis. Both of them write on it, tag-team style, their voices identifiable within a few words of a post. Mom is flowery and emotive, writing often of her children, her mix of emotions, God, and the many things for which she is grateful. Dad's posts read like this: *After a week of discomfort in the area of the gallbladder, Debbi underwent a series of scans that ultimately found a hypermetabolic right upper pole renal mass (SUV 6.5 peripherally, 4.3 x 5.8 x 5.2 cm in AP transverse and CC dimensions). No similar hypermetabolism in the right renal vein or IVC.*

Obviously, we all know exactly what he's talking about.

My father is a freak genius. Engage him in casual conversation, and you will likely hear words like "integer" and "control variable." As a kid, his idea of fun was dismantling TV sets and putting them back together. He has a PHD in Nuclear Engineering, and he can do math without numbers. My father is one of the few people on Wall Street with job security, as only three other people on the planet understand what he does and they live in Germany. Naturally, Dad was our go-to guy for math homework and science projects; Gabe became a high school legend with the potato gun he and Dad fashioned from PVC pipe. The entire class, including Gabe's physics teacher, watched, awestruck, as my father shot a half-dozen russets clear across the parking lot.

But for all of Dad's super-intelligence, he is the classic case of a super left brain eating the right brain. The first time my mother ever saw him at a Jewish youth convention in Pennsylvania, he was a gangly 16, with a helmet of brown ringlets and round, wire-rimmed glasses. Standing off by himself, he played with a set of clacker balls.

"It was typical Dad," Mom says. "He needed a prop in order to talk to people."

She was tall and green-eyed, with raven hair to her waist and a long line of male admirers. She didn't know it, but Dad saw her first, and had decided on a foolproof way to get her attention. Later that afternoon, she found him sitting on her bed, reading a Superman comic.

"What are you doing?" she asked.

He peered at her over the comic book. "Reading."

She looked around at the rows of empty beds that filled the girls' dormitory. "You're in my bed," she said, a double accusation: *And you're not even supposed to* be *here.*

"So?" he replied.

"I want to lie down."

He grinned cheekily at her and slid over. "There's room for the both of us."

She would have laughed at his *chutzpah* if she wasn't so annoyed. "Get out of my bed."

"Alright," he said, swinging his legs over the side. "But tell me your name first."

He was a pest, for sure, but he seemed harmless. Mom relented, and he disappeared.

Dad wrote her a letter every week for the next four months, and at the next convention, he bounded up to her to say hello. She had no idea who he was.

The only thing rivaling my father's intelligence is his stubbornness, which is what urged him forward in the face of flat rejection. At that convention, he parked himself behind Mom, eavesdropping on a conversation about her upcoming junior prom.

"It's a good thing you have a date already," he cut in. "Because I wouldn't take you even if you asked me to."

Mom and her friend turned back to him in disbelief. "Well, it's a good thing I didn't ask you."

She returned to her conversation - until Dad interrupted again. "I mean, maybe I'd consider it, but only if you asked me really, really nicely."

Mom glared at him. "Are you serious?"

"Well...I'd have to think about it."

"Listen," she said through her teeth. "I'm not going to ask you to my prom. I have a date already."

"Yeah, but you're going to ditch him and go with me."

Maybe it was the mischief in his brown eyes, or his ludicrous approach to romance. Or maybe it was his utter inability to accept defeat. Either way, something about him charmed her. She did indeed ditch her date and let Dad take her to the prom. She wore yellow chiffon and gloves. He wore a white jacket. They left after 30 minutes to walk around town, talking until dawn. She told him about the shambles of her family: a hypochondriac sister who manufactured crisis after crisis, a basketball star brother whose violent rages would land him in jail, an emotionally absent mother, and a father who was compelled to maintain appearances as the president of the local university. In the middle was Mom, flying under the radar, keeping quiet, and getting perfect grades so she could escape as soon as she graduated.

In response, Dad told her that he was a stoic.

"Like the people who don't have feelings?"

"No, they have feelings," he replied. "They just don't feel them."

"How is that possible?"

"I just decided to be a stoic, and now I am."

Not long before this conversation took place, Dad's father had moved out to live with a girl who was still in high school. Dad's mother, Rae, was left to support three sons. One year after this conversation, at age 36, she was killed in a car accident. The night of the memorial service, Mom held my weeping father in his bedroom, and the two of them promised to take care of each other for the rest of their lives. My father's stoicism was the survival tactic of a highly developed intellect, which, unable to quantify emotion, removed it from the equation. Since then, he's functioned much like a shark, constantly moving forward, because to stop means to drown.

So it was a shock when he said to me last night, "I'm falling apart, I think."

"Dad?" I said, looking down at my phone to make sure I hadn't called someone else by accident.

"I'm here. Can you hear me?"

"Yeah, yeah, I can hear you. You said you're falling apart?"

"I'm up all night getting my work done, I'm running back and forth to Urgent Care. I barely sleep. I don't know how much longer I can keep this up."

I was almost afraid to say anything, in case he remembered himself. "Do you want me to come? I can stay at the hospital so you can catch up."

"No. Stay where you are. Mom and I have been talking about maybe coming up to you."

"Is it because of what the doctor said?"

"That, and other things. A change of scenery will be good for her. And there's another oncologist up there, a colleague of our guy here. A fresh pair of eyes could make a difference."

"What do you mean? Mom made it sound like she's..."

"We don't know. The scans they ran here found more cancer, but they're going to run another biopsy up there. They might say that the cells are mostly infection. In that case, they can fight it and then start chemo again."

For a split second, it occurred to me that my father might be ignoring the facts, that maybe Mom knows something even the doctors don't. Then I dismissed the thought. Dad's not built that way.

Today, Mom announces their plans on the blog: *The journey has become very, very rocky at this point. My life feels like it is swinging on a pendulum....All I think about, all day, are my kids...I need to move to the Cape to be closer to my children and to see my grandson grow.*

She picks up on the first ring.

"So that's it?" I ask. "You're coming?"

"I'm done with New York. They don't know what to do with me anymore."

"What about the doctors? They're okay with it?"

"They think it'll be good for me. My shrink thinks so, too. I need to be around the baby."

"I can't believe Dad's game for this."

"Of course he is," Mom says. "I let him think it was his idea."

"Well, Ez will be happy to see you. He misses you."

"I miss him, too." Her voice breaks on the last word. "All I wanted was to watch my grandchildren grow up…."

Now she's crying.

I'm so confused. Dad seems to think there's every reason to hope, but here Mom is, talking like she's got a date with a guillotine. I have no idea what's happening here, but I do know that if I was in Mom's place right now, she'd get right in my face and tell me to cut the crap. "You're going to get better," she'd say, "and then you're going get out of this bed and go live your life. Now I'm going to make you some chicken soup."

I need to snap her out of this, but I don't know how. And that pisses me off.

"Stop it, Mom," I snap. "Self-pity is a luxury you can't afford."

I cringe as the words leave my mouth, reminded of my friend Avery, a piano teacher, whose most anxious student would panic at tricky notes and shut the piano, crushing Avery's fingers. This is essentially what I've just done. I might have told Mom that her despondence scares me, because it means she might actually be dying. Instead, terrified that it might be true, I slammed the piano shut.

I think Mom knows this, which is why she doesn't get upset. "You know," she says chattily, as if she hadn't been crying ten seconds before, "it's only two weeks to Passover. Everyone's coming to the house. Do you mind bringing all the seder stuff up from the basement?"

I mutter a contrite assent and hang up.

When I get home, Iris is reading on the couch. Ezra, she says, has been sleeping peacefully since I left.

"You okay?" she asks me, unfolding her body and standing up. "You look…something."

"I am something," I say, pulling her in for a hug. "But I'll be okay."
The minute she pulls out of the driveway, Ezra starts screaming.
Traitor.

Annie Blum brought Ring Dings in her lunch today. I saw them when she put her backpack in her cubby, which is right next to mine. She usually has the same lunch each day: peanut butter and jelly, celery sticks, a fruit cup, and animal crackers or a granola bar. Today must be special, though, because Annie has Ring Dings, those hockey-puck-shaped cakes with white cream inside, and covered with chocolate frosting that gets into the folds in your fingers.

I love Ring Dings more than I love Dena, but I rarely get to eat them. Mom buys boring snacks like pretzels, popcorn, and Wasa crackers, which taste like nothing and make my tongue bleed. Once in awhile, she'll come home with something exciting, like the Stella D'Oro cookies with the fudge dots in the middle, but they're usually gone before the groceries are unpacked. Mom never buys Ring Dings, Yodels or Devil Dogs, no matter how many times I ask. She says they're junk, and that we don't need it. What she really means is that I don't need it.

It's because I'm fat. Not cute, little-kid fat. Fat fat. I wear grown-up sizes because I don't fit in children's clothes. My thighs rub together through my tights and give me rashes. I have marks on my belly from where the buttons and zippers dig in, and there's a ring of dirt around my neck because my double chin gets in the way when I try to wash it. I don't eat like other people, who take a few bites and stop when they're full. I am never full. I'm hungry all the time – not hungry in my belly, but hungry everywhere, like an itch inside that always needs scratching. The only time it stops is when I'm chewing and swallowing. Then it starts up again. Even when I'm already full, even when I'm sick, I still have to eat more. Sometimes I eat things that aren't even food. Once, they called my mom from school to tell her I'd eaten the tights off my legs.

The other kids see me digging their pizza crusts and half-eaten sandwiches out of the garbage, and they say things. Every day during recess I wait for someone to let me have a turn at cat's cradle or kickball, but everyone ignores me. I eventually give up and walk around the parking lot by myself. Even my teacher, Mrs. Garcy, doesn't like me. She gets angry if I raise my hand too much and doesn't say anything when the other kids make fun of me. She sends me to do my work in the first grade as a punishment (for what, I don't know) and I have to act like I don't mind being in class with my little brother. All day, I hold every muscle in my body tight, feeling afraid and wishing I was at home with Mom.

There are other weird kids in my class, like Emily Fisher, who walks like she's holding a watermelon between her knees, Andrew French, who has an extra finger, and Joseph Lazar, whose parents are divorced. But they're still sort of normal, so no one says anything to them. I can't hide my fatness; I wear it on me all the time, like one of those Bison skins the Navajos wore in the winter to stay warm. I learned that in Social Studies, my second-favorite subject. English is my first-favorite subject. We get to read and write stories and talk about how to make nice sentences. I already know how to make nice sentences; they write themselves in my head when I look at things. Like when Dena crawled into a refrigerator box and fell asleep, and my head said, "Dena curls like a fiddlehead in her cardboard bed." The words just came to me, like someone else put them there.

Today, Mrs. Garcy teaches us about Haiku, which is a poem from Japan with five syllables in the first line, seven in the second, and five again in the third. After she shows us a few Haikus that other people wrote, she tells us to try and write our own. The other kids start chewing on their pencils and squirming in their seats. I put my pencil on the paper and watch the words come out:

Waves crash on the beach
Shining in the setting sun
Whispering, "Good night"

I put my pencil down on the desk and look around at my class. Most of them haven't started writing yet; a few are counting syllables on their fingers. I wait an extra minute so I don't look like I'm showing off, then I bring it to Mrs. Garcy's desk, where she marks Eli Baum's homework with a red pencil.

"Done already?" Mrs. Garcy asks with surprise.

I nod, excited, and hold my paper out to her.

Mrs. Garcy holds the side of her glasses while she reads the poem. I wait for her to smile. When she's done, she takes off her glasses off, but she isn't smiling.

"You didn't write this," she says.

I feel the air rush out of me like a whoopee cushion. "Yes, I did. I just wrote it. At my desk."

"I know you wrote it with your pencil. But this is not your haiku. Someone else wrote this."

Some of the other kids are watching us.

"No, they didn't," I say. "I thought the words in my head and then wrote them down."

"It's not possible. This poem is too advanced. You must have seen this haiku somewhere else and memorized it."

"But I didn't know what a haiku was before. How could I have memorized one before you taught me about it?" I'm talking in my upset voice, which is higher and louder than my normal voice.
All the kids are looking at us now.

"Go back to your seat, Rea," Mrs. Garcy says.

"But..."

"Go back to your seat. Now. We'll discuss this during recess."

I walk back to my desk, looking down at my paper to hide my hot tears. Everyone is watching me, but I won't let them see me cry. As I find my seat, I hear Mrs. Garcy praise Emily Rosendorfer's haiku about a brown dog named Ralph who ate pie. My haiku is better, but Mrs. Garcy doesn't believe I wrote it. She must think I'm not smart enough to write a good haiku.

I'm suddenly starving.

The egg timer on Mrs. Garcy's desk shows five more minutes until snack and recess. I don't know if I can make it five more minutes. Pretending I'm Matilda, the character from my favorite book who could move things with her mind, I send a message from my brain to the tiny cogs in the egg timer, telling them to turn faster. Finally, the bell rings, and everyone rushes to their cubbies to grab their lunch boxes. My apple and three Wasa crackers disappear in a few bites.

I'm still hungry.

Next to me, I see Annie take out her Ring Dings. I don't want to steal from her, but I can't help it; I have to have them. Before I can think, I grab the crinkly package from her hands.

"Give me that!" Annie says, trying to reach behind my back, where I'm hiding them.

I'm stuck now. If I give them to her, I won't get to eat them. But if I don't give them back, I'll get in trouble. I run for the playground, letting her chase me like it's all a game. Maybe if I keep it up long enough, she'll give up and let me have them. I sing the "Nah-nah-nah-nah-nah" song my mother hates as Annie's face turns pink.

"Give my snack back!" she cries.

But I don't. I open the package right in front of her, and wave one of the Ring Dings in her face. I already feel the chocolate melting onto my fingers. Annie's eyes turn to slits. I've touched them now, which means they have my germs on them.

"Give them to me," she says.

I shake my head.

"GIVE them to me!"

"Noooooooooo..." I open my mouth and take a bite, the chocolate melting and the cake crumbling to mush on my tongue. It's so good, I almost groan out loud. Then I swallow, and the good feeling is gone. Annie is staring at me, and so are some of the other kids who have been watching her chase me. They all look shocked, and a little scared. It's one thing to pretend you're going to eat someone else's snack. It's another thing to really do it.

I hold the other Ring Ding out to Annie. "Here."

"No. You keep it," she says, backing away like I might eat her, too.

Everyone walks away from me, whispering to each other. I look down at the package. The frosting is starting to stick to the cellophane. If I don't eat it, the chocolate will melt.

I swallow the first Ring Ding, then the second, in a few giant bites, pushing them hard down my throat.

I don't even taste them.

I have to stay inside for the rest of recess, which isn't so bad. I read my Judy Blume book about a girl named Linda that everyone calls "Blubber," which means whale fat. I thought the book might make me sad, but it doesn't. I'm just glad that it's Linda and not me who got that horrible nickname. She kind of deserves it, since she's so fat.

Mrs. Garcy sends me to the first grade for the rest of the afternoon. When I walk in, Gabe smiles and waves. I wave back, but sit at a table at the other side of the room. I do my work quietly, trying to keep as still as I can so everyone will forget I'm there.

When the last bell rings, I pack up quickly and hurry out of school. At the front of the carpool line is our gold minivan. Mom sits in the front seat, wearing jeans and a blazer with a pin Noah made for her. Just seeing her makes me feel better.

Then I hear a voice behind me: "Thief."

I walk faster, trying to ignore it.

"You're a thief," the voice says.

I look over my shoulder at Jordana Hoffman, Ring Ding Annie's best friend. She's small and skinny, with a pointy face and a voice that sounds like bees. Skipping next to me, she says, "And you're a freak. Do you know what that means? It means there's something wrong with you. You're a freak and a thief...."

I keep my eyes on our gold minivan, not looking at Jordana as she walks and talks next to me. "My brother says you probably weigh as much as our Dad, but I think he's wrong. I think you weigh more. Maybe you wouldn't be so fat if you stopped stealing other people's food..."

I'm almost running now, toward my mother. She's smiling at me through the windshield, but stops when she sees my face, which is all scrunched up from trying not to cry. Her eyes shoot to Jordana, who runs away just as I reach the car.

Throwing myself into the front seat, I drop my backpack and burst into the tears I've been holding back all day.

"What happened?" Mom asks.

I'm crying too hard to answer her.

"Rea! Tell me what she said to you!"

"She said I'm fat, okay? She said I'm a freak!"

Mom breathes out, hard. "You are not a freak."

"You have to say that; you're my mom. Everyone else tells me the truth: I'm disgusting!"

Just like that, Mom's finger flies up to my face. "Don't you let that little rat face make you feel bad about yourself!"

I'm so surprised, I stop crying. "Mom, you can't call someone a rat face."

"Why not? She looks like a rat."

"It's not nice," I say, but I can't help laughing.

Mom's shoulders drop from her ears, and she puts a soft palm to my cheek. "Listen, Cookie. People who say mean things to other people are not happy inside. They hurt other people so they can feel better."

I wipe my nose with the back of my hand. "Maybe they do it to get back at other people."

"Why? Did you do something?"

I think about Mrs. Garcy and the Ring Dings, and all the kids' faces when I took that first bite. If I tell Mom the truth, she might get mad. She might even say that I deserved what I got.

"No," I answer, looking out the window. "Can we go home now?"

The next afternoon, as I walk down to Mom's car, Jordana skips next to me again, singing, "Freaaak! You're a freaaak!"

This time, Mom waits outside the van, standing with her legs apart and her arms crossed, looking like one of those mother ducks that hiss at people who come near her babies.

The second Jordana sees her, she stops skipping and her song, "Freeee...." dips off tune.

Mom raises her eyebrows at her. You better beat it, *her face says,* before I break you in half.

Jordana runs away.

She never bothers me again.

Chapter Three

Mom's blog announcement that she's moving to the Cape has incited a flurry of emails from her readership, comprised of characters from every chapter of her life. One of them, a family friend of twenty years, sends me a message:

Being the oldest has its ups and downs, don't it? Please understand that our siblings deal with issues differently that we do. We are not necessarily right and they are wrong. It's just how things go. Just trust me when I say it is the time to just be there for Mom and Dad and let your siblings deal with things their way.

Dena calls. "It's not fair. She might not see me graduate or get married or meet my kids. I got the least time with her."

"Try to be positive," I reply, with a little more edge than I mean. "We don't know which way it's going yet."

"I prefer to assume the worst. Makes it easier in the long run."

As the queen of the worst-case scenario, I can't say I don't relate. When my husband gets lost for hours in the grocery store, I assume he's dead. But listening to my sister talk like the verdict is already in makes me want to punch her. "We still have to tell her everything is going to be okay, even if we don't believe it."

"I don't believe it," she says. "There are bad signs everywhere."

Her comment follows me around all day. On CNN they announce that the actor Ron Silver has died of cancer. I play a word game on my phone and spell, "nodule." Sorting through the Passover boxes in the basement, I open one of the Haggadahs to the passage: *The Lord took us out of Egypt with signs and wonders.*

"Do you think it means anything?" I ask Ben at dinner.

"Nah," he says. "There's no such thing as signs. You can read whatever you want into anything. What means one thing to you could mean something totally different to me."

"Like when I send you to pick up paper towels and you come home with ice cream?"

Ben points a green bean at me. "Exactly." He bites into it, then says, "I think it's good for Mom to come here, either way. Can you imagine sitting in that hospital all the time? Here, she'll at least get to be with us."

The *us* warms me. "Yeah, but it also means I'll be on double-duty, taking care of Ez *and* Mom. You might not see much of me for a while."

"Nah. We'll make time."

From upstairs comes the first strains of Ezra's impending wake-up cry. I raise my brows at my husband. "We shall see…"

"Don't worry," Ben says, smile flashing. "I'm not going anywhere."

Had you asked me ten years ago to describe my future husband, the character I sketched would have looked nothing like Ben. Back then, I was drawn to emotional paperweights, believing love was a game of trickery, a prize to snatch when my opponent wasn't looking. Then I met Ben, Mr. Kumbaya, who was as open and available as a 24-hour pharmacy. His optimism borders on delusional, he's allergic to negativity, and he wouldn't hurt a fly. (Like, literally. When he finds a bug in the house, he cups it in his hands, talks to it, and sets it free outside.) Ben sees the world with childlike wonder; he gets excited, about everything. The first time I brought him to the Cape House, Mom and I laughed as he raced around the tidepools on the beach, catching minnows with a net. After an hour or so, he proudly presented us with a full bucket.

Ben is always smiling, *always,* which would annoy me if it didn't stop my heart. That smile was the very first thing I noticed about him. Before we met, I was planning a year of study in Israel, though I had yet to decide on a program. I picked the brain of a young rabbi at Harvard named Avi who had lived in Jerusalem for a number of years and told me where to go. Then invited me over.

"It's no big deal, just a little *kumzitz,*" he said.

"A what?"

"Like a get-together. I do it every week for the college kids. We sit around, learn a little Torah, play guitar, sing. We do a barbecue. You'll love it."

The *kumzitz* fell on the first frigid night of the year, right before Thanksgiving, when the cold off the Charles River burrows into your bones to stay until May. I was wiped out from a full day of teaching, followed by a Hebrew School gig at a synagogue outside the city. All I wanted was my bed; the *kumzitz* would have to wait until the following week.

But something strange happened when I reached the two-way split on the Mass Pike. I don't know if it was exhaustion or Divine interference (possibly both), but I dropped into a semi-dream state. I mean, *checked out.* I was supposed to head left, toward Brookline, but my car steered itself to the right, toward Cambridge. Suddenly I was parked in front of the rabbi's with no recollection of actually driving there. But there I was.

The house looked dark and quiet, like no one was home. Maybe I had the nights mixed up. Maybe this was a weird rabbi prank. Then I noticed, at the back of the house, two figures in shadow sitting by a small fire. I stepped out into the cold, gasping as my cheeks went instantly numb. One of the figures looked in my direction and darted out of sight. Odd. I decided to play it safe in case those two weren't *kumzitzers,* and rang the bell at the front.

From the side of the house appeared a jovial fellow in a corduroy jacket and rastafarian hat - a fashion choice I wasn't sure was ironic.

"Hi," he said.

"Hi. I'm here for the *kumzitz?*"

"Oh, yeah! Ari said you might be coming. No one else showed up; all the college kids went home for Thanksgiving."

"Oh," I said, unsure of what to do. *Kumzitz* on? *Kumzitz* off?

"Ari and I were just 'cueing. He went inside to put on some pants."

"Ummm…"

"Come on back," he said, waving me around the porch. "I'm Ben. I'm Ari's roommate."

Then he smiled at me.

At that moment, I was struck by a sense of instant recognition - *Oh, there you are* - like I'd found the answer to a question I'd been asking all my life.

Kumzitz on.

Ben and I stole looks at each other all evening while Avi pontificated on the Torah portion. Then Ari talked. And talked. And talked. Ben told me he was raised Orthodox and had spent years studying in big-time yeshivas.

"You don't look like a yeshiva boy," I said, pointing to the rastafarian hat.

He laughed. "I don't fit the mold."

"Ha! Me, neither."

I wondered then if a former yeshiva boy, even one in tye-dye and jeans, would ever go for a girl with short pixie hair, skin-tight, red jeans and a t-shirt that said, "Buy Me Something."

I hoped so.

Ben walked me out to my car, where we talked some more, slowly freezing to death because neither of us wanted to go.

"I need to be around people I can tell the truth to," I said. "I need to be able to say, 'I really love God', and have that not be weird."

"Well, I love God," he said.

"*I* love God!" I cried, like we'd discovered a mutual friend.

What a couple of knuckleheads.

It felt safe to be around Ben because he was completely himself: awake, alive, exuberant. Also insecure and messy, but in a human, non-scary way. With Ben, there was no game; he didn't hide his need, nor his passion. He reminded me of a toddler I once saw at the grocery store who stopped to hug every person he passed. I didn't have to trick Ben or work to earn his love; he just held it out for me to take.

I didn't tell Mom about Ben right away. I held my sweet secret close, like a good poker hand. It all felt too new to talk about, and I needed some protection if it fell apart. I also didn't want to over-excite my mother, who would probably start calling wedding caterers as soon as I broke the news. But it was hard to keep it from her. For years I'd imagined the day when I could say those three magic words, "I've met someone," signaling to her that all would be well with me.

When I finally broke down, she laughed. "A yeshiva boy? Your father will be thrilled!"

I took Ben to meet my parents, and Mom greeted him with a huge hug and kiss. "Welcome to the family!" she said, like a mob boss. Ben said later he felt instantly like one of hers.

While Dad and Ben got lost in talk, Mom studied Ben's face.

"Great nose," she said, raising and lowering her eyebrows at me. "He's pretty."

I snorted. "Ma!"

"So tell me: what's so special about him?"

"He's good. He's the best person I've ever met."

She mulled that over, then said, "Marry him."

So I did. I joined that great human experiment of mixing two lives together, sticking them under one roof like a specimen in an incubator, and watching what grows. I have discovered quite a bit about "Rea, the Wife" that I never knew about "Rea, the Single Gal": My addiction to approval, for one. A penchant for picking fights when calm communication will do. Outbreaks of hives at the mere suggestion that I might be wrong. And a (slightly) unhealthy dependence on my family of origin. Two years in, I have yet to draw a clear line between where they end and where Ben and I begin. With a foot in both my old and new lives, I can revert from adult to child and back again as needed. When seas are calm, I dwell happily with my husband, but when gray clouds gather, my instinct is not to turn to him, but to run home. My family is my safe place, the model I try to replicate in my life with Ben. I pull him to join me in the shelter of my family, so we can have the protection we may not yet be able to give each other. But Ben pulls back, wanting to build a haven that is ours alone.

In my clearer moments, I remember that the family I cling to so fiercely began with two scared kids who could promise only to take care of each other as best as they could. And look what they made. Ben and I could do that, too.

All I have to do is let us.

The next morning, as I feed Ezra breakfast, I hear the rumble of the garage door.

They're here.

My stepdaughters, 7-year-old Naomi and 6-year-old Aviva, have hitched a ride from New York with my parents, and they run into the house in a scramble of noise and energy. They tip their heads up toward the living room's high ceiling, re-acclimating themselves to the wide and lofty spaces of a large colonial. Compared to their tiny Queens apartment, the Cape House is a castle. Dad comes in behind them with two bags slung over his shoulders. Mom brings up the rear, looking gray and tired, but happy.

I kiss Mom hello and ask, "How were they?"

"We had a blast. We left at three in the morning and sang the whole way up."

Ezra bounces in his high chair at the sight of his sisters, who climb all over the couches, waking their sleepy father.

"It's not even eight o'clock. How are they so wound up?"

"They just had a lot of fun," Dad says.

"And a lot of strawberry milk," says Mom.

Dad approaches Ezra, who presents his bottom lip at the sight of his grandfather. Dad and Ezra have been on the outs since the day Dad picked the baby up and growled at him, thinking it would make him laugh. Instead, Ezra wailed in abject terror. Since then, Dad has been trying to win back his affections.

"Hey, Ezra," Dad says. "Whatcha doin'?"

Ezra's face crumples.

"No dice, Dad," I say, taking the baby out of the high chair. "Better luck with the next one."

Dad and Ben go outside for the rest of the luggage as the girls chirp merrily behind them. Ez and I follow Mom as she shuffles to her room, her right arm holding the left to temper the pain from a long-ago excavation for cancer cells in her shoulder. My eyes go wide at the sight of her legs, which have swelled to the size of tree trunks.

"What happened to you?"

"Edema," she says. "My kidneys can't flush out the saline fast enough." As she settles onto the bed, her hips spread wide beneath her like the bottom layer of a wedding cake.

"Yikes."

"This is nothing. You should see my butt." She reaches out her arms. "Give me that baby."

Ez goes right to her and puts his lips on her face.

"Mmm…" Mom says. "You have kisses for Bubbles? Ooh, wet ones. Teeth in yet?"

"Any second, please, God."

"My mother used to rub Brandy on our gums when we were teething."

"That explains a lot."

Mom smiles, then burrows her face in Ezra's neck. He squeals, clamping his fingers in her hair, which Mom cropped short last month to preempt the next round of chemo. As long as I've known her, Mom's hair has always been long and dyed auburn. The salt-and-pepper pixie cut suits her, but it makes me feel like I've run into someone I'm sure I know, but can't quite place.

When Ez is calm, Mom puts him in her lap and gives me the up-down. "You look good, Re."

"Thanks. I'm going to the gym again."

"What are you doing?"

"The bike, mostly. Sometimes the elliptical."

I haul myself up onto the end of the bed, making kissy faces at Ezra. "Do they have spinning?"

"I think so, but I don't do it. It's no fun if you're not the teacher."

About ten years ago, Mom got addicted to spinning and became a certified instructor. Though she was twice the age of the other teachers, her class was the most popular. With the mike on her ear, she'd butcher

80's pop hits and yell at everyone like a drill sergeant. As her endorphins spiked, she'd shout, "WHOO!" quick and high, like a bird call. When Dena and I sat in on her classes, we'd laugh so hard we almost fell off our bikes.

"You hungry?" I ask. "You want some breakfast?"

"Nah."

I give her a long, hard look. "So what's the deal, Ma?"

"Nothing. Dad's going to run back and forth to the city and you'll cover while he's gone."

"So, what, I make sure you eat three square, give you meds, buy you trash magazines?"

"You'll keep me company, same as you did in New York. And take me to the hospital if I need."

The prospect makes me nervous. "You think you'll need to go?"

"I don't know. I hope not."

I reach over to squeeze one of Ezra's fat, silky feet. "I got a manicure at this place in Hyannis that does special facials for Cancer patients. Maybe we'll go this week."

"Mmm," Mom says, leaning her head back against the pillows.

"Tired?"

She nods and shuts her eyes. Her hands droop and Ezra squirms out of her lap. "The house looks good, Re…" she says sleepily.

"Thanks," I say, grateful that she noticed. The last time she was here, Mom was pissed at me for the newborn flotsam cluttering every flat surface, the cooked-on crust on the stovetop, and the dust bunnies I'd allowed to breed all over the house. I blamed my exhaustion, but the shameful truth was that a childhood with live-in housekeepers had trained me to leave messes for the magical cleaning fairies. But when they didn't show up, I was forced to face the fact that I am not a Disney princess. This time, I spent two days getting the place cleaner than when we moved in.

I scoop the baby up and shift quietly off the bed. "I'm going to let you rest. You sure you don't need anything?"

She doesn't answer.

In the kitchen, Naomi and Aviva munch on cereal.

"Can we go out after this?" Aviva asks, mouth full.

I laugh. "You just got here! But I'll tell you what: how about the two of you take a nap and then you can come with me to buy Shabbos food?"

"Can we make cupcakes?" asks Naomi.

"Very possibly."

She shoots a conspiratorial grin at her sister. "Okay."

We have a whole weekend to get through before Mom meets the oncologist in Hyannis to review the scans sent up from New York. Three days until we find out if there's anything he can do. It might be easier if we didn't have Shabbos, the holy day of non-distraction. Even before I became observant, I was drawn to places of calm and silence, rising before dawn to meditate and walk around my neighborhood when it was still quiet. It wasn't a stretch for me to start keeping the Sabbath, free of errands, work and electronic diversions, when I could just be in the company of family and friends. But today, with an invisible clock ticking in the back of my head, the empty hours stretch long and tedious.

While I clean up from lunch and Ben dozes on the couch, the girls play on the floor with Ezra and try coaxing him to crawl.

"Come on, Ezra," Naomi calls, holding her hands out to him. "Come to me..."

Ezra pushes onto his hands, drops down, then tilts his tush up to form a slide with his back. Up and down he goes, his torso and hips rising and falling like a seesaw. Naomi tries to motivate him with a Cheerio, but when he reaches for it, he collapses onto his belly.

"Why doesn't he just...*do it*?" Aviva cries, exasperated.

"He's still learning," I say. "He has to figure out how the parts work before he can make them go."

Dad sits at the kitchen island with his open Gemara, one of 63 tractates that comprise the Talmud. He is part of a worldwide network of people who study the *Daf Yomi,* the daily page, to complete the entire Talmud in a seven-and-a-half-year cycle. Reaching the end is one of the most respected accomplishments in Judaic studies, usually celebrated with a *siyum*, a party. (Four years ago, a grand-scale *Daf Yomi siyum* filled Madison Square Garden.) The first time Dad finished, a few friends threw a small *siyum* for him, which I heard was very nice; I had no idea it had happened until after the fact. When I asked why he hadn't mentioned it, he waved me off. "It was no big deal," he said.

As I lay out a plate of brownies for the kids, Dad leans back in his seat, pushes his glasses up, and rubs the bridge of his nose. Without a word, I hand one to him.

"So what do you think?" I ask.

"It's good," he says, chewing thoughtfully.

"I meant about the doctor. What do you think he's going to say?"

Dad shuts his Gemara. "I don't know. We'll go and he'll tell us whatever he's going to tell us and we're going to deal with it. We just have to pray for the best."

We just have to pray for the best. This has been my father's mantra during my mother's illness, which he has recited before every test, treatment, hospital stay, and blood transfusion. Each time I hear it, it gives me a chill: what if God's idea of "best" doesn't match ours, and we actually get what we pray for?

Mom's voice drifts in from her bedroom. "Willie....?"

"Yeah?" Dad says, eyes on his book.

She doesn't reply.

Dad turns toward the doorway. "What is it, Willie?"

My parents have shared a nickname since college, when, one afternoon, my father sat studying in a dormitory hallway where two maintenance men, one skinny and one fat, were working. Dad listened as the skinny man prattled on and on, stopping only to ask his silent companion, "Whatchoo thinkin' about, Fat Willie?"

"Nuthin'," Fat Willie said.

The skinny man launched into another monologue, until it again occurred to him to ask, "Wutchoo thinkin' 'bout, Fat Willie?"

"Nuthin'," Fat Willie said.

So the cycle repeated itself, to my father's great amusement.

That evening, Dad went to visit my mother in one of his pensive moods, adding little to the conversation.

"What are you thinking about?" she asked.

Dad laughed, and told her about the exchange in his dorm. From then on, my parents called each other "Willie." In fact, I have never once heard my father address Mom by her real name.

"Will you bring me a brownie?" she says.

Dad and I smirk at each other. The dessert radar in our family is foolproof.

"Didn't the doctor say no sugar?" I call.

"He said a lot of things," she mutters.

Amused, I slap a brownie on a napkin. "I got it," I tell Dad, and head to my mother's room. Aviva and Naomi, who holds Ezra, trail behind me.

Mom's face is hidden behind the cover of a celebrity magazine, which features the newest reality TV stars: "Octomom" and her eight newborns. I recall my sleepless nights with Ezra and shudder.

"You know you're getting old," Mom says, flipping the pages, "when you don't know who half these people are."

This is her way of saying she's above celebrity culture, which is a big, fat lie. These magazines are my mother's heroin. If you want free entertainment, hand one to her, sit back, and watch. She lights up with each bloody chunk of gossip, and weighs in with baseless authority. The day she saw Brad Pitt and Jennifer Aniston's wedding photos on the cover of People, Mom's face split in an oracle's smile. "He was ready," she said, like she was Brad Pitt's conscience.

The girls clamber up on the bed and flank themselves on either side of my mother. As they sink deep into the pillows, Ezra wriggles around their feet and grabs one of the magazines.

"Who's that?" Aviva says.

"Her name is Suri Cruise," Mom replies. "Her father is famous."

Naomi's eyes brighten. "Suri's a Jewish name! Is she Jewish?"

"Not exactly," I say.

The sound of ripping makes us look up: Ezra has mangled Christina Aguilera's face.

Mom grins at me. "That's nothing. One time, you destroyed an entire phone book."

As Mom and the girls turn back to the magazine, I run my fingers along the bed's intricately carved mahogany. This bed, a high, king-sized platform you alight with steps, is majestic, with a downy mattress that invites you to disappear for a while. Mom's bed has been the hub in every home we've lived in, the place to be held, to find company, and to unload your worries. If you happen to come by, even for the first time, there's a good chance you'll be invited to take off your shoes and climb in.

Turning to a picture of Johnny Depp, Mom dips her head back and moans. "Oh my *God*. I cannot believe how gorgeous this man is. Look at his face. He's unbelievable."

Ezra pukes all over his magazine.

"They're all so pretty," Aviva says.

"It's makeup, honey," I say. "And computers."

"They have nice hair," Naomi says, her hand absently wandering to the bald spot on the back of her head. When she was born, her scalp didn't fuse properly, and now there's a patch of skin where hair will never grow.

"So do you," says Mom.

Naomi shakes her head. "Some kids at school were making fun of my bald spot."

A mixture of fury and sadness well up in my throat. "You know something about kids who make fun of other kids? They do it because they're not happy inside."

From the corner of my eye, I see Mom's knowing smile. I pretend I don't notice and rescue Patrick Dempsey from Ezra's gums.

"Don't you know this guy?" Mom says, flipping the magazine around to show me the host of a cooking show.

"Friend of a friend," I reply. He was one of the group I went with years ago to chase the dream in Los Angeles. A good number of them are making it happen: one does stand-up at all the big festivals and just signed a contract with MTV. Another hosts a Sirius radio show. My old roommate is a producer for a daytime talk show, and one of my best college girlfriends is a writer on tour. Sometimes, seeing my peers move up in the world makes me feel like a dog tied to a tree, watching frisbees whizz by. But I bet none of them can change a diaper in less than ten seconds.

Dad wanders in, and Aviva wraps herself around his chest. He takes her hand and dances with her, half-singing and half-humming. *"The way you wear your hat, the way you sip your tea, hmm, hmm, hmmmmm...no, no they can't take that away from me..."*

Laying on my side, I take in the quiet scene, Mom and Naomi with the magazine, Dad and Aviva cheek-to-cheek, and I wonder, not for the first time, if God was having a Coen Brothers moment when he made me a stepmother.

Not long after Ben and I started dating, he sat me down and told me there was something I should know: "I'm divorced."

Okay, I thought. *Not a dealbreaker.*

"And I have two kids."

Oy.

It's not that I didn't like kids. At the time, I made my living as a teacher. But having my own children was a milestone way, way ahead on the timeline I'd mapped out for my life. If I was serious about this guy, it would mean swapping out my plans for instant parenthood.

"Do you have a picture of them?" I asked.

He produced a snapshot of two little girls in matching dresses, one three and one four, smiling brightly at the camera. The older one had dark hair and a sweet-cheeked Eskimo face. The younger one was lighter and still round with baby fat, but she had the same smile as her sister. Had they looked like hairless cats, I might have been able to run for it. But they were *so cute*. And I couldn't defy the force, powerful and elemental as gravity, that had pulled me into Ben's orbit. I looked from the little faces in the picture up to his, and decided to give my vision of "happily ever after" an overhaul.

It didn't take long for reality to blow the romantic bubbles away. When the girls came to stay, Ben and I switched from blissed-out newlyweds to wiped-out parents, with barely any time to exchange a word. I found myself rooted to the east coast, where the girls lived, a veritable jail sentence for a gypsy like me. Then, of course, there was the money. I knew the girls deserved every penny their father sent them, but my inner kindergartener didn't like to share. I thought stepmotherhood would be like a mindless part-time job; instead, it was a monolithic commitment that bled into my full-time life. Like a thief, resentment crept in. A few months after our wedding, I found myself on hands and knees in the middle of the night, scrubbing the bathroom after one of the girls had an accident. While my husband facilitated a quick pajama change in the next room, I looked down at the sponge in my hand and thought, *This is so not what I signed up for.*

The girls, meanwhile, were much more adult about the whole thing than I was. They volunteered to help me cook and curled in my lap like kittens when I read to them. They even brought projects and cards they'd made for me at school, which made me feel like a pygmy.

It was my mother who righted my thinking. From the moment the girls entered their world, Mom and Dad transformed into fantasy grandparents. They took the girls to the circus, on their first-ever subway ride, to buy American Girl dolls that cost more than my car payment, and to the Cape House, where Naomi and Aviva splashed the in low tide with Ben. One Sunday morning, Mom covered the dining room table with Dora the Explorer wrapping paper and woke the girls up, to their sleepy delight, for a "Dora pancake party!" I was dumbstruck by how easily my parents absorbed Naomi and Aviva into their lives, especially when my adjustment was so bumpy. It seemed like everyone in my family had left the station, while I was throwing a tantrum back on the platform.

Then, last year, my parents decided to take the girls for a late-night run to Toys R' Us. Mom had just spent most of the day sleeping off a chemo treatment, but she roused herself from bed, put on her coat, and hustled them out the door. When I urged her to stay home, she told me to zip it. "I told them we'd go," she insisted.

When they got back, the girls were mad with excitement over their presents, while Mom looked like she'd left her entire blood supply in the cab.

"I'm fine," she assured me. "We had fun."

"Thank you, Ma."

She gave me a puzzled look. "For what? They're my granddaughters."

It was as simple as that. She had made the decision, and now they were hers. True, our positions were different; she had the luxury of spoiling them, while I had the responsibility of co-raising them. But still. I had made the grave mistake of thinking of them as the catch in the deal, when really, they were the bonus.

After that, I got on the train.

By Monday, I'm desperate for quiet. I ask Ben to take the girls out, my patience draining as I wait for Mom and Dad to come back from the doctor. To nudge the time along, I play on the floor with Ezra, who squeaks and blows raspberries at me, liking the vibration on his chin. These are happy raspberries, unlike the ones he makes before he starts fussing, like a flight attendant's warning to expect turbulence. When I got him dressed this morning, I was compelled, inexplicably, to button the collar of his polo to the neck, like a little ivy leaguer. It just seemed to suit him. I never thought I'd have a buttoned-up-to-the-neck kind of kid; I expected a dark, spiky-haired punk rocker to dress in suspenders and clashing plaids. But when I met Ezra, my little blonde recessive gene, I knew immediately that he was too sweet for that kind of thing. Once I put him in a t-shirt with graffiti on it, and he looked like he was having a midlife crisis. I had to concede that my little guy is more Mr. Rogers than Joey Ramone.

After I get him down for a nap, I sit down and write. About Mom. About the waiting. About the swing between fear and numbness. I sense that this convergence of new motherhood and Mom's illness is a cocoon of time I am duty-called to record, too precious to be trusted to memory alone.

It's 3:50. Mom's appointment was almost an hour ago. Dena calls to ask if I've heard anything, which I haven't. I tell her to call back in an hour. She does, at 4:50 on the dot, but they're still not home.

Just shy of 5:00, Mom and Dad walk in, grave and quiet. Mom goes right to her room and climbs into bed.

"What happened?" I ask, following her.

"It's exactly what we thought. There's no treatment for me. The best they can do now is keep me comfortable and try to fight the infection."

"You mean like Hospice?"

"Like Hospice."

"So you're dying."

"Yes."

"Like...soon?"

She smiles sadly at me. "I asked him if I have two weeks. He said probably. Two months, he couldn't say."

It's the most unnatural thing I've ever heard anyone say.

To me, death has always been theoretical. I knew it lingered out there somewhere, but it was far enough away for me to avoid thinking much about it. My allotment of time, I assumed, was ample and long-lasting, like a keg of pistachios you keep around for decades of Super

Bowl parties, until the day you reach in and realize there's only a handful left. My friend Rosie, a therapist who had both her breasts removed, told me that most people think like that. "We push death away because we don't want to deal with it," she said. "We all assume we're going to die a long time from now, in some fluky way, like a car crash or a stroke. But death doesn't always come suddenly. The lucky ones get time to look it in the face for a while."

I crawl into bed with Mom and curl up at her side, which feels so like home that I ache. "Are you scared?"

"I was," she says, stroking my hair, "but I'm not anymore. I used to have panic attacks about what will happen to you guys, how painful it will be for you, but then I realized there's nothing I can do about it. Then it was okay. I know God has a plan. It pisses me off, but He does."

I watch her hands as she talks, her fingers drawing back toward her palm, then stretching out again in a staccato rhythm. Her wedding band and engagement ring are gone. She must have already returned them to my father.

After dinner, Ben leaves to drive the girls back to New York, and I dig through the pantry for my favorite tea. When I shut the door, I find Dad standing behind it. He wordlessly wraps his arms around me, and I rest my cheek against his chest.

I repeat the question I asked my mother: "Are you scared?"

"More numb," he says, his voice vibrating under his shirt. "It's hard to see her in pain."

"Yeah."

Dad takes a step back, but leaves a hand on my shoulder. "It seems like you were appointed to help take care of her here. I'm not dumping her on you, but a lot of it's going to fall on your shoulders."

"It's okay, Dad. I want to help."

He gives my shoulder a quick squeeze, then walks into the little shul with strides long and swift, the pace of traffic on the sidewalks of New York. Before I can say anything else, he's gone.

An image floats to the surface of my memory: a portrait of my grandmother, Rae, not long before she died, wearing pearls and a white pillbox hat. Her wide moon face was my father's exactly. The painting was stored, for some unknown reason, in my bedroom closet, where I would often sit and stare into her black-brown eyes until it seemed like she was staring back at me. Caught just so, her gaze would give me goosebumps. But I never looked away. I searched her face for the right angle that would reveal a deeper glimpse of who she was, and who my father was before he lost her.

As I head up to bed, I pass by Mom's room. She sleeps with her mouth open, twitching occasionally from all the drugs. I retreat from the doorway, suddenly needing more than anything to hold my baby.

In the middle of the night, Ben slides into bed. "I told Naomi about Mom," he whispers.

"What did she say?"

"Nothing, at first. She just looked down and kicked the back of my seat for a minute. Then she said, 'But I like Debbi.'"

I know how she feels.

Chapter Four

It's day one of Mom duty, and within hours of Dad's departure for New York, she's already spiked a fever.

"I thought things were going to be calm for you, " Mom says in apology.

The doctor on call told us to sit tight, so we pass the time sorting through Mom's jewelry. I label each box with either my name, Dena's or Sammy's, so we'll know who gets what.

"This is *mine*," I tell her, holding up a necklace of turquoise and silver I've lusted after for years.

"Of course."

I slip the necklace over my head, then open a small velvet box containing a pair of amethyst earrings. "Whose are these?"

"You can have them. Dena's not into the colorful stuff. I'm giving her the diamonds."

I write my name on a label and stick it on the box. "What about your hats?"

Over the years, Mom has amassed an enviable hat collection. Topped with feathers, bows, and sashes in every imaginable color, they crowd the top of her closets in fancy wicker boxes. She wore them to synagogue, mostly, looking elegant and dramatic with her long hair flowing out from under them. Every time she put one on, she'd say, "You know, someone once asked me to be a hat model."

"Really?" I'd say, even though I'd heard it a hundred times. "Why didn't you do it?"

In response, she'd make some disparaging noise and brush her hand away, sweeping off hat modeling as frivolous nonsense. I bought that move until I pulled it myself in college, quitting a "stupid" play because I was afraid, come opening night, that I'd be laughed offstage.

"You want them all?" Mom asks.

"Obviously."

"So take them."

"Yes!" I lift my hands in victory to make Mom laugh, but she's too tired. It's possible she didn't even hear me, with a mass of hair cells in her ears wiped out by chemo. It's an eerie parallel to her mother, who went deaf in her 50's after a stroke.

"So what about the shiva?" Mom asks, alluding to the seven ("shiva") days of mourning.

"What about it?"

"Well, I'm going to be buried in Millis with the rest of the family, but all our friends are in New York." She holds a rhinestone bracelet up to the lamplight, then tosses it onto the "miscellaneous" pile. "It's not going to be easy for them to pay a shiva call if you guys are sitting in Massachusetts."

"Mom. Are you trying to plan your own shiva?"

Her smile is sheepish. "You gotta think about these things."

"I guess we'll sit here a couple of days, then sit the rest in New York?"

"The kids have work."

"When your mother dies, work takes a backseat."

It's a bizarre conversation, with the casual tone we have when discussing dinner menus or sleeping arrangements. It's almost rude to discuss it with her, like we're planning a party she won't be invited to.

"What are we gonna do with this guy?" I ask, holding up an awful geometrical pin from the early 90's. "Please say, 'Donation.'"

Mom responds by bursting into tears.

"Ma? What's wrong?"

"I've been robbed!" she says. "Just when you guys are starting to blossom!" She gives into crying for a minute, then stops herself, takes a deep breath, and fixes her jaw. "God has a plan for me. He gave me 55 years. I had a husband who loves me more than anything, four children I wasn't even supposed to have. I had a charmed life."

"Yeah, and it's not over yet. Stop talking about yourself like you're dead already. It freaks me out."

"Sorry," she says, dabbing her eyes. She points to the white teddy bear behind her neck and says, "Can you fix Ralph?"

Ralph is named after Mom's physical therapist, who gifted Mom with the bear to help her get comfortable after surgery. He'd done the same for his own mother when she was dying of cancer, and it helped both women finally get some sleep. "It really works," Mom marveled when she first sank her head onto the bear's belly. Now Ralph lays horizontally behind my mother's neck, his face curved up to hers like he's kissing her. He's slipping up a bit, though, so I tug on his foot and ear to get him back where he should be.

"I'm glad you don't have to watch me age or put me away somewhere," Mom says thoughtfully.

"And you'll save a fortune in facelifts."

Mom shakes her head and chuckles. "You still don't think this is happening, do you?"

"I don't know what I think."

"Rea, I'm dying."

I look down at the comforter, tracing a blue flower with my finger. "I know, Ma. I just don't believe it."

"Is there anything you want to say to me?"

"Can you tell me what to do with the rest of my life?" I make it sound like I'm joking, but I'm not.

She thinks about it. "Find a place to have a home."

I was hoping for something loftier, but Mom's aspirations for me have always been simple: to be settled somewhere, fulfilled and content, with a family of my own. To settle anywhere has been the struggle of my life, driven as I am by the need to be more, have more, do more. I've run from city to city, country to country, chasing the pervasive lie that happiness is a destination, a possession, or a circumstance. Really, it's a state of being, no matter what the circumstance. But for a mind like mine to make that switch, to abandon a lie for the truth, it takes a whole lot of Grace.

"Is there anything you want to say to me?" I ask.

"Yeah. Remember me as I was."

I don't like when Mom says she wasn't supposed to have children. Clearly, that isn't true, or we wouldn't be here. But I'll give her this: we did take our sweet time showing up.

My parents got married when they were twenty, and they'd barely left the reception before they were trying for a baby. Seven years later, they were still trying. In those days, people only said the word "infertility" under their breaths, and "reproductive technology" meant a turkey baster and some Vaseline. Mom had dreamed of motherhood since she was a little girl, and with every month that passed without a pregnancy, the weight of disappointment and failure grew heavier, and crushed her.

People asked questions. One tactful uncle slapped Mom on the rear in the middle of a dinner party and said, "What's the matter, you don't know how to do it?"

The doctors ran my parents through a humiliating litany of tests, while their bedroom turned into a laboratory. To transport a sperm sample to the doctor, my mother held the cup between her thighs to keep it warm, like a penguin with her egg, because their van had no heat. In the end, the tests revealed nothing. The doctors advised Mom to tuck her dream away, because she and my father would never have children.

At this devastating news, my parents created a cooperative coping system they called the "Eat Your Way to Happiness Program." All you had to do was choose your favorite high-calorie treat and eat as much of it as you wanted, forever. It was a successful enterprise until neither of them could fit into their pants.

After this came a series of failed adoptions that almost always fell apart at the last minute. But my parents were determined, sitting through countless meetings with social services, filling out reams of paperwork, and waiting hours for the phone to ring. For a year and a half, they fostered four siblings caught in a bitter custody battle, but it was a temporary arrangement, and my parents eventually had to send them home. In the interim, Mom got a positive pregnancy test. My parents were over the moon...until the follow-up test came back negative. A trip to the doctor confirmed that the positive test had been a fluke. Dad took to the nursery's mahogany rocking chair, where he rocked in silence for three days, wrapped in a blanket. After one last thwarted adoption, my parents gave up.

Then Mom got pregnant.

To this day, no one can explain how it happened. How after seven years, Mom's womb was suddenly occupied by a bona-fide fetus - a girl, my mother knew, with that cosmic instinct exclusive to pregnant women.

Mom bloomed in pregnancy. In one picture, she stands at a right angle to the camera, holding a green satin tunic tight against her bowling-ball belly. Her small smile belongs to someone with a delicious secret. Her skin glows, her eyes sparkle, and her hair falls in shimmery waves past her shoulders. Dad swore she was never more beautiful. As the months passed, Mom nested with a vengeance, scouring, scrubbing and vacuuming every inch of the house with superhuman energy. My father dreamed that he was back on the navy ships, feeling the sea spray in his face. The mist he felt was actually paint, which my mother was rolling onto the ceiling over their bed at 3 a.m..

One night late in the pregnancy, Mom started bleeding. They rushed to the hospital, terrified that she was losing the baby. In the tense stillness one feels in a bomb shelter during an air raid, my parents waited as the doctor moved his stethoscope like a chess piece around Mom's belly, listening for a heartbeat. There was nothing.

And then, high up in the uterus, there was a flutter.

At that time, neither of my parents were spiritually inclined. But both of them, and their doctors, thanked whatever God was up there for saving this baby, who was not even born yet and had already beaten nature twice.

On a rainy December night in 1981, my mother's obstetrician and all of the nurses stayed past their shifts to help this baby make her entrance into the world. The labor was long; Mom played cards with the doctor while Dad tinkered with the IV and documented the progression on graph paper. His notations show the contractions, timed to the minute, getting closer and closer together. On the last few rows of the graph, my father writes, in his number-like script, "TIME TO PUSH!!!"

I was born with a full head of black hair that stuck out in all directions, and, according to my mother, violet eyes. ("From the minute I saw those eyes," she said, "I knew I was in trouble.") I gave the requisite cry, then surveyed the place with the cool expression of a mafioso shrouded in cigar smoke. After they placed me in the baby bed next to my mother, I promptly ripped my little hat off, picked up my head, and shot my parents a look of amused condescension: *Synthetics? You must be joking.*

They named me Rea Miriam, after Dad's mother, Rae, and Mom's grandmother, Mary, a ballsy Lithuanian who, orphaned and destitute at 20, brought herself and her five siblings to America, speaking not a word of English.

My parents, finally, had their own little family. They were so grateful, they barely noticed how exhausted they were. When I was a few months old, they made a video of themselves singing to me, both of them goofy from sleep deprivation and falling all over each other with laughter. They were young and happy, without a clue that within the year, I'd have a brother.

Gabe was born the color of a bruise, with the umbilical cord wrapped around his neck. The doctors whisked him away before my parents could see him, returning the baby only after he'd been unraveled, suctioned, cleaned, swaddled, deposited in an incubator and placed under warming lights, where Dad stood over him.

"How does he look?" Mom called from the bed.

Dad looked at the baby's long, skinny limbs, the imperious nose, and the purple face mashed into a Popeye grimace, and wondered how to break it gently to his wife.

"Hello, Celia," he said, referring to his aunt with the face of a sturgeon.

Mom, in a postpartum crying fit, begged him to switch Gabe for one of the other babies.

After a while, Gabe's chicken legs fattened up, a spring of brown curls bloomed on his head, and Mom fell in love with her little boy. Whereas I was temperamental and active as a windup toy, Gabe was a little Buddhist monk. Around his first birthday, my mother heard a strange banging coming from the nursery, interspersed with grunts of frustration. Running down the hall, she found me trying, with olympic effort, to pull him through the crib rungs by the straps of his overalls. My fierce yanks pulled Gabe tighter and tighter against the wood, but instead of crying, he smiled placidly, entertained by his big sister. Gabe's easiness naturally attracted people to him, and he was popular for the right reasons, always with a good word, even for people most had no time for. At the same time, he had a quiet drive that would compel him to pick up a banjo and, through sheer persistence, teach himself to play it.

My parents barely had time to register that they had two children before Mom was pregnant with the third. She decided that if it was a girl, they would name her Ariel, Noah if it was a boy. When the baby finally arrived, it was hard to tell what it was. There was the china doll face, the thick sweep of lashes, the rosebud lips, the strawberry-golden curls. From the neck up, there was no doubt it was a girl. But below the bellybutton, he was clearly a boy. "He was," Mom insists, "the most beautiful child I have ever seen." He was also a Mama's boy, attaching himself to my mother's side until she peeled him off for nursery school. His scientific brain, however, was entirely my father's, constantly running numbers and facts and writing code for kicks. From as young as ten, he was fluent in Dad's computer-geek language. Noah tried to dumb it all down for me once, when I asked him to tutor me in math for the GRE's.

"This is a triangle," he said, drawing one on a piece of paper. "But for you, we'll call it a 'funtangle.'"

It didn't get any more ironic: the woman who would never have children needed birth control. She got on the pill and nursed Noah like the milk was on sale. But even after Noah was well into his eighth month, she could barely keep herself awake. She started feeling strange, hazy, like she had a mild flu.

"It's not the flu," the doctor told her when she finally got herself to his office. "You're just five months pregnant."

Her first thought was to get an abortion. How could she possibly handle another baby? But, like her first pregnancy, this one had happened against incredible odds. And, like me, this baby was a girl. Mom knew it the second she learned she was pregnant. So she prayed for only one thing: that this baby and I look nothing alike.

When Mom was young, people would often compliment her good looks, to which my grandmother would reply, "You should see my other daughter." Comparison between Mom and her older sister, Esther, was almost inevitable, as their features were so similar. Esther was the petite, delicate version, often sickly and therefore, coddled. Mom was the galumphing giant, hitting 5'8 in the seventh grade, bigger in both body and personality and so expected to fend for herself. It would be better for everyone, Mom reasoned, if my sister and I shared no resemblance at all.

She got what she asked for. While I am black-haired, blue-eyed and olive-skinned, Dena has brown eyes, thick, chestnut ringlets, and the creamy complexion of an English heiress. I never grew past 5'4, while Dena stands a good head taller. If you saw the two of us together, you'd never know we were sisters. Actually, it's Dad she resembles the most. One year on Purim, the Jewish combination of Mardi Gras and Halloween, she taped on a beard of brown construction paper and donned Dad's signature polo, jeans and glasses. Though she was missing the rock-hard belly protruding over the belt, the likeness between the two of them was spooky.

From the beginning, Dena was averse to anything remotely feminine, wearing her hair in a short mushroom cut, affecting a stooped, tough-guy strut, and elbowing her way into my brothers' street hockey games instead of playing Barbies with me. Getting her to wear a dress required weeks of threats and high-stakes bribery; just two years ago, Mom had to special-order a pair of Converse to match Dena's dress for my wedding. As the baby, she was Dad's pet, going with him on special excursions that made me stew with jealousy. With five years between us, and complete opposites, Dena and I grated against each other until I left for college. Then I came home from winter break and discovered that there was no one in the world who could make me laugh like my sister. And while she had grown as tall as my mother, with the same strong build, there was no heart more gentle than hers.

So yes, the doctors may have told my parents that they'd never have children, but they were wrong. They had four of us in less than five years. The wolf pack, Mom likes to call us.

Our family history is full of medical miracles like these. My great-grandmother Anna left Yom Kippur services one year with stomach pains so intense she thought she had a tumor; a few hours later, she gave birth to my grandmother, Libby. Anna had been so preoccupied with her other eight children (and her alcoholic husband), she hadn't even noticed she was pregnant. My Uncle Charlie almost choked to death when he was seven, but he was saved at the last minute by an emergency tracheotomy performed on the dining room table. There are plenty of tragedies in there, too, like the consumptive aunt on my mother's side who threw herself into the Harrisburg River. And my grandmother, of course, who didn't live to see 40. But the happy endings are consistent enough to make me believe that luck is on our side, and that Mom's prognosis will somehow reverse itself.

It's hard to keep the fantasy going, though, when she insists she's going to die.

Gabe calls.

"I need to ask you a favor," he says, his voice grave. "You've got to try and keep a positive attitude around Mom."

I'm instantly defensive. "What do you mean?"

"I just think she has a better chance if she stays upbeat."

"A better chance of what?"

"You know..."

"She's dying, Gabe. I don't think my attitude is going to make a difference one way or the other."

His exasperated sigh swells in my ear. "I don't really know what's going on over there. I'm getting conflicting messages from her and Dad. Mom says she's got weeks. Dad says they're treating the infection so that they'll be able to do something for her later."

"That's sort of true. He's hopeful that things can still turn around."
"Do you think they will?"
"Honestly? I have no idea."
He says nothing.

"Listen," I say, trying to sound soothing, "I can be positive, but I can't decide for her. Even if they could do another round of treatment, which they can't, she doesn't think it's worth being sick all the time. It's a quality of life thing now."

I'm test-driving that expression, *quality of life*, which has popped up a few times since Mom got here. Before now, I'd only ever heard it used in reference to money, which, ideally, improves the way you live. But when you switch money out for death, the meaning changes entirely. "Quality of Life" is no longer about a timeshare in Miami, but how willing you are to stay alive. It suggests a bottom line, and we all have it, at which you are willing to go no lower. Like my friend Julie's father, who said, when he was diagnosed with early-onset Dementia, "The day you have to put me in Pampers, tell them I'm ready to pack it in."

"I know that," Gabe concedes, "but just...don't let her get too down."

He sounds so helpless, it makes me sad. "I'm scared too, you know."
"I was scared before, but now I'm really scared."

We both sit with that for a minute, then I ask, "When are you coming?"

"Not sure yet. We have a month before we move into the new place in Boston, but only two weeks to get out of this apartment. We have to pack up, then drive cross-country. The plan was to camp a little, but now it looks like we're heading to the Cape as quickly as we can."

"Do you think you'll make it for Passover?"
"No idea," he says. "I wouldn't count on us."

Late in the morning, Mom receives her first official visitors: our cousins Rhona and Bette, who climb onto Mom's bed to chat. Invigorated by guests, Mom entertains with jokes and stories, even mustering the energy for a catty remark or two. Watching her, you'd never believe she was dying.

"She looks great," Bette whispers to me as they leave. "She just needs to change her attitude."

Hearing her echo Gabe's words, doubt twinges in the back of my throat. Is it really a question of attitude? If it is, maybe the prognosis isn't as bad as Mom is making it out to be. My mother doesn't lie, exactly, but she has been known to add sparkle to the truth. To this day, she insists I was reading highway signs at 18 months old, while Dad assures me I was just chirping in my carseat.

I call Dad at work. "I need you to tell me what the doctor said. I've heard it from Mom. Now I want to hear it from you."

He lays out the conversation with the doctor, clearly and logically so that I understand. The biopsy came back positive for cancer, he says, but her system can't take any more chemo. The most important thing now is to fight the infection and keep her comfortable. As he speaks, I'm transported back to the night before my 9th-grade biology final, when Dad taught me the form and function of Mitochondria. Fifteen years later, it's one of the few things I remember from high school.

"So she's dying?"

"She's dying. Not right now, but she is. Our job is to make her as comfortable as we can."

Despite the heaviness those words carry, I'm relieved to hear something definite. "Okay."

"But, listen. They told Judy Rubin's husband he had six months on Hospice and he lived for two and a half years. The doctors don't know everything."

My relief dissolves. While I don't like the idea of Mom dying, I do like knowing what to expect. Dad's hopeful addendum just muddles everything, like water turned murky by a dirty paintbrush. It's a fitful, back-and-forth feeling, like unrequited love.

In the living room, I hear the floor creak under Mom's stocking feet. Slowly, she creeps into view, hunched over and cradling her arm. "That's it, you got it," she murmurs, cheerleading herself through the pain in her bones until she reaches her favorite overstuffed chair. Sinking down with a small moan, she shifts, inch by inch, until she's comfortable.

"Shhh..." she says to herself, like she's soothing a baby.

After dinner and bathtime, I bring Ezra to Mom's room for what has quickly become our nightly routine.

"Hi, Bubbles," I say, making the signs for "hi" and "grandmother."

Mom waves back to him, then signs "E" by curling her fingers into claws. "Hi, Ezra."

"Ezra, say, 'I love you.'"

Mom holds up her pinkie, pointer and thumb. "I love you."

"Night-night Bubbles. Give kisses..."

Ezra opens his mouth against Mom's cheek, and she closes her eyes like she's savoring a fine wine. "Night-night, my angel."

Ezra smiles at her.

"Beautiful child," says Mom, stroking his face.

"We'll see you tomorrow," I say, wondering how many more times that will be true.

Whenever I tell people my father has a plane, they get all excited. "Like a real plane?" they ask.

Yes, like a real plane, I say.

Then, every time, they ask: "Who flies it?"

"He does."

"What do you mean? Does he have a license?"

"Of course," I say, remembering the weekends he spent taking lessons. The day he passed his pilot test, Mom filled the living room with balloons. He walked in the door, smiling with his whole body, and Mom threw her arms around his neck and kissed him.

"Aren't you scared to fly with him?" some ask.

"Why would I be scared?"

"I don't know. He's not, you know, professional."

These are usually people who have never met my father. If they had, they would never say something like that. My father knows everything. He's a doctor, but not for sick people. I don't actually know what kind of doctor he is, but I do know that he went to college for 100 years and he used to fix submarines in the Navy. Not only can he fly a plane, but he could probably build one if you asked him to.

Dad's plane isn't like one of those jets you take to Disney World. It's a small double-engine with six seats, one for everyone in my family. The pilot and co-pilot sit in front, and the other four seats are huddled together in the back, two facing forward and two facing the tail. If it's not your turn up front with Dad, you want to sit facing forward, next to Mom, because her legs are long and there's not much room if you're stuck across from her. Sometimes we move our legs over so everyone can put their feet up on the seat across. We spread blankets over our laps to make a giant bed, like Charlie Bucket's grandparents, and then it's cozy.

When I sit up front with Dad, he lets me wear a pair of chunky green headphones like his. I can hear him talking to the man in the control tower: "This is 1127-Tango. How do you hear me?"

When you fly a plane, you have to know how to speak pilot language. It's like English, only you use words for letters so the people in the control tower don't get confused. Alpha for A, Golf for G, Tango for T. My name is Rodeo-Echo-Alpha. Dad taught me how to make the plane go up and down by using the steering wheel in front of my seat. I give a little push and the plane dips, making my stomach leap up to my throat. When I pull back on the wheel, we rise up again, and my stomach drops down to my knees.

Pilots also have to know what all the knobs, switches and dials on the control panel do. Sometimes I'll ask Dad about one of them, but as soon as he starts to answer, I wish I hadn't asked. My father doesn't give simple answers; he likes to explain how everything else works first. He thinks it's important that I get the whole picture, but it takes him a long time get there. Once I asked him about the wing panels that move up and down, and he started talking about wind trajectories. After a couple of minutes I realized I wasn't listening anymore; I was reciting "The Lorax" in my head.

The last time we flew together, I pointed to a thin, white button on the control panel. "What does that one do?"

"That's the ejector seat," Dad said. "Touch that and you'll fly right through the roof."

For the rest of the flight, I couldn't keep my eyes off that button. I itched to push it, just to see what would happen. But I was also terrified I might bump it by accident and shoot into the sky without a parachute. By the time we landed, I had flattened myself against the door, as far away from the button as I could get.

As Dad parked the plane, I said, "That's not really an ejector seat, is it?"

He grinned at me. "What do you think?"

Today it's Gabe's turn up front, so I push past Noah and Dena to get to the seat next to Mom. The inside of the plane smells like industrial-strength chemicals; Dad had to have everything cleaned after our last, windy flight, when Mom, Noah, Gabe and I threw up all over the back. They must use the same stuff at Daughters of Miriam, the old age home my class goes to visit once a month, because that place smells exactly the same. The last time we went, they had a Chanukah party in the cafeteria. There were streamers and balloons with gold Stars of David on them and it looked sort of nice, but every so often one of the balloons popped and scared everyone who could hear it. I sat with a woman named Ruth who grabbed my boob and held onto it like a leash. I wondered if I should ninja-chop her, but I felt bad because her hair was purple and she had to live in a nursing home and she kept calling me

Dora. So I didn't say anything. I just helped her put blue icing on the dreidel cookies with her free hand.

I have the biggest boobs in fifth grade. Mine aren't actual boobs, like the ones you get from puberty. The doctor said I'm nowhere near puberty. My boobs are just two extra fat rolls that grew over my belly. They bounce and jiggle like real ones, though, so I have to wear a bra, which cuts my back and belly fat into segments like an earthworm. I'm not excited about my bra the way those girls are in "Are You There, God? It's Me Margaret," who think that having boobs means you're all grown up and special. I don't feel special. I feel like a mistake.

I've tried losing weight so many times I've lost count. I've been on every diet there is: Weight Watchers, Diet Center, Jenny Craig, Optifast, NutriSystem, and a whole bunch of others I've made up. It starts like this: Mom and I join a diet program together because she always wants to lose weight and I can't drive. We walk into a big room at the Women's Club or the shopping plaza with the frozen yogurt place. The walls are painted bright pink and a smiley woman named Wendy or Patrice or Lisa is there to greet us. She's always wearing a pantsuit. She acts like she's known us forever and is always extra-nice to me because I'm young. She tells us about the program, which is the same as all the other ones: buy their food, eat it when you're supposed to and you will lose weight. If you drink lots of water and exercise, you'll lose more.

Then she makes me step on the scale.

This is the worst part, especially when the scale is in the middle of the room, in front of everyone. Whenever I let the woman weigh me for the for first time, her expression is always the same, the eyebrows lifting higher and higher as she slides the weight past the 100 mark, past 150, past 175. When she finally stops around 180, her eyebrows have disappeared into her hair. Then the woman catches herself, blinks a few times, and smiles at me, like it's so great that I'm eleven and weigh as much as a man.

"Don't worry, Sweetie," she says. Sometimes, she'll wink. "In a few months, it'll all be gone."

I usually say something like, "I hope so," because I do, even though she's wrong.

Then there's a big meeting where everyone listens to the lady talk about how she used to be "overweight" - no one ever uses the word "fat"; it's like saying "fart" - but she followed the program and now she's thin and her life is perfect. The women in the room get so excited, like they can't wait for their lives to be perfect, too. After her talk, the lady gives out pins to the people who have lost 10, 20, 30, or 40 pounds. Everyone claps as they charge up to the front of the room, smiling like Miss America.

Sometimes, I can stick with the program for a month or two. Once, I even lost twenty pounds - it was the only time I ever got a pin - but for that month, I was ready to tear my skin off. All I want, all I think about, is more food. Eventually, I break down and have a bite of something that's not on the diet, like ice cream or the crumbly Kiddush cookies at synagogue, and then it's all over. One bite becomes two, two becomes the whole box, and then I'm sneaking up and down the stairs all night again, taking food from the kitchen and hiding the wrappers behind my bed.

Other times, I can barely make it a few days. After my first visit to NutriSystem, I ate all the desserts we'd bought for the week in the car on the way home. Whether it takes a month or a day, I always end up fatter than I was before.

It might be easier if I was the only one who knew about this, but Mom goes on every diet with me. We tell each other what we eat, what we wanted to eat but didn't, and how much weight we lost. She usually does better than me - she can hold out longer - and when I fail, she's watching. Mom never says anything, but she doesn't have to. The sad looks she gives me when I take an extra slice of garlic bread say enough. As soon as I give up, she usually does, too.

The only thing I haven't tried is Fen-Phen, the pill Mom's doctor gave her that kills your appetite but gives you lots of energy. It's like magic. When Mom took it, she started running five miles every morning and zipping around the house like she was in fast-forward. She lost so much weight her eyes bugged out and you could see the bones in her chest. I begged her to let me take Fen-Phen, too, but the doctor said I had to be at least 16. I have never been more jealous of anyone, not even Dena when Dad took her alone to the fair at the Meadowlands, or the boys when they go with Dad to hockey practice. But then they found out that Fen-Phen makes holes in your heart and Mom stopped taking them.

I wouldn't have stopped.

Dad shuts the doors and turns on the engine. The plane starts humming underneath me. By the time we charge up the runway and into the sky and I swallow past the pop in my ears, I've forgotten the chemical smell. Outside, I watch the airport, the streets, the cars and the rooftops all turn into specks, then disappear. Dad pulls us into the clouds, which bat gently at the plane like a puppy with a ball. I am always surprised at how solid they feel; by the look of them you'd think they were as thin as smoke, something you could make disappear with a wave of your hand.

We fly most weekends, usually small trips to upstate New York or skiing at Camelback Mountain. Sometimes we take bigger trips, like when Dad flew us down to the Bahamas. We stayed on an island called Treasure Cay where there were no cars, only golf carts. Dad let me drive one, only me, since I'm the oldest. Every day, I drove into town with Gabe next to me and Noah and Dena in the back, feeling like a grown-up. We always stopped at Miss Clare's Bakery, a cement house painted the color of a flamingo. Miss Clare was a fat woman with shiny, black skin and colorful scarves wrapped around her head. She would wave to us from the door, her dress flowing out from her body like a tent, and smile, showing the gap between her two front teeth. It didn't matter that Miss Clare was fat; she looked like a beautiful, happy queen. She'd give each of us an apple turnover wrapped in wax paper, the crust flaky and buttery, and the filling like sweet gold.

After our drive, we would go to the beach behind our little house, just Gabe, Noah, Dena and me, and peer down at our feet through the clear, turquoise water. We spent hours on that beach, pretending we were abandoned children trying to survive in the wilderness, hiding behind trees so we wouldn't be discovered by poachers.

Today is a short trip: we're going to visit my grandparents in Pennsylvania. We don't go so often; whenever we do, Mom gets jumpy and snaps at everyone. When she was young, her father was the president of the University in their town and everyone knew them. All kinds of people would visit their house, and Mom had to get dressed up and be quiet.

"It was like being a Kennedy," she said.

That didn't sound like a good thing.

My grandparents are already at the airport when we land, standing on the tarmac where the other planes are parked. They hold their collars up against the cold, looking like one of those cartoon couples that are complete opposites. My grandfather, whom we call Zadie, is tall and thin, like a tinker-toy person in a houndstooth jacket. A paperboy cap covers his white hair, and his green eyes sparkle like Mom's. Bubie, my grandmother, reminds me of a mushroom, squat and round at the shoulders. She wears a green raincoat and a clear plastic hood that ties under her chin, like the ones from the beauty parlor. They're both smiling, but Bubie looks like she doesn't know why.

Dad ties the plane down, and we scramble out of our seats.

"Two hours, then we're out of here," Mom says.

As my feet hit the tarmac, the wind slaps me in the face. I burrow into my grandfather's jacket, less to hug him and more to protect myself from the cold. The wool itches and smells like something burnt. So there will be room for all of us, Bubie and Zadie have brought the matching Toyota Camrys Mom forced them to buy last year because she said they'd had their Cadillacs since Vietnam. Dad, Noah and Gabe go in Bubie's car. Dena and I fight over who gets to sit in Zadie's front seat.

"I WANT TO!" Dena screams in my face.

"It's illegal for you to sit up front," I tell her. "You could go to jail!"

Zadie looks at Mom like we're a couple of monkeys who have escaped our cages.

"Forget it," Mom says. "I'm sitting in front!"

She throws herself into the front seat and slams the door, hard. Dena and I crawl quietly into the back. We drive through Wilkes-Barre, Mom's hometown. It was once a busy place filled with coal-mining families, but now it's just a bunch of gray, empty buildings, rusty store signs and houses that look as old and tired as my grandparents.

Bubie and Zadie have lived in the same house for over forty years. Mom told me they bought it for $16,000, shaking her head in disbelief. I couldn't imagine a house costing that much money, especially one that's not so big and creaks a lot. The floors are thin like paper and you can always hear people moving around upstairs. The only fancy things are the windows, which have bowls of fruit cut into the glass that make prisms when it's sunny. The rest of house is dark and smells like boiled cabbage.

There is the attic, though, where Bubie keeps all of her old clothes and shoes and purses. The wood is moldy, but she has stuff up there from the '60s, a lot of it still with tags. Bubie doesn't buy things to use, just to have. And she doesn't throw anything away. All the extra closets and the basement are filled with stuff she won't get rid of: dishes, furniture, and broken appliances. Mom says she dreads when Bubie dies because it will take months to clean out all the junk she's kept for fifty years.

You'd think Bubie wouldn't mind sharing her stuff since she has so much of it, but she does mind. A lot. She locks away her silver and won't tell anyone where she keeps the key. It's because she grew up when everyone in the country was poor and starving. Bubie's father drove a delivery truck that got stuck in the ice and everyone had to get out and push. Her mother, Anna, made gin in the bathtub but people weren't allowed to have gin then so the police would raid their house all the time. Bubie was still a little girl and would hide under the stairs when the police came. Now she keeps everything because she's afraid someone might take it away.

Off to the right of my grandparents' cold stone entryway, a familiar, woody smell floats through the slightly open door to Zadie's office. I peek in at the high shelves that display his model train collection. Zadie has trains of all different sizes and colors, each one perfectly shiny, some with fake black coal on the back. He likes trains because his father carried bags for the Pennsylvania Railroad and brought him on rides as far as Chicago. Last year, Zadie took Gabe and I on a tour of the old mines, where trains were once loaded with coal and sent all over the country. He smiled like a kid the whole time. It was freezing down there, my nose dripped, and all I wanted was to go home. But Zadie went deeper and deeper into the mine, the darkness growing around his beige-coated body like he was walking into the belly of a giant whale. He used to take his trains down and let me play with them, but now he says they're too delicate.

I drop my coat with everyone else's on a green velvet bench by the door. Right away, Gabe and Noah start jumping on the couches. I follow Bubie into the kitchen, where she lights a fire under a big pot. Probably more cabbage.

"Bubie," I ask her. "Can I go up to the attic?"

She doesn't answer me.

I forget that if Bubie isn't looking at me, she doesn't know I'm talking to her. Before I was born, she had a stroke that made her almost completely deaf, and now she wears a hearing aid that works only if she's looking at me, and even then I have to talk loudly while she mouths the words along with me. Sometimes, Bubie's hearing aid will make a high-pitched shriek, like a dog whistle, that everyone but she can hear. When it happens in a room full of people, I'm embarrassed for her, but then I think it's okay since she doesn't know the difference. Mom says it's sad because Bubie used to have a beautiful voice, but now when she sings it sounds like she's crying.

I tap her on the shoulder. "Bubie?"

"Ehh?" She turns to look at me, her eyes on the same level as mine.

"Can I go up to the attic?"

She wrinkles her nose at me. Over her shoulder, in the living room, her and Zadie's wedding picture hangs over the fireplace. Bubie was a slim and pretty bride with big, round eyes. She told me once that she weighed 108 pounds that day, like it was the greatest thing she'd ever done. Fifty years later, Bubie's shoulders curl over her lumpy chest, her skin is spotted and her hair rises off her head in old-lady curls. She doesn't weigh 108 pounds anymore.

"UPSTAIRS," I say, pointing to the ceiling. "TO THE ATTIC."

She looks up, then back at me. "What are you going to do up there?"

"I don't know. Look at stuff."

Her eyebrows crawl toward each other like two caterpillars, but she doesn't say no.

That's good enough for me.

The stairs moan under my feet as I run up. I make a sharp right at the top into my Uncle Lewis's room with the Scottish plaid carpet, and throw open the door to the attic. I take these steps gently; they looks like they're about to collapse. Then I'm at the very top of the house, where it's dark and damp, with rotting wooden beams along the walls and roof. But all I see are the racks of colorful clothes and the piles and piles of shoeboxes.

I walk to the closest rack and reach for something purple and shiny: a blouse with creamy white buttons and a bow around the neck. The material is slippery and rises in a little bubble at the shoulders. I lay it next to a round wooden mirror to try on later. I find a long, pleated skirt the color of a Nilla Wafer that floats like a cloud, and place it on top of the purple shirt. Picking through the rest of the racks, I pull off skirts and sweaters and dresses of every color, all of it smelling like polyester and mold, but I don't care because they're beautiful. Sucking in my belly, I try each piece on, struggling to close the buttons and zippers. Sometimes I can do it, sometimes I can't. I pose in front of the mirror, pretending that everything makes me look like a movie star, even though I really look like a balloon about to pop.

When I'm done, I wander around, touching the sewing boxes and old dressers and needlepoint signs. "Love makes a house a home," one says, in the shape of a heart. I find a box with the word "Debbi" written on the bottom, and a pair of dirty white baby shoes inside. I can't imagine my mother, with her size-ten feet, wearing these teeny little shoes. But then I look at the scuffs on the sides and the worn bottoms, and I remember how Mom told me that when she was little, she would put on her shoes and her hat, walk to the door and say, "Out? Out?" She always wanted to go and do things, but Bubie never wanted to; she tried to keep Mom inside with her. Mom said that was why she left for college at seventeen and never came back.

A pattern of blue and green flowers catches my eye from the rack: a dress with long sleeves, a high neck and a chunky rhinestone pin on the waistband. I know this dress; I've seen it in pictures. It's the one Bubie wore to Mom's wedding. I lift the dress from the rack and bring it down to Uncle Lewis's room to try on at a better mirror, pulling up the zipper with my eyes squeezed shut. It goes as far as my back and no higher.

I face the mirror, hiding the half-open zipper from view. From the front, the dress gives me a waist, and the periwinkle flowers match my eyes. If you ignore the double chin and the outline of my belly, I could almost be pretty.

If I lost weight, I could wear this dress and be pretty.

I change back into my clothes and carry the dress downstairs, praying that I can convince Bubie to let me take it home. On the way to the kitchen, I weave past my brothers, jumping from the top of the stairwell to the bottom. They crash to the floor and laugh as the whole house shakes. Zadie grips the arms of his chair.

Bubie is still in the kitchen, looking at a yellowish poster on the wall with a long list of foods and their calories per serving. Flying above the list is a fat baby with wings and a halo, and red letters beside it say, "Be an Angel!"

She sees the dress in my arms, and her eyes go wide. "What's that?"

"I found it upstairs. Do you think I could bring it home?"

As I speak, Bubie mouths the words with me, telling herself what I said. But then she says, "What?" like she didn't hear me.

I know she did.

"CAN I BRING THIS HOME?" I say, pointing to the dress.

Bubie presses her lips together so hard they turn white, then shakes her head.

"Please?"

She shakes her head harder and says, "No", then walks back to the stove.

I follow her. "But it's just sitting up there. You haven't worn it in twenty years!"

"Why do you want it?" she asks.

"I want to wear it."

"What?"

"I WANT TO WEAR IT!" Yelling makes me feel angrier than I already am.

Bubie looks me up and down and points her ladle at my belly. "It'll never fit you."

She doesn't say it in a mean way; she says it like that's how it is: she's deaf, and I'm fat. But I still turn to water inside.

At least no one else heard her say it.

Then I see Mom charge through the doorway, staring laser beams at her mother. "How dare you say that to her?"

A ripe red anger sweeps through me. I hate Mom for hearing. I hate her for seeing. But I lower my eyes to my shoes, hoping I look sad so she'll feel sorry for me.

Breathing hard, Mom get right up close to Bubie's face. "She's eleven. She's eleven, Mother."

Bubie looks somewhere over Mom's shoulder. "What?"

"YOU HEARD ME!" Mom booms.

For a moment, the entire house, even the living room, is silent. Then Mom says, "If you have to say those things, say them to me. Don't say them to her."

My grandmother makes an odd "hmmm" sound, then turns back to the stove.

I walk out to the living room, still holding the dress, just as my grandfather grabs Noah by the collar and throws him down the stairs.

"We're leaving," Mom tells Dad. "NOW."

On the flight home I stare out the window, my anger growing so big, my body can't hold it. I'm not angry at Bubie - at least, not as angry as I am at me, for being fat, for not fitting in Bubie's dress, for not having any friends. But I'm most angry at Mom, because I can't hide any of it from her, and because she keeps trying to make it all better.

"She's not mean, she's just ignorant," Mom says. "She doesn't know she's hurting anyone."

"So? She still did." I stab her with my voice, trying to push out the anger before it chokes me, but it keeps getting bigger, especially when Mom looks at me like I'm the saddest story in the world.

"I wish I could make it better for you, Honey" she says.

"Well, you can't, so stop saying that."

Mom sees I'm trying to make her angry, so she starts humming to show I'm not getting to her.

"Look at this day," she says, peering out the window. "Not a cloud in the sky."

"Actually," I say, pointing out my side, "There's one right over there."

Mom slams her hand on the armrest. "Knock it off, Rea. I'm not your punching bag."

My anger is so big, I have to get it out. It doesn't matter how.

"You know what, Mom? You only had kids just to prove you could."

As I say the words, my mother flinches like I've thrown acid in her face. All the big anger rushes out of me, and for a few seconds, I'm empty and calm again. Then I see that Mom is crying.

I've never made my mother cry before. It's a dark, scary feeling, like I've discovered a secret power I don't know how to control.

For the rest of the trip home, Mom doesn't speak. She just looks out the window with tears running down her face. And all I can do is sit across from her and watch.

It's torture.

But it's what I deserve.

Chapter Five

The first knock comes at 9 am. It's the cleaning crew we hired to tackle a year's worth of dust and *chametz*, leavened foods that must be out of the house before Passover begins. Fifteen minutes later, we get an Edible Arrangement, our third this week. The phone has trilled six times already this morning, and the activity has Ezra glued to my hip. When the third knock comes, it's barely past ten, and I'm ready for bedtime.

At the door stands a woman no taller than five feet, round as an apple and draped in a leopard-print tunic. Costume jewelry adorns her neck and wrists, and her tiny feet shine in patent leather flats. The black bag slung over her shoulder bears the insignia of The Cape Cod Visiting Nurses' Association, and an official-looking clipboard rests against her pillowy bosom.

"Della Grasso," she says. "I'm the head nurse on your case."

Shaking her hand, I say, "I'm Rea. The daughter. This is Ezra." I tip the baby up on my hip, hoping he'll score me some points. On cue, he flashes Della his winningest grin.

The smile that breezes across her lips disappears so quickly, I wonder if I imagined it.

"Cute," she says, looking past me. "Is she awake?"

"Yeah, yeah." I step back to let her in. "Follow me."

I lead her into my parents' room, where Mom knits placidly on the bed, tree-trunk legs crossed at the ankles.

"Hey, Mama," I say. "Nurse is here."

Della wastes no time. After a quick introduction, she runs rapid-fire through Mom's treatment history, stopping only for clarification. Mom opens with one of her one-liners, but sees quickly that this woman is not open to being charmed. She downshifts to business mode, returning Della's quick questions with equally quick answers, until they fall into a rhythmic ping-pong. While there's none of the warm fuzziness I'd prefer in the people caring for my mother, I get the feeling that Della is the one to have around when things start getting interesting - which, I'm starting to see, they will very soon.

Della turns to me. "What were her last counts?"

I look dumbly at her. "I've been on Mom duty for, like, a day. My Dad would know."

Della writes something on the clipboard (probably, "Daughter: Useless") then looks back at Mom. "You having trouble in the shower?"

"Yeah. I'm having a hard time keeping myself standing."

"You are?" I exclaim, then look apologetically at Della. "She makes me stay outside the bathroom door."

Della is too busy writing to respond.

"I would have helped you..." I say to Mom, though we both know she never would have let me. My mother would rather swill tar than admit she can't do something herself.

"We can't risk you slipping," Della says, pulling a phone out of her pocket. "I'm calling for a shower seat and a wheelchair."

As Della places the order, I picture Mom slouched and pruney in the shower seat, and an inky black dread fills my chest. Hearing the request for a bedpan, it takes everything in me not to grab the phone from Della's hands.

"You don't need that," I murmur insistently to Mom, hoping she'll agree that Della is going overboard. But she just waves her knitting needles at me like it's no big deal. I stare at her like she's lost her mind.

Della whips out a blood pressure cuff and starts on Mom's vitals, then arranges her weekly meds in a box with rows of tiny compartments, like a mini-vending machine, but instead of cellophane sandwiches and off-tasting apple juice, each square holds an array of candy-colored pills: Augmentin, Lasix, Oxycontin, Levaquin, Ativan for when she freaks out about dying, Lyrica, Clindamycin. If she wanted to, my mother could sell her prescriptions on the black market and retire in Anguilla. As Della pops them into their places, she talks me through the chart where the dosages are listed, along with the times they need to be taken. The numbers lock in my brain.

"I got it, though I think Mom can handle this herself."

I see a flicker of something behind Della's officious gaze. "For now," she says.

The dread in my chest creeps up to my throat. Everything is suddenly too noisy: the baby fussing, the vacuum upstairs, Ben tapping at his computer right outside the door.

Della notices. "This house is busy."

"We're getting ready for Passover."

"When does that start?"

"Two weeks from today?" I look to Mom for confirmation. She nods. "Two weeks from today. My brothers and sister are all coming down."

"Something to look forward to," Della says.

Mom sighs. "We'll see if I make it that long."

I need to get out of the house.

As soon as Della leaves, I get Ez down for a nap and drive to the gym. I run hard, wondering how none of this seems to faze my mother. In fact, she seems relieved. I suppose I can't blame her, worn down as she is after a year of uncertainty, pain, fear, discomfort, and decline. If there's really no chance she'll get better, then having an end in sight, any end, would be a relief. And even if there is a chance, perhaps a person can only take so much before they give up.

But.

Give up? Really? Mom *can't* give up. That's not how the story is supposed to go. The hero always rallies at the last moment to vanquish the enemy. Giving up is French New Wave bullshit.

Since Mom first told me she was coming here, I've had a huge cry brewing that has yet to come to a boil. It ekes out in little spurts, like drops from a leaky faucet, starting at random then stopping abruptly. Small things set me off: the curve of notes in a song, the catch in a friend's voice, morning sun through the trees. I wander through the supermarket, wondering if the other shoppers can sense the sorrow coming off me like a stink. No one seems to. What would they do if I gave into a big, sloppy cry in the middle of frozen foods? Would they stare, or pretend it wasn't happening, fearful that I might be contagious?

When I get home, Mom's eyes are glassy and she's not quite lucid. Something isn't right.

Dammit. Why couldn't she short circuit when Della was here?

Ben and I watch her through the afternoon. Around 10 p.m., she spikes a fever and can't stand up.

"I don't care what you say, Ma," I say, pulling the thermometer from her mouth. "I'm taking you to the hospital."

She doesn't argue.

Ben and I line the dining chairs in a row so she can sit her way from her bedroom to the garage. It takes a while; every movement sends pain shooting through her bones. When she reaches the garage, Ben picks her up under the arms and guides her to the car. Mom grunts in discomfort as she drops into the seat, and I try to maneuver the belt around her without hitting her shoulder, where her pain is the worst. As we pull out of the driveway, my husband watches us from the garage, a silhouette framed by a block of light, small and solitary against the pitch-black sky.

I drive gingerly, easing into the turns instead of cornering the way I usually do. I force myself to focus on the immediate details: the bright orange light of the speedometer, the yellow lines on the road stretching into the darkness. Mom's shadowy form in the passenger seat. I recite each image in my head, like I'm narrating someone else's life.

A thought comes and goes in a second: *A car accident. I'd be fine, but she wouldn't make it. So quick, she wouldn't feel a thing...*

"Remember what's her name?" Mom asks.

"Who?"

She starts, as if jolted out of a dream. "What?"

"You just said, 'Remember what's her name?' Who were you talking about?"

"Oh. I don't know…"

We drive in silence for a minute.

"Remember what's her name?" Mom says again.

"Who, Mom?"

She looks hazily at me. "What?"

In our room at the ER, Mom lays on the gurney, floating in and out of coherence. One moment she's awake, alert, and the next she floats, twitching, into a drugged sleep. Sometimes her face crumples and her mouth falls into the open frown of a sad theater mask. It's like watching someone possessed.

During one of her lucid spells, the doctor strides in, blonde and rugged, his face creased and worn like an aging surfer. He leans in close to Mom and looks her in the eyes with a pure goodness that makes me want to hug him.

"I remember you," he says. "You were here Christmas Eve. How you doing, honey?"

"Not good," Mom replies hoarsely. "I've only got a few weeks left."

Her matter-of-factness breaks something in me. I start crying and can't stop. The doctor acts like my tears are nothing out of the ordinary, shaking my hand with both of his. He speaks reassuringly to us, explaining that the fever is probably from the infection in her chest. They're going to admit her, and give her a strong antibiotic drip overnight.

"Can I stay with her?" I ask the doctor.

"You're not staying," Mom says. "You have a baby at home."

I'm almost relieved to hear her argue with me. "I'm not leaving you here alone."

"Dad's coming back in the morning. He'll be here by the time I wake up."

"Then I'm staying until they admit you. I want to make sure your room is okay."

The nurse accesses her port, a tube in her chest that feeds the medication directly into her bloodstream. I reach for Mom's hand and talk to her about the old stores we used to shop at and lunches at Joe's Cafe. We would go there just for the bread, crusty on the outside and doughy on the inside, slathering it with butter and stuffing ourselves before the entrees arrived.

"Remember when I used to call you from the nurse's office? You knew I wasn't sick but you always came to get me."

She smiles. "I knew…"

"I think you just liked hanging out with me."

"I did…"

She fades away, then comes back.

"What do you want me to tell Ezra about you?" I ask.

"Tell him that I loved him more than anything in the world, no matter who he turns out to be. And that I'm sorry I didn't live long enough to walk with him in the tide pools." She begins to cry. "I would have loved to read to my grandchildren and play with toys and stuff. I would've really liked that."

To pass the time, I read aloud from a poster-sized list of languages for which the hospital offers interpreter services. Three of them I've never heard of before: Khmer, Urdu and Tagalog. I look them up on my phone.

"Listen to this, Ma. Tagalog is spoken in the Philippines. Khmer is spoken in Cambodia and Urdu is spoken in Pakistan, India and Fiji. But Fiji has its own Urdu Dialect."

But Mom has slipped away again, murmuring sleepily to herself. I sit by her bedside, watch the fluorescent light catch the yellow in her skin, and miss her. For a moment she wakes and reaches for me, running her hands along my face and hair. Her hands are large and warm and soft. I shut my eyes, wishing I could tattoo her touch on my skin. Then she fades again, and the moment is gone.

It's 1 a.m. when they are ready to admit Mom. I hold onto the gurney as we ride the elevator to the third floor, and all the way down the hall to Mom's room. It's the size of a shoebox. Mom is still wobbly; two nurses have to help her from the gurney to the bed. I run my hand along the sheets, the cotton rough and thin against my hand.

"Will these be warm enough?" I ask no one. "Will she be comfortable?"

The nurses ease her into the bed and she curls up, oblivious to the quality of the sheets. I tuck a blanket around her shoulders and give her a kiss.

"Sleep well. Pleasant Dreams," I whisper, the same goodnight words she said to me as a child. At the doorway, I look back, afraid that this will be the last time I see her.

One of the nurses walks out with me, a doe-eyed pixie around my age.

"You'll take good care of her?" I ask.

She puts a reassuring hand on my arm. "Like she was my own mother."

As I leave the bleach-white of the hospital, it takes a moment for my eyes to adjust to the crisp, still night. I locate my car less by sight than by memory, and drive the long, empty road toward home. Riding through the darkness, my heart vibrates insistently in my chest, its rhythm steady despite my shaking hands. While a disaster unfolds on the other side of my skin, this body continues to operate with astounding efficiency. The human survival instinct is a fascinating mechanism, enabling us to withstand all sorts of horrors and still keep going, like one of those inflatable clowns that pop back up, no matter how many times you punch it. Amid the brutal getting-through, the helplessness and terror as the bottom drops out, our hearts keep beating, our lungs keep breathing, one foot steps forward, then another. As my friend Jen says, "Things happen that you think you can't survive. Then you wake up the next morning, get dressed, and put on the coffee."

So that's what I do. I creep into the quiet house and check on husband and baby, both sleeping soundly. I text my father an update. I pull out chicken to defrost for dinner. I make a cup of tea, steam rising in wispy shadows as I climb the dim staircase. I sit in meditation and pray for help. And then, when my mind is calm again, I fall asleep.

Chapter Six

The antibiotics break Mom's fever, and by the time Dad arrives at the hospital in the early morning, she has energy enough to "noodge" him, as he describes it on the blog, about how to set up his blankets on the guest chair in her room, and even tries to get out of bed to do it for him. Dad brings her home in the afternoon, then spends half an hour calculating the optimal placement of pillows and blankets under her legs to help drain the edema.

"You hungry, Ma?" I ask. "I'll make you something."

"Nah, everything tastes like metal."

She looks exhausted, so I leave her to rest. Meanwhile, the house, which has seen only my tiny family for the past six months, begins to fill with people. Noah and Sammy come for the weekend, as do Dena and her boyfriend, Alex, hauling bags of clothes to feed the washing machine. And apparently, my grandfather, aunt, and uncle are arriving for a visit tomorrow morning. A stream of other visitors flows in and out: deliveries of flowers and food, Della, to hook more antibiotics up to Mom's IV, and Tess, our blazer-clad social worker, assigned by the VNA to prevent anyone from having a nervous breakdown. I'm tempted to tell her she might be too late. The phone hasn't stopped ringing, between check-ins with the nurses and doctors, well wishes from blog readers, and the inevitable telesales calls. Because all we really need right now is faster internet.

The noise and activity has Ezra all freaked out; he superglues himself to my hip, where he cowers until naptime. I'm right there with him, with bonus exhaustion from the late night at the hospital. Anxiety mounting, I brace myself against the kitchen counter.

Noah opens his cup of coffee over the sinks, preparing to pour it out.

"The left one," I say.

"What?"

"The left sink is dairy. The right one is for meat."

My brother stiffens: I have breached our family's unspoken code of diplomacy when it comes to all things religion. The topic is a loaded gun, which over the years has sent more than a few bullets whizzing through this house. Our family represents the wide spectrum of Jewish observance, from the strictly law-abiding right wing, to the "modern Orthodox," to the Conservative branch, to the unaffiliated. It is understood that no judgment, no attempts at coercion, and absolutely no pressure in either direction will be abided. Though strictly a practicality - Dad asked me to debrief everyone on the sinks - directing anyone with a different standard of kosher not to pour their milky coffee into the meat sink is also an imposition.

I don't have much time to dwell on it, though, with the kitchen in pre-Passover chaos. The cabinets, the pantry and the refrigerator hang open like gaping mouths, their contents spewed all over the room. Food that needs to be packed away covers the kitchen island, and a pyramid of pots and pans crowds the countertops. The magnitude of the task ahead looms over me like a monolith.

Making *Pesach*, Passover, is an olympic undertaking. Imagine spring cleaning your entire house, then shopping for and cooking the equivalent of six Thanksgivings. It's not difficult to see why, come April, Jewish women all over the world lose their minds. Before one egg is cracked, every corner of the house must be stripped of leavened substances, or *chametz*, which a Jew is not even allowed to *own* on

Passover. That means no bread, no pasta, no cookies, no crackers, no cereal - not even the rogue Cheerio your toddler tossed behind the dresser. For eight days, we eat flat crackers called *matzah*, the food our ancestors ate on their hasty retreat from Egypt, when their bread had no time to rise. Even foods that aren't leavened but have been used before Passover get the boot. That half-empty bottle of ketchup? Out. Those spices you used to make chicken soup last week? Sayonara. Even your kid's unfinished baby food is *verboten*. Refrigerators, freezers, pantries and cupboards are emptied, scrubbed clean, and re-stocked with kosher-for-Passover food. The pots, pans and utensils you cook with the rest of the year are packed away and replaced with new ones designated only for Passover use. Same goes for dishes, silverware, cups, and even hand towels.

Only once the kitchen is completely "turned over" can the cooking begin. This year, of course, has to be a "three-day *Yom Tov*," when the first and last two days of the holiday go right into Shabbos - three days in a row when the use of electricity is forbidden. While cooking is allowed on *Yom Tov* if there's a pre-existing flame and the oven is left on, it's too complicated when I'm trying to take care of Ezra and Mom. Which means I have to pre-cook enough food to fill eight bellies for three days. Twice.

So I'm a little on edge.

It doesn't help that Dad has been sulking since Mom's family said they were coming. He snarls at everyone all morning, then stalks out of the house, returning after a couple of hours with a slew of cheapie disposable paper goods and plasticware.

"What are those for?" I ask as he unloads them on the island, pushing cereal boxes over to make room. "We have *Pesach* dishes."

"We can use these for the seder. It'll be easier."

"But I just said this morning we should use the china."

He hears the annoyance in my voice and meets it with his own. "If you don't mind, I'd rather take those fifteen minutes of washing dishes and spend them with your mother."

He spins hard on his heel and walks out, ending the conversation.

"Is it such a big deal to use the plastic stuff?" Sammy asks, peering over the mess on the island with wide, crystalline eyes.

"No. But Mom's tables are always so perfect. With this stuff, I might as well serve dinner in a trough."

"It wasn't the plates that made it nice..." she says.

In my head, I finish her sentence: *It was her.*

My tension dissipates, and I'm suddenly really, really sad - precisely the feeling I've been trying to avoid by fixating on stupid details like plastic plates. I think that if I can perfectly recreate my mother's Passover, we can pretend things are how they've always been. But they aren't.

As a peace offering, I invite Dad to the beach with me to *tovel* our Passover pots, pans, and utensils, immersing them in a natural body of water to spiritually purify them before use. He agrees, loading the lot into two milk crates which he stacks on a handcart.

We walk side by side on the gravel path leading to the ocean, my short-legged steps quick to keep up with Dad's long ones.

"How long are you here now?" he asks.

"Five months. Ready to get rid of us?"

"No. It's obvious you were supposed to be here to take care of Mom."

That observation sounds like one my mother would make, and probably did, and it rang so true that Dad assumed it was his own.

We ease the cart down the steep wooden steps to the beach as the wind whips cold around us. The tide is heading out, and Dad has to wrestle the cart through the dense, wet sand, leaving two jagged tracks behind him.

At the water, we kick off our shoes and roll up our jeans to the knees.

"Look at these babies," he says, pointing to his pasty white legs, which are hardened with muscle from three decades of walking Manhattan. He bends his knee inward like a coquette. "Haven't seen the sun in months."

"Oh, please. They'll be tan again in ten minutes." My father's skin contains magical melanin that, within minutes of exposure to the sun, transforms him so completely that after three weeks at sea with the Navy, my mother walked right by him at the port. As a toddler, he lived in Alabama, where his father was stationed, and my grandmother was forced to sit at the back of the bus for holding a baby the driver assumed was black. One year, on Martin Luther King Jr. Day, I told that story to

83

my students, hoping to illustrate the absurdities of racial segregation. In response, one of my favorite students raised her hand.

"Hold up, Miz B," she said. "Your father is a black baby?"

It was an inspirational moment for everyone.

The ocean is so cold it bites my skin. I can stand it only for a few seconds before I run out, laughing, but Dad ploughs in without blinking. As he lugs one of the crates into the ocean, I yell the Hebrew blessing into the wind: *"Blessed are You, O God, King of the universe, who commanded us concerning the immersion of a vessel."* He dunks with efficiency, covering every piece completely with water, then looks back at me to make sure he's done it right. I give him a thumbs-up.

I could laugh aloud at the picture we must make, two wacky Orthodox Jews praying over their pots in the frigid Atlantic - and not even to clean them. To Dad, customs like this one are the practical application of methodical Torah study, the scientific exactness of *halacha*, Jewish law, that hooked him on Judaism in the first place. But my intention here is different. I want to access the spiritual music behind the laws, the deep wisdom that sits right with my soul, and to discover God behind the mask of the physical world. Some would argue that both approaches are vehicles to the same destination. I'm inclined to agree, but there's a reason that highways have more than one lane.

The truth is, I shouldn't be Orthodox. I resigned from the religion of my birth at 14, with no intention of ever uttering a Hebrew prayer or setting foot inside a synagogue again. A seeker by nature, I explored a long list of other religions, meanwhile ignoring my Judaism like it was the socially awkward kid I'd known since preschool who yelled my name across the cafeteria on the first day of ninth grade. But in my early twenties, to my horror, I began envisioning Shabbos dinners like those of my childhood, only with a family of my own. I would go to Barnes and Noble for a biography and find myself perusing a shelf of Jewish books. At the news of an Intifada in Jerusalem, I had the nonsensical urge to book a ticket and go there. Exasperated, I went to Yom Kippur services at the Harvard Hillel, where, at the pinnacle of *Neila*, the holiest moment of the year, I looked up at the ceiling and said, "Alright. *Fine.* If that's what You want, I'll do it. I'll become Orthodox. But You make it happen; I'm not doing anything."

Three weeks later, I met Ben.

Mom saw this coming long before I did, and at first, she was nervous. When I called her from Israel with plans to extend my three-week stay to a year, she trounced the idea in one whip-crack syllable: "*WHAT?!?*"

Looking back now, I should have called my father first.

"It's not forever, Ma," I said. "It's only a year."

"A lot can happen in a year, and you're in the middle of grad school. "

"So I'll take a break, finish when I come back."

"It's not a good idea. You have a path here. I don't think you should abandon it."

"Who's abandoning anything? I'm just taking a detour."

There was quiet on the other line. I could just imagine her in bed with a book on her lap and a pointer finger hooked over the bridge of her nose, trying not to panic.

"What would you do for a year?" she asked.

"There's a school here, for women. It's called a seminary. They teach you about Judaism."

"Is it Orthodox?"

I considered lying, then decided against it. "Yes."

"Charlie Rosen's son went to a school like that. They brainwashed him and now he's married with 18 kids and learning in some yeshiva in the West Bank."

"Maybe he wasn't brainwashed. Maybe he wanted to be Orthodox."

"Do you?"

I hesitated, not yet ready to acknowledge it out loud. "I don't know. Maybe."

"I think you need to come back and finish what you started."

"Is that really it," I said, "or are you afraid I'm going to flip out on you, like Dad?"

"Rea, you can wear a wig and have a million kids, for all I care, if that's what makes you happy. But come home first, then make your decision. I'll put you back on the plane myself, if it's what you really want. Just come home. *Please.*"

Neither of us could have known then that within a few years, she'd be the one dragging me to the most exclusive *sheitel macher* in Crown

Heights for a custom-cut wig. Time had softened her by then, as had the realization that the life I'd chosen for myself made no demands of her to change. At the time, though, I took her advice and came home, partly because she was right, and partly for the excuse to delay my jump into Judaism. I often think of what might have happened if I'd stayed. Maybe I'd be living in the Golan Heights with a gaggle of kids, a Torah-scribe husband, and a herd of goats in the backyard. It feels like unfinished business, despite my belief in a God that makes no mistakes. But if I hadn't come home, I never would have met Ben, or had Ezra, and I definitely would not be able to care for Mom the way I am now.

You were supposed to be here.

As we hauling the handcart back to the steps, Dad says, "Della thinks that August is pushing it."

I'm not sure if he's telling me or himself.

"But you never know," he continues. "Judy's husband was supposed to be in Hospice for six months and he ended up living for two years and six months."

This is the second time he's mentioned this. He must be working the numbers to slant the odds in Mom's favor, comparing data to buy her more time.

"I don't know, Dad," is all I can say.

We wheel the cart home and kick off our sandy shoes.

"Well done, Sir," I say with mock formality, offering him my hand to shake.

He kisses my cheek instead. "Well done, Beez."

I light up inside at the sound of my childhood nickname.

He must have forgiven me for the plates.

"Might want to rinse those off," Dad says, pointing to the pots with a half-smile. Then he leaves me to check on his wife.

In the morning, Mom's family arrives, chipper and laughing like they've just popped over for a Sunday barbecue. Zadie shuffles in behind his walker, much more befuddled since I saw him last. He tells me a story, then tells it fresh a few minutes later. Mom's brother, Lewis, saunters into the house, his six-foot-seven frame clad in starched Ralph Lauren, and talks up his new BMW 7 Series. To illustrate its speed, he brushes his palms together and shoots one of them forward. Noah smiles obligingly, then looks at his phone like he's willing it to ring. Lewis's two daughters ride my girls' bikes in the driveway while Lane, his wife, admires the hydrangeas. Aunt Esther, Mom's sister, bounces around with surprising energy for a woman who has lost both breasts, a uterus, and uses an ostomy bag. She's the vaudevillian version of my mother, speaking with the roller-coaster inflection that engages children, her face shifting from one exaggerated expression to another. By the time they leave, everyone is exhausted. Especially Mom.

"You need to cool it with the visits and the calls," Della says, adjusting her hibiscus-print blouse as she checks Mom's oxygen. "You have to be the gatekeeper, man the phones and decide if she's up for visitors."

"Look who's in charge now," I tease Mom, who is tucked into bed with the covers up to her chin, as I feed her a slice of Swiss cheese. "You know I love power trips."

Mom barely smiles. Her grumpy spirits match today's blustery weather. Breathing hurts, she says, in her chest and back. Every part of her body is tired.

"It makes me sad to see everyone," Mom says. "It was easier when it was just Dad and me. And my father looks old."

"It must be strange to see him as an old man."

"He was so handsome. And *stature*. He carried himself so beautifully."

"I'm glad I'm not going to see you get old. I want to remember you just as you are."

Her eyes suddenly lighten. "Me, too. And on your 56th birthday, you'll say, 'I'm a year older than she was.'"

I smile sadly at her. "I'll have a cupcake for you."

I smooth a wrinkle in the sheet and shift over for Della to line up the new round of meds.

"Time to flush your port," Della says, handing me a pair of purple surgical gloves. "Want to do it?"

I look at the gloves, then back at her. "I don't know. Do I?"

"It's easy. And you should know how."

With trepidation, I slide on the gloves and, following Della's instructions, unfasten the yellow clamps on the tube that connects

Mom's port to the bag of meds. After swabbing the hookup with alcohol, I screw on a syringe full of saline and push it through. Della directs me to draw back a little when it's empty to make sure there's blood flow, and I'm morbidly pleased when a cloud of blood swims back into the saline like a scarlet jellyfish. Drawing my mother's blood feels over-intimate, like when I saw her pee into a commode at the hospital. But it doesn't scare me like I thought it would. I'm surprisingly composed around the unlovelier aspects of caring for an adult human, an ability I didn't know I had until now.

Once the port is flushed, I unscrew the syringe and attach the meds. Done.

"That was way easier than I thought it was going to be," I say.

Della gives my shoulder a pat. "You're a natural."

I have a nightmare in which I'm chained to a hot kitchen and forced to cook meal after meal for ravenous company. Jolting awake, I realize it's not a nightmare; with Passover in less than 24 hours, the cooking marathon is real, and it starts right now.

I creep out of bed to the kitchen and leaf through Mom's cookbooks, studying her notes in the margins. The Roasted Herb Chicken is "Excellent!" and the Balsamic Tomato salad is "Quick and easy." Best to avoid the scallion soup, though, to which Mom says, "Yuck!" Small post-its with menus from holidays past peek out between the pages, and help me piece my own menu together. Mom's clean, familiar handwriting soothes and encourages, like breadcrumbs on the forest path. All I have to do is follow.

As my mother tells it, her cooking was once so dismal, she would burn water. I found this hard to believe as she whizzed about the kitchen making one of her expansive Shabbos dinners, throwing in this and that without a glance at a cookbook, bypassing the measuring cups for her own intuition.

"How do you *do* that?" I would ask.

She'd shrug casually and say, "It's easy."

When Mom baked challah, it was my job to "punch" the dough after it had risen, to release the excess air. It was a small but crucial job, and one I took seriously, powering my fist into the yeasty mound with a satisfying *thud*. After setting a traditional piece of dough aside for burning, Mom would split the rest into groups of four, roll the pieces into tubes, and weave them into perfect braids. With a beaten egg, she would paint the tops of each challah and sprinkle them with cinnamon-sugar before committing them to the oven. Within minutes, the smell of baking dough and hot cinnamon would mingle with the chicken soup bubbling on the stove. When Dad walked in the door late Friday afternoon, he would stop, close his eyes, and breathe in deeply.

"Ah," he'd say. "Smells like Shabbos."

It was like magic. And Mom had barely broken a sweat.

The one thing my mother did not do well in the kitchen was delegate. She had to do everything herself. On the few occasions she let me help, I struggled with a peeler or got delayed by a stubborn jar lid, and I would inevitably feel the pressure of Mom's hip easing me out of her workspace.

"Let me…" she would murmur.

For this reason, I found myself a single twenty-something with no clue how to cook. In fact, when it came to most things domestic, I considered myself a genetic misfire. Just turning on the oven was overwhelming, the code of "broil" and "convection bake" uncrackable. Whenever I used the stove, the smoke alarm provided dinner music. My lack of culinary skill became glaring when Ben and I got together, but we had enough Shabbos invitations that I could coast for a while on my challah-punching skills alone. Then an unexpected snowstorm kicked me into a crash course in cooking.

Ben and I had been invited out for dinner one Friday night, but a fluke blizzard pummelled Boston and our plans. From the first snowflake, I paced at my windows like a tigress, chewing on my nails and praying for a reversal that would let me use my "Get Out of the Kitchen Free" card. But three hours before sundown, the storm was still going strong, and I faced the harsh reality that I would have to make dinner myself.

I called my mother in a panic: "Tell me how to make chicken soup!"

She talked me through the ingredients: a chicken in eighths, carrots and parsnips, cut into chunks. Peel an onion and cut an "X" into the top. A generous amount of fresh dill, salt, and pepper to taste. Cover it all with water, bring it to a boil, and let it simmer for an hour and a half, at least. As I peeled and chopped and spiced, I felt calmed by the meditative rhythm of the knife as it struck the cutting board, the mix of aromas in my nose, and the weight of the vegetables as I scooped them into the pot. Soon enough, the smell of my mother's chicken soup filled my one-bedroom hovel.

Ben walked in right before sundown, brushed the snow off his jacket, and inhaled deeply. "Smells like Shabbos!"

Magic.

While not the most sophisticated meal, that Shabbos dinner marked an auspicious beginning in my cooking career. Since then, there have been hits and misses ("This soup tastes like burning"), but under Mom's tutelage, I've learned to cobble together a pretty decent meal. With time I've became more adventurous, and the anxious grip in my throat has given way to a sense of ease, even excitement, as I plan a menu. I've discovered that cooking, when not terrifying, can actually be fun.

I try to keep that in mind as I embark on a culinary epic that last for the next eleven hours. As the rising sun streams pink and gold through the windows, the house fills with the smell of frying onions, browning brisket and apples stewing in cinnamon. Ben and Ezra come down in pajamas and watch me, bug-eyed, as I zoom around the kitchen like Speedy Gonzales.

"How are you doing this?" Ben asks.

"Adrenaline," I reply over my shoulder as I spice a Vilna Tzimmes. "I'm sure I'll pass out at some point."

When Ezra goes down for a nap, Dad and Ben run to the store for last-minute ingredients. While they're gone, I man the phones and check on Mom intermittently. She's sleeping hard today. Then I run back to the kitchen to make sure the moussaka doesn't burn. Somewhere between the potato kugel and chicken soup I hear the front door open and assume the menfolk are back with the goods. I'm shocked when Gabe and Erin walk into the kitchen. I squeal with excitement, rushing around the island to hug them.

"I thought you weren't coming for seder!"

"We got bored," Gabe says. His eyes don't quite meet mine, and instantly, I know it wasn't boredom that rushed them up here, but the fear of losing time.

After a year without seeing him, I give my brother a good look up and down. "You look great!"

"So do you," he replies with amazement, surveying the activity in the kitchen: pans sizzling, pots boiling, trays of food cooling, and me at the center. My brother hasn't seen me since I became a mother, let alone one holding the reins of two households. Now he stares at me like an apparition.

Erin's tight hug is all affection, with a trace of her New England stiffness. Her hazel eyes shine above a smile that crinkles her freckled nose. I feel a swell of pleasure at seeing her, anticipating spot-on book recommendations and good conversation. In true Erin fashion, the first words out of her mouth, after complimenting my top, are "How can I help?"

I put her to work chopping vegetables for the soup while Gabe goes to see Mom. In moments I'm swept away in a frenzy of spicing, mixing, and pouring, blind to everything but what I have to accomplish.

Hours later, as I stuff the last of the labeled entrees into the fridge, Dad asks me to take a ride with him to grocery store.

I look into the packed refrigerator, then back at him.

"I just need to get out of the house," he says.

The hour is late, and the store is mostly empty, save the insomniacs and night-shifters. Dad wanders the aisles, asking if I need this or that, but we've already bought everything. We leave with a carton of milk and some bananas, more of a gesture than a necessity. On the way home we drive by the airport where Dad used to keep his plane. Through the holes in the wire fence, I watch the rows of lights along the runway, planted in the ground like electric flowers. I used to watch those lights shrink away as Dad pulled us up from the ground, and on return trips, wink in assurance that we were almost home.

Once, flying back from a weekend trip, I woke up to the sound of my mother sobbing.

"Please God," she said, "Please let him land us. Please get us home okay..."

The plane's electricity had gone out, cutting off Dad's radio contact and navigation system. Years later, my father would tell me that this was not a life-threatening emergency, more like an inconvenience slightly more alarming than a flat tire. The engine and landing gear were intact, and Dad's battery-operated radio kept him connected to air control. But my mother, knowing nothing of aeromechanics (or the backup radio), was certain we were all going to die.

My siblings slept peacefully as Mom wailed, begging God to save us. My mother's hysteria was jarring, but I watched it with atypical detachment, confident that Dad would figure it out. I stared out the window, waiting for the runway lights to appear, which they did soon enough, growing larger and larger and whooshing past us as Dad brought the plane gently down.

"Where do you think we should sit shiva?" Dad asks as the last of the lights fade from view. "Hypothetically, of course. We could do it here at the Cape, or at the cousins' in Lexington. Or we could go back to New York."

I think about it for a minute, then say, "I think we should stay here. Then we can all be together."

An hour before Passover begins, Mom comes into the kitchen to taste everything.

"You're messing up the food," I say, half-annoyed by the dents she's made in my perfect presentation, and half-pleased that she's up and out of bed.

Mom takes a spoonful of potato kugel and moans with pleasure. "I love this," she says with her mouth full.

"I'm going to take a shower, Ma. Don't eat everything while I'm gone."

As the sun sinks low behind the trees, I come back downstairs to find the table beautifully set. Gabe and Erin have unearthed some blue seashell placemats that perfectly compliment the turquoise plates. A bouquet of hydrangeas adorns the table in a pearly glass vase, courtesy of Erin's mother. Simple, relaxed, and welcoming, it lacks Mom's finesse, but with the golden light angling in through the windows, this seder table is nothing to sneeze at.

Everyone arrives and the seder begins. The old songs and Haggadah readings are more than familiar, but this year, every word is heavy with meaning. "*Mah Nishtana Halaila Hazeh?*" Dena, the youngest, sings.

What makes this night different from all other nights? Tonight, the question is rhetorical.

When we come to *Hallel*, a selection of psalms, we grow quiet in honor of Mom's passage, which she always reads aloud: *He makes the barren wife a glad mother of children.* There's a catch in her voice, but no tears. We make giant matzah sandwiches with lettuce and horseradish. Gabe piles on enough spicy stuff to make his eyes water.

Holy Moses, I think as my family digs into dinner. *I made a real seder.*

Mom tastes my Vilna Tzimmes, then turns to me. "Rea, you have exceeded any expectation I've ever had of you by 1000 percent."

Guess that makes two of us.

Elijah the Prophet freaks me out. They say that on Passover, he comes to every seder on the planet to drink a cup of wine poured especially for him, like Santa Claus, but with no presents. And unlike the cushiony, white-bearded grandpa they put on Coke cans at Christmastime, I picture Elijah as a combination of shtetl peddler and ninja, with a ragged coat hung with pots, birdcages, and rolling pins, and a samurai sword on his back. When I was five, I spent the entire seder under the dining room table, expecting Elijah to burst in, all smoke and hellfire, to chop our heads off. Now that I'm twelve, I don't really believe the story anymore, but my back still tingles whenever it's time to open the door for him. And I never, ever volunteer to do it.

But if he would appear anywhere, a Passover resort in Phoenix is as good a place as any. I mean, it is the desert, and there are a lot of Jews here, celebrating their freedom by eating all day. If Elijah came, he could kill 200 birds with one stone.

As far as I'm concerned, Arizona is the best place on earth. It's everything that gray New Jersey isn't: open space, flat-topped mountains shining red and purple, the days passing hot and bright and slow. I could see us living here, in a long ranch of smooth, white stone, with a couple of horses and a view of the mesas. Dad would teach high school math and come home before the sun goes down. Mom would paint. The four of us could run free outside, our feet dusty and our skins toasted to coconut. It'll never happen, though. As long as Dad works in New York, we're stuck with long, depressing winters, scratching ice off of the windshields with credit cards and waiting for Spring like a kid waits for their birthday. So a ten-day vacation will have to do. We've already gone to the artists' colony in Sedona, a Suns game, on a jeep tour of the red mesas, and seen the Grand Canyon. (It was nice enough, I guess. Big.) But I prefer staying put. I don't like being too far away from home base, even if it's a hotel room. I'm afraid of getting lost and having nothing to eat.

I don't like the kids' program at the hotel, either. They make us pray and listen to the same boring Torah stories I've already learned in school. I'm supposed to be on vacation, *far away from the stupid teachers who say that Hashem (God's Jewish name) punishes people for using electricity on Shabbos and eating* treif, *non-kosher food. We watch Urkel every Friday night, and our house never burned down. We eat cheeseburgers and clam chowder and no one got food poisoning. Last year, Mrs. Malachi told us that if a Jew walks into a church, he'll turn into a pillar of salt, like Lot's wife. Then I went to an acting class at St. Peter's in Livingston, one of the churchiest churches I've ever seen, with old stone, stained glass windows, and a red wooden door with a cross on it. As I walked in, I shut my eyes tight, waiting for God to turn me into salt.*

He didn't.

I was hoping for a break from all the Jewish stuff while we were away, but it's tough to do that on Passover - especially when Dad acts like there's nothing more important in life than having a Seder. He insists on reading the whole Haggadah out loud, including all the commentaries. Dad wasn't always like this. He used to play us ragtime music on the piano after Shabbos dinner while we danced on the couches, and drive us to synagogue on Saturday morning. My father grew up knowing almost nothing about Judaism, which was one of the things Mom liked best about him. She ditched the religion when she was six years old, and a crusty Sunday school teacher told her that "girls shouldn't ask so many questions." Sending us to the Jewish Day School five minutes from our house was their compromise, because Dad wanted us to learn what he didn't get to. Now we know most of the rules; we just don't follow them.

Except Dad, that is. All of sudden, he started going to Torah classes and hanging around the city with men in black hats. He wears a yarmulke all the time now and lugs around big, heavy books with Hebrew on the covers. Yesterday, I walked by one of the lectures and saw him in the back, the only one in jeans and a baseball cap in a room full of dark suits. He listened to the rabbi speaking with the same laser-beam attention he has when he's working and doesn't hear Mom when she talks to him.

"We were slaves to Pharaoh in Egypt," Dad reads aloud, "but God, our Lord, brought us out from there with a strong hand and an outstretched arm. If the Holy One, blessed be He, had not taken our ancestors out of Egypt, then we, our children, and our grandchildren, would still be enslaved to Pharaoh in Egypt."

Mom sighs loudly. "Can we move it? The kids are hungry."

I'm with her. We all know the story: The Jews were slaves in Egypt. It stunk. God commanded Moses to tell Pharaoh to free the slaves, but Pharaoh wouldn't listen. God sent ten plagues, and Pharaoh agreed to let the Jews go. They left Egypt so quickly, their bread had no time to rise and the dough cooked into flat crackers on their backs. Boom: matzah. Then Pharaoh changed his mind, gathered his army, and trapped the Jews at the shore of the Red Sea. Just when the Jews thought they were done for, God made a miracle and the sea split. The Jews walked through to freedom, and the water crashed down on the Egyptians and drowned them. Hooray. We win. Let's eat.

As Dad reads on, I shove a fork under my hat to scratch my head. The inside band itches like crazy from the heat, but I refuse to take my hat off. I don't want anyone to see my hair.

My haircut isn't my fault. I got it last summer at this program I went to at Wellesley College, where middle school kids take classes and travel around Boston. It was fun, except my room was on the top floor of a huge dormitory called Tower Court with no elevator and no air conditioning. At least once a day, I almost died. During the first session, a group of blonde, shiny girls from Iowa lived on my floor, and for some reason, they wanted me, the dark, fat Jewish girl, to hang out with them. My friends were obsessed with two things: Herbal Essences and boys. They had a gazillion boyfriends, picking up one and dropping another in less than a day. They would sigh over dreamy eyes and cute butts, while I quietly picked the strings off my cutoffs and tried not to eat them. I wasn't going to tell them that the most attention I'd ever gotten from a boy was when Tommy D'Amato yelled "FAT ASS!" while I was batting at a softball game, and my mother pulled mace out of her purse and bolted at him.

After weeks of listening to their dating dramas, I got tired of having nothing to add. So I said, "I have a boyfriend," and watched the girls go all atwitter.

"You DO?" asked Lisa, her blue eyes going round with surprise.

Megan leaned in closer. "What does he look like?"

"Blue eyes. Black hair. Tan. He's really cute."

"He sounds it," sighed Gina.

"I can't believe you didn't tell us you had a boyfriend!" Lisa pouted.

"We just started going out. He's been asking me for a while, but I didn't say yes until now."

"Why not?"

"A lot of girls like him, even some of my friends. I didn't want to make anyone jealous."

They actually believed me; I could see it in the way their eyes gleamed. If I didn't know better, I would have believed me, too. There are tricks to lying: look them in the eyes, use a couple of good details, and stick to the story, no matter how many times you tell it. I've gotten good at it, and now I lie more than I tell the truth. I'll even lie when the truth works better. Lying lets me be someone else and do things I'm too afraid to do as me. I like the thrill of getting away with it. One time, though, I told a lie that made Mom cry for a year. She thought something bad happened to me that didn't. I wanted to tell her it wasn't true, but by then she had told too many people and it was too late.

"What's his name?" said Gina, who had just dumped her last boyfriend for his identical twin brother.

"Andrew Medesta."

This wasn't technically a lie. Andrew Medesta is an actual person, and I've had a crush on him since I was eight years old. He's a year older than me and has silver-blue eyes. Whenever I see him at synagogue, my body turns into molten lava. I don't know much about him except that he's the youngest in his family, that his father is the candy man at our synagogue, and that his oldest brother died in a car accident. But how much more do I need to know? Someone as beautiful as Andrew Medesta must be a deep thinker, and he's probably sad because his brother died. He needs someone to love him so he can be happy again. It doesn't matter that we've exchanged maybe fifty words in the four years I've known him. Our connection is spiritual; words aren't necessary.

"He's really into music," I told my friends, because talking about it made it feel true. "Nirvana's his favorite."

"My mom doesn't let me listen to Nirvana," said Megan.

"Well, he's older. He's fourteen. And he goes to public school."

A shot of excitement rippled through them. I knew for a fact that all of them went to posh private schools, and anyone who goes to a posh private school thinks that public school kids are all drug dealers. Their eyes went dreamy as they imagined a tough guy with a cigarette dangling from his mouth, like Johnny Depp in "Cry Baby." They actually believed that someone like that would want me, which made me feel like a real person. But underneath, there was a dark feeling, like syrup so sweet it makes you nauseous.

After the first session, my friends went back to Iowa while I stayed on. In their place came a group of girls from Atlanta with deep chocolate skin they slathered with Shea butter. They danced to TLC and shouted a lot and had the coolest clothes I'd ever seen.

One night, their ringmaster, Dynasty, pointed at my purple Doc Martens and asked, "Those your boots?"

I looked down at my feet. "Uh...yeah?"

She jutted her head forward and back, like a rooster. "Those are niiiiice."

That was Dynasty's way of inviting me to join them, almost. I was allowed to sit a foot outside of their circle and speak only when spoken to. Like the rest of the group, I didn't even think to question her. Though she could have passed for a second-grader in her overalls and thick glasses that reduced her eyes to onyx beads, Dynasty was as vicious as a honey badger. One of the other girls told me that back in Atlanta, she'd almost gone to juvenile hall for scratching out another girl's eye. But she also had powerful charisma, and everyone, even the counselors, did whatever she said.

I studied Dynasty like a school subject, puzzled by how this tiny person, whose pinched expression made her face look like a raisin, could demand such respect. Even her lies were impressive; just by saying them, she made the most unbelievable things true. Like the afternoon she told us that her aunt was Whitney Houston's hairstylist: "Aunt Bess been doing Whitney Houston hair since they were both in choir together. Even did her hair for that movie she was in."

The other girls murmured their approval.

"Yo' aunt ain't no Whitney Houston hairstylist," said LeNay, right on cue, not because she didn't believe her, but because it was her job to give Dynasty a leg-up for the rest of her story.

"Mmm-hmm," Dynasty replied, satisfied. "Bessie taught me everything she knows. She says she gonna take me to Hollywood to be her assistant when camp is over."

"What about school?"

"Don't need school," said Dynasty, puffing out her concave chest. "I got talent."

"Dynasty Harold," said Yuki, "you full of shit." Yuki, whose father was black and mother was Japanese, was the only one not afraid to talk back to Dynasty. She had the eyes of a geisha, caramel skin, and could turn herself into a human pretzel by tucking her legs behind her head, the very position she was in just then. "You ain't going to no Hollywood. And you ain't no hairstylist, either. You had the same cornrows since first grade."

"This my look,*" Dynasty shot back, pointing at her medusa braids with pastel baby barrettes fastened to each end. "I'll show you I can do hair. I can do y'all hair better than Janessa at House of Curlz. I'll do it right now. Who wants?"*

All the girls' eyes looked elsewhere.

Dynasty stared them all down. "Ya'll afraid to look like an African queen?"

Until that moment, I had never thought about cutting my hair. The thick, black waves that flowed down my back were one of the few things about myself I actually liked. But for some reason, I raised my hand. Dynasty smiled, and the other girls turned around to stare at me in shock. LeNay shook her head ever so slightly, channeling me a message with her eyes:

Girl, you better run.

I still don't know why I volunteered my head as the stage for Dynasty's "talent". Maybe I wanted to be brave. Maybe I thought a new hairstyle would distract everyone from the rest of me. Maybe I hoped the drastic change would get me some attention. Or maybe I just liked the thrill of doing something risky and sudden; it made me feel like I was having a life, instead of watching life happen to everyone else. Whatever the reason, within two minutes I was standing in front of the bathroom mirror with Dynasty, who held a pair of heavy kitchen shears over my head (I have no idea where she got them). All of her friends, plus a few other curious girls from the floor, gathered around us.

"You'll see," Dynasty said as I heard the scrape of the metal blades opening. "You gonna look fly."

I watched numbly as my hair fell in long pieces at my feet. Dynasty chopped it almost completely, but left one long piece next to my face. It was a cool haircut, when it was wet. When it dried, my Jewish hair frizzed into mushroom with a limp little mudflap next to my cheekbone. I was too excited by the change to know if I actually liked it or not. I popped on a hat and strutted around campus, pulling it off like a magic trick to show the counselors my new 'do. Everyone's reaction was the same: surprise, then horror, then the fake smile the doctor gives you after he says he has to take the leg.

When my mother saw me two weeks later, she took me right to the salon for an emergency appointment. But all they could do was cut off the Snoopy ear and tell me to wait for it to grow out.

"You had to do this eight months before your bat-mitzvah?" said Mom.

All I could do was shrug. "Oops."

After that, I started wearing hats all the time, floppy ones with big flowers, like Blossom.

I packed every single one I have for our trip here, switching them up throughout the day after I sweat through the bands. Whenever I put one on, I think of Dynasty, pointing at her cornrows: "This my look. *"*

I put down the fork after a good, long scratch, and join my family in dipping our fingers in wine. We dot them ten times on our napkins, saying the name of each plague God sent to Egypt. When we're done, the napkins looks bruised.

Dad raises his glass. "He took us from slavery to freedom, from sorrow to joy, and from mourning to festivity, and from deep darkness to great light and from bondage to redemption. Let us therefore recite before Him Halleluyah, Praise God!" He looks at Mom. "You're up, Willie."

Mom smiles for the first time all night. This is her part of the Seder, which she reads every year because of the line at the end: "He restores the barren woman into a joyful mother of children." She looks at the four of us with her eyes all gooey.

Finally, it's time for dinner, which waiters bring in on big trays. I eat everything in each course, plus Dena's leftovers.

"Who wants to open the door for Eliyahu?" Dad asks.

Gabe leaps up from his chair. "Me!"

I barely notice everyone singing to welcome Elijah, focused as I am on scraping the last of the chocolate mousse from my plate. But when the song abruptly cuts off, I look up, and a shiver runs under my skin.

In the doorway stands a round man with a bushy gray beard, a silky black jacket and tzitzit strings hanging low from his hips. His black hat is askew, as if he's just blown in on the desert wind. As he waddles into the room, my mouth falls open.

Maybe there is a Jewish Santa Claus.

"Gut Yontif!" he says, in a voice that sounds like a giggle.

We all stare at him.

In high-pitched blend of Israeli, Yiddish, and Brooklyn accents, the man introduces himself as the hotel mashgiach, *who ensures that the kitchen is kosher. "I just wanted to make sure everything was good for you here."*

Dad clears his throat. "Everything is wonderful, thank you. We just thought you were...when we opened the door for Eliyahu Hanavi, you were standing there."

The man makes a strange, whispery sound, "Psshhh...", and looks up at the ceiling like Dad's words have fallen from heaven. Then he laughs in a twinkly sort of way.

"I'm no Eliyahu," he says. "Just Itzik."

So the long-dead prophet hasn't magically come back to life. But looking at Mom, you'd think this Itzik (Rabbi Itzik, he says) is some kind of demon. She eyes his black hat and jacket, straight out of the shtetl, with wariness. Dad, on the other hand, is starry-eyed, like he's meeting a celebrity. He chats away with Itzik for long minutes while Mom taps her fingers against the table.

Eventually, Itzik looks at his watch and says, "Oy! So late! I have to start my Seder now, before it's past midnight."

"By yourself?" says Dad.

Itzik shrugs.

"You shouldn't have a Seder alone. Come, join us."

"You're almost finished," Itzik says as Dad scrambles for a chair. "I have start the Seder from the beginning."

"So we'll start over again."

I look in horror at Mom, who coughs loudly and says, "The kids are tired, Willie."

Dad waves her off. "They can wait. Or they can go back to the room and sleep."

Dad ushers Itzik into a seat, flips his Haggadah back to the beginning, and the two of them start singing.

A wave of anger swells in my throat. We've already done all this! Why should we do it again just because there's a chasid in the house? And why is Dad more excited to be with a stranger than he is to be with us?

Dad and Itzik pour each other wine and tell stories for hours. Around the time they start dipping their fingers, I fall asleep across a row of chairs.

At three in the morning, Mom shakes me. "Wake up, Beez. We're going back to the room."

As we file out, Dad and Itzik's seder still going strong. The two of them sit catty-corner at the table, Itzik swaying back and forth with his eyes closed, like he's in some kind of trance. Dad's face is close to his Haggadah, knitted in concentration.

He doesn't look up to say goodnight.

New Jersey is just as gray as we left it, though the air is starting to smell of Spring. All my parents talk about is my bat-mitzvah, which is coming up fast. Dad taught me how to read from the Torah, to chant the Haftorah, and to lead the services. He sits with me in my room, looking over my shoulder as I sing the Hebrew words, repeating them over and over again until I hear the melody in my sleep. Mom makes a thousand phone calls, confirming menus with the caterers, the band, the DJ, and the hotel rooms for out-of-town guests. She sits up at night writing lists and drawing seating charts on graph paper. It's a lot of work, but Mom never seems to get tired. She's like a battery that feeds itself energy the longer it runs.

A few weeks before the big day, I come home from school to find Dad's car in the driveway. He's never home this early. Maybe someone died.

Mom stands at the kitchen island, stirring something in one of her metal bowls. Dad faces her on one of the stools, a half-dozen plastic containers open before him. The walrus-like body beside him is unmistakably Itzik's.

"Rea'le!" he cries, opening his arms for a hug.

I run to him. "Itzik! What are you doing here?"

"I came to see you."

"Dad brought him home," Mom says. Her spoon makes a harsh scratch-scratch sound against the bowl.

"Come, come," Itzik says, gesturing toward the island. "I brought treats from Brooklyn."

I peer over his shoulder at the containers, catching the scent of fried onions and something smoked. The only thing I recognize is the gray-brown of chopped liver, which I tried once and will never eat again. Itzik dips his white plastic knife into a golden goop that looks like raw honey.

"What's that?" I ask.

"Shmaltz!"

"Chicken Fat," Mom explains.

I wrinkle my nose.

"My Bubbe used to make it fresh," Itzik says. "It's all she cooked with."

"You're going to have a heart attack if you keep eating that stuff," Mom says, waving her spoon at him. She looks like she wouldn't mind that so much.

Itzik smiles, smears a glob of shmaltz on a cracker and pops it in his mouth.

It's strange to see Itzik in our kitchen, with his long, gray sidelocks and black hat, while the rest of us are in jeans and t-shirts. But he doesn't seem uncomfortable; he just eats his chicken fat with admirable gusto. I eat like that, too, but I don't have the guts to do it in front of other people.

"How is preparation for the bat-mitzvah?" he asks me.

"I need a little more practice, but I think I'm ready."

"She's going to be great," Dad says with a pride that makes me glow inside. "I wish you'd be able to hear her."

I turn to Itzik. "You're not coming?"

"Shabbos!" he sings out as explanation.

"Brooklyn's a long walk," Dad says.

"Our shul isn't Jewish enough anyway," adds Mom.

Itzik makes the same sound he did when we first met him, that "Pssshhhh...", only this time, it's like he's trying to blow Mom's words away.

"A Jew is a Jew," he says, looking straight at her.

Mom ignores him.

Itzik gives me a smile that's both cheerful and mischievous. "Don't worry, Rea'le. You'll see me at the party."

Dad looks at his watch. "We have to go."

"You're leaving?" I try not to sound disappointed.

"We have a wedding in Passaic."

"Whose?"

"Who was it again, Itzik?"

"My friend, his daughter," Itzik explains.

"Oh." I love weddings. I want to ask if I can come, too, but I don't.

Itzik gives my hand a squeeze and says, like he's reading my mind, "My daughter is getting married in June. You'll come to her wedding."

"Where is it?"

He laughs. "Where else? Boro Park."

I watch from the window as Dad pulls his motorcycle up the driveway to Itzik, who hitches himself over the backseat, his weight half-flattening the wheels. Dad hands him a helmet, revs the engine, and they zip off, Itzik's black coat tails fluttering behind him like wings.

"Why is Dad going to the wedding of someone he doesn't know?" I ask Mom.

She sighs. "Why your father does what he does is a mystery."

"When do you think he'll be home?"

"That," Mom says, "is the $64,000 question."

My bat mitzvah day finally arrives. In front of the whole congregation, my extended family, and friends, I recite the prayers Dad taught me and chant from the Torah. Starting out, I'm nervous, but it fades quickly. I like being up here with everyone's eyes on me. I smile at Dad and whisper, "This is fun!"

Before the big party on Sunday, Mom and I get our hair and makeup done. Dena can't because she has pink eye, which makes her look like one of those poor kids in Africa who blink flies. (Not that she'd let anyone near her with makeup; Mom had to promise her new rollerblades just so she'd wear a dress to my party.) All made up, we look at ourselves in the mirror. Mom stands like a queen in her sleeveless white gown, hair long and loose down her back.

My gown is white, too, with poofy sleeves and a big Cinderella skirt. The bodice and hem are embroidered with white willows that shimmer when I move. It's gorgeous.

I wish I could say the same for me. My mushroom hair, dough face and balloon body are even more obvious when I try to camouflage them with a beautiful dress. It reminds me of a woman I saw in the mall who used pancake makeup to cover her acne scars; the makeup caked along the creases and made the scars look worse. As I frown at my reflection, Mom pulls at my skirt, fluffs my sleeves and plays with the wisps of hair at my temples. She says over and over again that I look beautiful, forcing me to believe it.

"You love your dress?" she asks with pleading eyes, because all she wants is for me to be happy.

"I love my dress," I say, forcing myself not to cry.

At the party, the DJ has everyone form a long aisle and clap as I walk into the room. It's like a movie: the cheers, the music, everything for me. I'm the Velveteen Rabbit becoming real. But it ends quickly, the guests disperse to dance and eat, and I feel the hole inside me empty again.

My blonde friends from Iowa are gushing over my dress when Mom comes over. "The Medestas are here," she says. "They want to say hi to you."

"Like Aaaandrew Medesta?" squeals Megan. "Where is he?"

"Over there," Mom says, pointing to the sushi bar, where Andrew stands beside his parents, hands in the pockets of his gray suit. His cheekbones are visible from across the room.

"Ohmigosh, Rea, he looks just like you said!" Lisa cries. "You are so, so lucky!"

Mom's eyebrows go up.

I look at the floor.

As Mom leads me away, she leans in close. "What was that about?"

I consider lying, but it's pointless. She already knows. "I told them he was my boyfriend."

Mom's lips press together. "Well. That's a big one you got yourself into."

I say a quick hello to the Medestas, barely looking at Andrew before I slip away. Mom stays and talks with them, standing extra close, their eyes locked on hers like she's saying something important. Mr. Medesta looks over at Andrew, then turns back to Mom.

She's telling them.

The humiliation makes my palms tingle. I want to run across the room stab Mom with one of the centerpieces, but the blood would ruin my dress.

Now Andrew is walking toward me and my friends, and I feel my whole body go floaty, like I'm turning into vapor. I talk extra loudly with my friends, pretending not to see him until I feel his tap on my shoulder.

"Oh, hey, Andrew," I say, twisting my face into surprise.

"Hey," he says, looking shy and uncomfortable and perfect. "You want to dance with me?"

"Sure," I say, cool and casual. Because it's no big deal that the boy I love is asking me to dance. Because people ask me to dance all the time.

Andrew holds my waist with his arms extended, putting two feet of space between us. I rest my hands on his shoulders. We sway back and forth, saying nothing, while Whitney Houston sings "I Will Always Love You."

Maybe I should tell him I know her hairdresser's niece.

As we dance, I keep my eyes on the blur of people around us, watching them watch me dance with a boy. I try to pretend that this isn't just a favor, that this beautiful person I'm dancing with is really my boyfriend. But I know the truth: he would never have danced with me without Mom's help. That sweet-sick feeling comes over me again, like I've won the game by cheating.

As the last of the guests leave, a familiar figure waddles in from the lobby.

"Itzik! Dad, Itzik's here!"

"Must be on Brooklyn time," Mom mutters.

I run down the hall to greet him. He smiles, but when I open my arms for a hug, he steps back.

I search his face for a clue of what I've done wrong.

Then I realize: I'm a bat-mitzvah now, a woman according to Jewish law, which means Rabbi Itzik, who is not a blood relative, can't touch me.

I suddenly feel like a stranger in my own body. Although I carried the Torah around the synagogue, made a big speech in front of hundreds of people, and had a big party in a fancy dress, I didn't understand until this moment that my childhood was ending. All at once, I want to crawl into my mother's arms and dash from the hotel to discover the grown-up adventures that await me.

I stare at Itzik. Maybe he is Elijah the Prophet after all.

"Mazel Tov, Maideleh," he says with his Disney-elf grin.

I smile back at him. "Thanks, Itzik."

A month later, my parents and I drive into Brooklyn for the wedding of Itzik's daughter, Mishket. Boro Park is a strange place, with everything and everyone right on top of each other. There are stores with Hebrew painted on the windows, and lots of men who look like Itzik: sidelocks, yarmulkes, black jackets and short pants with white socks pulled to their knees. It's like we've entered a foreign country.

"Do I look okay?" Mom says, checking her lipstick in the mirror. She hasn't stopped talking since we left New Jersey.

"You look beautiful," Dad says.

"I mean, am I modest enough for this thing?"

"No one cares."

"My neckline is too low."

"I'm telling you no one cares. Itzik'll just be happy we're there."

Mom looks out the window at the crowded streets. "God, I haven't been to Boro Park in years. My uncle Meyer used to live here. He knew everyone. Walked the whole neighborhood every day 'til he was 92."

We pass a line of women pushing baby strollers, most of them wearing kerchiefs on their heads. A few wear those wigs they call sheitels.

Mom turns to Dad. "I'm not putting anything on my head."

"No one asked you to."

She sighs in frustration. I'm not sure what she wants to hear, but whatever it is, Dad's not saying it.

Mom looks at me through the mirror and says, "Look, Reez, I'll show you a trick." She gives a little tug on her hairline, moving her scalp forward. "See? It's a sheitel*!"*

I laugh.

We pull up to the wedding hall, where a team of valets stand in a row. I didn't think there would be valet parking; I expected a VFW with shag carpeting and herring on paper plates. But this place is nice. *There's rich red carpet in the foyer, gold-framed mirrors along each wall, and an actual coat check. Chassidim in long black coats and* shtreimels, *those round, furry hats, stream in with wives that twinkle with diamonds and could stop traffic in wigs more beautiful than most real hair I've ever seen.*

Mom, in the white suit she wore to my bat-mitzvah, grips my hand like she's using me as an anchor. As we move toward the main ballroom, she fidgets, tucking her hair back, smoothing her skirt, shifting her purse from shoulder to shoulder.

At least a thousand people fill the crystal-draped ballroom, right up to the gold wallpaper. I can barely see over the crowds, nor hear my father, who stands a foot away and points to the front of the room.

"The bride is up there!" he shouts. "We're supposed to say hello to her!"

He leads us through the sea of black hats and sweet-smelling wigs, the buzz of English and Yiddish thick around us. We stand out from this crowd, Mom with her hair long and loose, me with bare legs under my short chiffon skirt, and even Dad with his dark gray suit and tie. I wait for someone to kick us out, but no one seems to notice us. We join a long line that leads to the bride, snaking past a smorgasbord overflowing with food: pink roasts, miniature veal chops, franks in blankets, sliders, fries, and all kinds of fruits and desserts. I stack as much as I can on a Barbie-sized saucer, wondering who I have to kill for a dinner plate.

After about ten minutes we reach the bride, who sits in a white wicker chair surrounded by flowers. I gasp at the sight of her stunning face: sparkling blue eyes, high, rosy, cheeks, and creamy, luminescent skin. And her dress. *A simple cloud of white with long sleeves and a high neck, elegantly draped to make her look like a princess.*

"Mazel Tov, Mishket!" Dad says. "This is Debbi, my wife."

"Mazel Tov!" Mom echoes. "You look gorgeous."

Dad gestures to me. "This is my daughter, Rea."

I can't speak. She's too beautiful.

"Thank you for coming!" Mishket says, smiling into my eyes. "I'm so happy you're here. I know my father is, too."

Suddenly, shouts erupt from the entrance, and the band, which until now has been playing soft cocktail music, launches into a loud, upbeat number that gets everyone clapping. Mishket's bridal party flutters excitedly around her as the crowds part, making way for a cluster of men who jump and sing at the top of their lungs. Behind them enters a young man, blushing bright pink and smiling, Itzik on one side of him and another man, probably the groom's father, on the other. They lead him toward the bride, who has moved to the edge of her seat in anticipation.

It's too loud to ask my father what's going on, so I just watch the groom approach the bride as everyone claps around them. The two of them smile at each other. Itzik leaves the groom's side and places his hands on Mishket's head, blessing her the way my parents do us every Shabbos. The groom's father does the same but is careful not to touch her, keeping his hands an inch or two above the veil. Someone hands the groom what looks like a cream-colored napkin, with which he covers Mishket's face. Then the singing crowd swallows him up and dances him away.

The current of people turns for the doors.

"That's it?" I ask. "It's over?"

Dad laughs. "That was the Badeken. The groom hides the bride's face like Rebecca did before she met Isaac. He'll take it off during the chuppah ceremony."

"When's that?"

"Now."

Every wedding ceremony I've ever seen has taken place in a hall or synagogue, or under a tent outside. But Mishket gets married in the middle of the street under a portable chuppah, walking around her groom seven times while taxicabs and moving trucks wait with their motors rumbling. Though it's sunset, it's as hot as it was at noon today - and it's even worse with everyone pressed up close together. I shift from foot to foot as sweat drips down the backs of my thighs, scanning the crowd for Dad, who had disappeared on the men's side. I can barely see the chuppah over the rows of heads and shoulders, and the ceremony is drowned out by the two women next to me who swap kugel recipes and argue over where to find the best price for a whole chicken. Mom watches the bride the whole time, right up to the tinkle of breaking glass and booming "Mazel Tov!" that makes me jump.

"What are you thinking?" I ask her as the crowds start heading back in.

Mom shakes her head. "She's so young."

"So? You and Dad were both 20 when you got married."

"It's different," she says.

Back in the air conditioning, I can breathe again. Mom and I head straight for the bathroom to dab our faces with water, but five other women have lined up at the sinks with the same idea. They all look at us as we walk in. Mom tosses her hair and throws back her shoulders in a way that makes her look confident and comfortable. She leads me to an empty mirror and reaches into her purse.

"Want?" she says, holding out her tube of Tea Rose lipstick. I shake my head, wiping beads of sweat from my upper lip.

As Mom paints her lips and brushes her hair out with her fingers, the woman at the next sink steals looks at her. Mom pulls on the front of her suit jacket and gives the woman a half-smile.

"I'm sorry," the woman says, laughing nervously. "I just love your sheitel. *I've never seen one so natural-looking."*

Mom's gives her hairline a yank. "Thank you."

I bite my lip to keep from laughing.

Back in the ballroom, the party is wild. Everyone dances, the men on one side of the lattice mechitza *dividing the room, and the women on the other.*

"Good luck finding your father," Mom shouts over the music.

I peek through the partition at the sea of men in black suits dancing in concentric circles. Toward the middle, I see Dad, one of the few without a hat on his head, with his arms thrown around the shoulders of men next to him. His face is bright red and glistening with sweat, and he's dancing like he's forgotten everything in the world except the music and the hundreds of strangers around him.

I've never seen him so happy.

On the ride home, the wedding plays back in my head like a movie: the huge crowds, the angelic bride, the wild dancing and my father in the middle. I fall asleep to the echo of music, as the lights along the Lincoln Tunnel throw shadows across my face.

Chapter Seven

Dena arrives for the weekend with Alex, and Noah and Sammy appear just in time for dinner. After we eat, they, along with Gabe and Erin, slip on their jackets.

"Where you off to?" I ask.

"Getting a drink," Dena says. "You should come."

I look at the clock. It's barely past eight, but the thought of leaving the house makes me seize up tight. What if something happens?

"Go," Dad says from the dining room.

"What about Mom?"

"She's sleeping."

"What if Ezra wakes up? Ben's not back from New York until tomorrow."

"You think I've never taken care of a baby before? Go out."

Fighting a riptide of anxiety, I quickly change my clothes, swipe on lip gloss and slide into the back of Dena's car. We drive to an old Irish pub in Harwich, a fixture on the Cape where Erin used to work. On the small stage, a fat man strums a guitar and sings ballads in a rich baritone. He tips his hat to Erin as we head to our table.

Dena, Alex, Gabe and Erin order beers, while Noah, Sammy and I stick with water.

"You guys are so married," Gabe teases.

"Someone's gotta drive home," says Noah, mildly ruffled.

I don't say anything. They all know why I'm not drinking.

We chat about everything except Mom, trying to enjoy being out together in who knows how long. Sammy, Alex and Erin watch the four of us jam in our shorthand of movie quotes and inside jokes that no one but we can speak. After his third beer, Gabe beats me in a laughing contest with his signature move: crossing his eyes, which slightly bulge so he looks like a Muppet. I laugh hard, and it feels so good I almost cry.

I've missed my brother since he moved to California. Our paths have led us in starkly different directions, and yet, when we are together, it's easy for me to remember a time, long past, when Gabe was my center of gravity. One of the first dreams I remember is of he and I discovering we could fly, so long as as we stayed in our playroom with the door locked. No one else could join us, especially not the grown-ups; only we could float up like bubbles, eyes wide with delight, to flip and swim through the air like giggling fish. The dream stayed with me long after I woke, as did the sense that, without Gabe, I couldn't have done it.

This was probably true. In one of our old home videos, five-year-old Rea gingerly climbed up to the monkey bars at the top of our swing set, a perch I'd avoided until then because of my crippling fear of heights. Gabe had crawled across plenty of times, as had Noah, who was barely two. Shame and pride compelled me to finally try it myself. Grimacing as my knees hit the first rung, a reedy voice called from below, *"You can do it, Beezie!"*

It was Gabe.

I reached a shaky hand to the next rung, followed by a tentative knee. Another hand, then another knee. My progress was slow and halting, but Gabe cheered me on. *"You can do it, Beezie! You can do it!"*

In the middle of the monkey bars, I looked down and froze, petrified. Gabe's voice became even more insistent. *"You can do it, Beezie! I know you can do it!"*

I gathered my reserves and crawled the rest of the way across. As I reached the end, Gabe was wild with excitement. *"You did it, Beezie! I knew you could do it!"*

In pictures from those early days, we're always together: fresh from the bath in matching Winnie the Pooh pajamas, wet hair combed and shining; wearing Raggedy Ann and Andy costumes on Halloween; sharing a pair of headphones with a book-on-tape across our laps; laughing as a magician produces a bouquet of flowers from his top hat. Our world was small then. All we needed was each other.

Then we started school. From day one, I got the feeling there was an instruction manual for life that everyone else had read, while all I'd gotten was a wadded-up Bazooka wrapper. All I wanted was a sense of belonging, that ease and comfort that enveloped me at home. But my efforts at connection were clumsy; all my fancy parlor tricks fell flat.

One morning when I was in third grade, I was one of the first in my classroom. A few other kids were there, too, ones whose friendship I'd been trying to win since kindergarten. As usual, they ignored me as we unloaded our backpacks, chatting only with each other until there was a knock at the door. It was Gabe, holding a brown lunch bag in my direction.

"You forgot this on the bus," he said.

I felt the others looking at me, and their crumbs of attention, however paltry, flipped on a sinister switch. I wanted to keep them watching.

I strode over to Gabe and snatched the bag from him, the paper crackling sharply in my hands.

"O-*kay*," I said, louder than I needed to. "You can *go* now."

What are you doing? Gabe's eyes said.

With mine, I silently pleaded with him: *Please. Don't blow my cover.*

Then my brother gave me a look which, twenty years later, still breaks my heart. There was no anger, no hurt, just sadness. Sadness for me. He gave a little nod, and left.

I don't know what I expected to happen after that. There was the hope, of course, that my big show of toughness would earn me some points with my classmates, and possibly a parade around the classroom on their shoulders. But after a second or two, the other kids turned back to each other, back to acting like I didn't exist.

For weeks afterward, the acid taste of shame was in my mouth. I had long suspected that deep belowdecks, I was all darkness and ugliness and rot. And now I'd proved it: I was the kind of person who would throw her own brother under the bus in exchange for a scrap of attention - which in the end, I didn't even get. I withdrew from Gabe, unable to trust myself, like my mutant alter-ego could jump out at any moment and eat him alive.

Gabe, on the other hand, acted like nothing had happened. He still sat with me to watch Looney Tunes before bed, still asked me to jump with him on the trampoline. He didn't say a word about it to Mom, so I held the secret like a weighty stone in my stomach. One afternoon, riding in the car with Mom, the story burst out of me on a wave of tears.

"There's something wrong with me," I wailed. "I'm a bad, bad person."

"You're not bad," Mom said. "People hurt each other sometimes. Even the ones we love. It's what people do."

"But what if I...broke it?"

"You can't break family. They're family forever, no matter what happens."

I took comfort in that, despite my suspicion that I could hurt people badly enough to ruin them. But if what I'd done had hurt Gabe, I never knew, because he never mentioned it. Not once. Such was his way for the remaining years we lived under the same roof, watching me with an expression of helplessness as I spun more and more out of control. But Gabe never held it against me. He simply stood by, unsure of what to do but brave enough not to run. His presence was a dim glow from a far-off lighthouse, just as his cheers had been when I'd trembled on the monkey bars, dangerously high off the ground. Years later, before I left for a trip abroad, Gabe gave me a journal with a note written inside: *If you are ever homesick, I hope this will remind you that the family that loves you is proud of you and not far from you. We are just a quick, eleven-hour plane ride away.*

That was when I knew that Mom was right.

"I feel guilty leaving her," I say to Gabe now, breaking the evening's unspoken rule not to talk about our mother.

Gabe understands. "It's okay. She's asleep."

"You know what I mean."

"She doesn't want us to drop everything and crowd around her all day. She wants us to go on."

"If you figure out how to do that," I say, "let me know."

When we get home, everyone drops their keys on the kitchen island and collapses on the couch, except Sammy, who empties the dishwasher. Sammy is like Mom in her constant busyness, never quite sitting still. But where my mother is fueled by creative energy, Sammy needs activity to burn off steam. Movement is comfort and distraction, which is why her pleasure is running marathons.

When I first met Sammy, she struck me as an adult in a young woman's body, polished, organized, and tense. I assumed that, beyond my brother, we had little in common, she of the Ann Taylor and pearls, I of the hippie dresses and nose ring. She carries Purell in her purse, while I've been known to wipe my baby's nose with my sleeve. Then Noah told me about Sammy's mother, who was diagnosed with MS when Sammy was four and moved into a nursing home within a few years. Sammy had only a few brief years of childhood before her petite shoulders were saddled with adult responsibility. Her freshman year of college, she met Noah, who brought her home to meet my parents. At once, Mom took her on as a third daughter. Sammy dove into her affections, grateful to have a mother again. So we had that in common, too.

Mom was thrilled when Noah and Sammy got engaged, and bought herself a fabulous mother-of-the-groom gown (plus two backups). Six months later, she was on chemo, and the gown that had fit perfectly at the boutique now pushed painfully on the port in her chest. Unfortunately, Mom did not discover this until the day before the wedding. She was forced to make a last-minute switch, and needed a matching wrap to wear under the *chuppah*. Sammy, who was getting married in less than twenty-four hours, ran from store to store to find one for her. Now, I was a pretty relaxed bride, but I would never have had the wherewithal to go shopping for *someone else* the day before my wedding. But Sammy did, and from that day on I was humbled by my quick misjudgment of her, by how good of a person she'd proven to be, and how clearly she had needed what Mom had to offer.

Of course Sammy can't stop moving; she's losing a mother for the second time. In some ways, I feel worse for her than I do for the rest of us. I want to go over and hug her, to tell her it's okay, but I feel foolish. Instead, I watch her wipe down the countertops until they're shining.

So apparently the KGB has been stalking my mother for the last forty years.

"It started with Kathy Kabee," Mom explains. "She moved here from Russia when I was in fourth grade. My parents made me become friends with her. There were other things, too, but I can't say."

"We're taking her off the morphine," Dad says.

I had no idea that Hospice would look like this. When Dad told us that Mom was being "moved up" from palliative care, I pictured the soldier's hospital in *Gone with the Wind*: skeletal patients croaking for water, and nurses in origami hats shuffling from bed to bed with Dixie cups. But Hospice is not that much different than palliative care; you just get better drugs.

Dad is quick to point out, however, that receiving Hospice care makes no difference to Mom's life expectancy. "There's been no growth of the cancer cells in the past couple of weeks," he tells us at dinner, "and her infection seems to be improving. Hospice just gets her oxygen and meds without having to go to the hospital." He sounds like someone watching his house burn down, and noting that the ash will do wonders for the garden.

Not that Hospice has made much difference either way. Mom has settled into a strange plateau, neither improving nor deteriorating, and the waiting is starting to wear on all of us. Noah snaps at everyone. Gabe wanders from room to room, looking lost. Dad buries his head in work. Dena can barely stay in the house for more than a few hours. I pick at Ben like a scab, starting arguments as an energy release. But it's hardest for Mom, who's saying more and more that she just wants this to be over. She's tired of being sick.

"I wish things would get better or get worse," I tell Tess, our social worker, whose thick Texas accent and rotation of 90's blazers are oddly comforting. "Just *something*."

"Something will happen soon enough," she says. "I guarantee you that."

Pacing the little shul, I absently touch the colored spines of books and wipe dust off the shelves with my finger. "Ben left this morning. He went to New York to see the girls and his parents. I was supposed to go with him, but I changed my mind."

"Did you want to go?"

I shrug. "I felt like I should have, but I didn't want to leave Mom. Even if she sleeps the whole time, it's still time I can have with her."

"How did Ben feel about that?"

"He was fine with it. He even offered to take the baby with him."

"And?"

"I said no."

This is partially true. What actually happened was that I burst into tears at the thought of letting Ezra go. Even though it was only for a few days, I was convinced I'd never see him again.

"It's good that he went," I say. "One less person to need me."

"What about you? What do you need?"

I cross my arms in front of me in a protective shield. "I can't even think about what I need. I can't think past the next meal, the next phone call, the next round of meds..."

"It's a very specific time you're in," Tess says.

"Part of me wants it to be over, and part of me wants to stay in it forever."

Tess nods her understanding. "But the world keeps turning."

That expression makes me picture the globe as a giant steamroller, burying everything under a smooth cement finish. "It sucks. Shouldn't the world stop for a second, at least, when someone dies?"

"People die all the time. If we stopped for everyone, there'd be no time to live."

"What about when Princess Di was killed? The whole world shut down. Heath Ledger was all over the news after he OD'ed. Celebrities always get a big send-off. There are people rescuing women from the slave trade, midwives delivering babies in refugee camps. When they die, no one ever hears about it. My mother taught inner city kids; they're not going to put her on CNN."

"Does she have to be on CNN? You recognize her. Your family recognizes her. That's more than many people get."

"It's not just about being recognized," I say, "although that's part of it. It's like, what if time just sweeps forward and everyone forgets? It'll be like she was never here."

"As long as you remember her, she'll be here."

"But that's my point. One day, I'm going to die, too. So will Ezra, and so will his kids. Eventually, my mother won't exist in anyone's memory. None of us will." I grow heavy at the thought of it, the same heaviness I felt years ago, watching a sand sculpture contest in Ocean City. People with tool boxes and magnifying goggles arrived before sunrise to build elaborate castles with turrets, buttresses, arches and balustrades. Some of them had indoor lighting and moats, and one even had plastic sheets in the windows that made them look like stained glass. Each castle was a miracle. But as I watched the sculptors at work, the wonder I felt gave way to mourning: in only a few hours, the tide would come in, and everything they'd built would be gone.

"What does your faith have to say about that?" asks Tess.

I ponder that for a minute. "We believe that the good deeds we do while we're alive - they're called *mitzvot* - survive forever in some esoteric way. That's our legacy: bettering the world. And our children."

"Do you believe that?"

"Yes."

"Does it comfort you?"

"Not today."

Tess smiles kindly at me. "We all ask questions in times like these; there's a comfort in trying to puzzle out things that arc beyond our comprehension. But I promise you, even if you have the answers, it won't hurt any less. The distance between the head and the heart is too far."

Like a mist, the words of C.S. Lewis rise up in my thoughts. After the death of his wife, he said, "Talk to me about the truth of religion and I'll listen gladly. Talk to me about the duty of religion and I'll listen submissively. But don't come talking to me about the consolations of religion or I shall suspect you don't understand."

"Just be in the pain," says Tess. "Sit with it. Because the pain we feel is directly proportional to how much we love."

Ezra slithers around the floor while I make lunch, pushing himself up on his knees now and then to trick me into thinking he's about to crawl. Dad saunters in, whistling.

"Hey, Ezra," he says. "Want to come play with Zadie?"

Ez hides half of his face behind my leg.

"We're having lunch now," I say.

"I can feed him."

"Seriously?"

"Why not?"

I shrug. "Okay."

Dad pulls a stool beside Ezra's high chair and says, "What are we having, Ez?"

I read from the baby food jars. "Lentil Dinner and Peach Oatmeal Banana."

"Yum." Dad leans close to the baby and says in a stage whisper, "Maybe I'll give you some ice cream when the mama's not looking."

I leave them to it and bring Mom a plate of food she's not going to eat. In the background, Dad sings to Ezra, "A peanut butter sandwich made with jam…", spinning a Yiddish twist on the word "jam" that makes it sound like a Klezmer song.

Mom's ears perk up. "What's that?"

"It's Dad. He's singing to Ezra."

"He used to do that for all the babies." She starts singing, dreamy and hoarse. "*Hit the road, Jack, and don't you come back no more, no more, no more, no more...*"

"I guess the baby is working some kind of voodoo on him."

"God is prolonging the agony for a reason: Dad's getting to see there's more to life than work."

In the afternoon, we set Mom up in a lounge chair outside and sit on the grass around her, listening to the Beatles on Dena's iPod. Ezra plays at Mom's feet while she sways in time to the music, her gray face turned up to the sun. The circles around her eyes glow copper. She looks like a dying person now.

"Sgt. Pepper's was my favorite," she says. "I bought it when I was sixteen and listened to it over and over again. Then I went on this trip to

Provincetown and came home in a pair of bell-bottoms. My mother went crazy."

"Mom's such a hippie," Dena says, and we laugh, because our mother is hopelessly square. The big joke about all this is that she never touched cigarettes or drugs (at least, that's what she tells us). She ate well(ish). She exercised. But cancer got her anyway.

"Maybe we should get you a prescription for pot," Gabe suggests. "It might help with the nausea, get your appetite going. Maybe it'll chill you out."

"I could bake it into brownies for you," I offer, to a hearty thumbs-up from Dena.

"I asked the doctor about it," Dad says. "It won't help the way the other drugs do."

"Too bad. That would have been fun to watch."

A few hours later, Mom burns with a fever of 103. She's delirious, talking nonsense, fading in and out of lucidity.

"Ivanika Trump is carrying a baby for Aunt Suzie," she says. "She'll be by later to visit."

"You mean Ivanka Trump?" I ask her.

"No. It's Ivanika."

Dad and I exchange a glance.

"You want something to eat?" he says. "You haven't eaten in 24 hours, at least."

She shakes her head, half-dreaming.

"How about some water?"

"...Makes me sick..."

Out of nowhere, she bursts out with the Star Spangled Banner, hitting the last lines with gusto: "Oh say, does that Star Spangled Banner yet WAAAAAVE..."

Dad and I laugh, though underneath I feel dangerously close to sobbing.

When Della comes by, she takes one look at Mom and calls all of us into the kitchen. "She's started her decline. A decrease in appetite is one of the signs."

Finally, I think, with a relief that's so shameful, I want to hide my face. "So what are we talking here? Weeks? Months?"

"More like weeks," she replies. "I'd say less than a month."

Dena starts crying. Noah looks like he's just been slapped. I can't look at them, so I peer out the windows at the the grand old tree hugging the house, now just starting to bud.

Mom can't die now, when Spring is finally coming. And Summer. All she wanted was to walk with Ezra on the beach.

Della softly outlines what we can expect, and the steps we can take to make Mom more comfortable. As she speaks, I steal glances at Dad, whose eyes are slowly draining of hope.

"But the scans in her lungs say there hasn't been a change," he insists. "The fevers may not have to do with the cancer…We've changed her drugs so much, her body may just be going haywire…"

Dena and I meet eyes across the table: *He's not getting it.*

"She's dying," Della tells Dad, with a gentleness that cuts the poison of her words. "It's going to be hard, not just for her, but for you. Just like the dying have their process, so do the living."

Dad stares at her in stunned silence.

Della walks us through the box of emergency meds they've brought us, which include pills that are administered rectally. At the word "suppository", I see Noah bite back a smile and a horrible giggle swells in my throat. He catches my eye and we dissolve into hysterical laughter. Unable to stop, we stumble out of the kitchen and into the garage, shutting the door behind us.

"We are terrible people," I say, wiping my eyes.

"Dude," says Noah, "I am not sitting next to you at the funeral."

After Ezra's nap, I pack him up for storytime at Barnes and Noble.

"Can I come?" asks Erin.

Ez grins at her.

"Guess it's a date," I say.

Storytime turns out to be a dud. An elderly woman gives lukewarm reading of "The Little Engine that Could" that is barely audible over an orchestra of squirmy toddlers. When they disperse, I read Ezra the deceptively long "Green Eggs and Ham", which leaves my mouth dry. Erin takes the baby and shoos me off to wander the shelves alone. As always, I find myself in the Religion and Spirituality section, where I stumble across a familiar title: "The Jewish Way in Death and Mourning" by Maurice Lamm. I've seen it in more than one rabbi's office, but never, until now, had reason to read it.

I flip it open. *The study of mourning observances is not likely to be undertaken until it is absolutely necessary,* Lamm writes, *and when it is necessary, mourners will be in no mood to do so.*

I laugh darkly. *You're telling me.*

But the crisis will come, ready or not, Lamm continues ominously. *If thinking on the subject is to be deferred, if there is to be no education before the crisis, what chance is there that we shall know how to handle the crisis when it comes?*

If you ask me, there's no chance. I can learn the customs my religion would have me perform as a new mourner, but I don't think we can ever be fully prepared for a death. It's like trying to prepare for a car accident: you can watch the telephone pole come at you in slow motion, lock your muscles, and shut your eyes, but your body doesn't really know the shock it will endure until the moment of impact. And it may take years, long after the sirens fade and the road is cleared of glass and blood, before you realize just how hard you were hit. But I'd be lying if I said I wasn't trying to brace myself. Since our talk with Della, I've been composing Mom's eulogy in my head. I've chosen the outfit I'm going to wear to her funeral. I've even pictured the moment when I call out to tell her something and remember she's not there. Some instinct is pushing me to anticipate the loss, to lay track for a runaway train, so that maybe it will hurt less when it actually comes.

Defeated, I slide the book under my arm and head to the checkout.

Erin and I wander around the mall, poking through racks while Ezra plays with his feet in the stroller. We talk about clothes, books, California, and Mom. I'm refreshed by Erin's smart-funny company, realizing that this is the first time we've ever spent time together without Gabe. As the hours pass, the slightly awkward in-law dynamic relaxes into the first dance of friendship. A few times, she begins a thought, then abandons it, and I begin to suspect that there's something she wants to say to me.

Ez grunts hungrily, so we walk to the food court to feed him. He's taken with a brightly lit merry-go-round, watching it spin with fascination. As turns his head to follow it, his cheek collides with the spoon of baby food.

"Come on, Ez," I say, wiping a glob of plum off his face, "you're too young for ADD."

"He's doing really well, with everyone coming in and out," Erin says.

"Thank God. I was worried he was going to pick up on my stress."

"He's got it together," Erin says, squeezing his thigh. "I don't know about everyone else."

I raise my eyebrows in question.

"Gabe freaked out last night, crying. After what Della said...it's hard to cope with."

"What about you?"

Erin shifts in her seat. "I tend not to cope with things."

Just like that, her eyes well up and spill over. She brushes the tears away, shaking her head in apology.

"I need her," she says. "I know that's selfish…"

"It's not. We all need her."

As Erin gives into her tears, I reach my hand across the table for hers. Her eyes are down, though, and she doesn't see it. Quietly, I draw it back.

As Ezra gnaws on the rim of my empty coffee cup, a large family stops right by our table to survey the restaurants.

"Heah we ah at the food caught," says the beer-bellied patriarch in a Red Sox cap. "Go to town, kids!"

Erin and I smile in amusement. As the teenagers beeline for a nearby yogurt stand, the wife flips open her cell phone.

"We-ah at the mall," she says. "All of us. It's a family affair."

"That's right," I say to Ezra. "A family affair."

Everyone heads back into Boston for the week, Dena, Noah, and Sammy for school, Gabe and Erin to move into their new apartment.

Dad leaves for a twenty-four-hour run to New York. I'm on my own again with Ben, Mom, and Ezra.

Dad sends me an email about the custom of making a key-shaped Challah for the Shabbos after Passover, or baking a key inside a regular one, to open the heavenly gates of sustenance. I figure it can't hurt. As I slide a silver key into my challah dough, I picture it unlocking the door to a mystical future where reality is shaped to my desires: Ben and I have found a place to land, with a community of people around us we count as family. My parents, Gabe, Noah and Dena all live nearby. Dad has quit his job and is the favorite chemistry teacher at the local high school. And there's Mom, walking up the beach, holding hands with Ezra.

Mom's oxygenator kicks up with its low rumble. I creep into her room to watch her sleep. Her mouth hangs open, her lips dry and cracked, as a plastic tube feeds oxygen into her nostrils. For a long time I take in her strong nose, the olive planes of her face, her skin soft and supple as a sea sponge. Years ago, the aestheticians at Elizabeth Arden swooned over Mom's complexion. She scandalized them with her secret to ageless skin: Dial Soap.

The speed with which that memory bubbles up makes my eyes sting with tears. That story, like the thousands of others Mom has told me, are so familiar it's like I lived them myself. Her memories are intertwined with mine, who I've become shaped by who she's been.

Who will I be once she's gone?

I lay beside her in the bed. She stirs awake and moans softly in pain.

"This whole thing sucks," she whispers.

"Mommy, what happens when I have to make Passover again? Or when we move into a new house? How will I know what to do?"

Mom shakes her head in sympathy, but she can't speak anymore. The pain is too intense, just the slightest movement makes her wince.

In the middle of the night, I hear her calling for me. Her voice is not so loud, but my sniper hearing, honed by new motherhood, has primed me to wake at the slightest sign of trouble. I rush out of bed, heart pounding, and run to her.

She's scary-pale, and her forehead is burning.

"I don't feel well," she says.

Pushing off panic, I call my father, who should be on his way back up to the Cape.

"Hulluh...?" he says, voice is fuzzy.

"Mom has a fever. I don't know what to do."

He's instantly sharp. "I had to stop and rest for a few in Mystic. I'm coming now."

I hang up, unsure of what to do for Mom. "Water...Do you want water?"

She nods, and I rush to fill a cup with the coldest water the tap will give. I'm relieved when she takes big swallows of it, along with an Ativan to head off the anxiety. She sinks, worn, against the pillows.

"Do you want me to call the VNA?" I ask.

"I was going to an hour ago, but now I feel better."

"You've been up for an *hour*? Why didn't you call me?"

"I couldn't call out on my phone," she says, lifting her finger in the direction of her cell.

She's lying. She didn't call because she didn't want to bother me.

Once she's calm and drifting off, I slip back upstairs, desperate for sleep. But as I lay down, my mind starts racing: *What if the fever goes up? What if she dies on my watch?*

I come back and take her temperature again, just to be sure.

It's gone down.

Relieved, I kiss her hot, flushed cheek and go up to bed, lingering in the in-between place for the rest of the night, not awake but never fully asleep.

Mom and Dad both wake up later than usual; she's wrung out from the fever and he needs to sleep off two four-hour drives in one day. When I bring her breakfast, she lays flat on her back, too weak to sit up.

"Why am I still here?" she asks.

"I guess God isn't done with you yet."

She laughs bitterly through her nose. "I wish He would just leave me alone."

Then she turns her face away from me.

In the last few days, there have been several calls and emails from Mom's devoted readers regarding the blog. The hopeful tone of Dad's recent posts have been hinting at the chance that Mom could get better.

"But if she's doing okay," asks one friend, "why can't we visit her?"

I have to say something.

Dad sits at the dining room table, staring intently at his laptop, as I slide into the seat across from him.

"Dad?"

"Hmmm?"

"We need to talk about the blog."

He looks at me.

"People are getting the impression that Mom is doing better than she is. We need to tell them the truth."

Dad's chin drops a fraction of an inch. "I'm actually writing something a little more negative today."

I sit with him in silence as he taps out the rest of his post, and listen as he reads it aloud:

As we pass the door to Debbi's bedroom, we take note of her as we go by. Time was that she would hear a particular floor board creak just a bit, even from a gingerly placed footstep, and wake to see who was there. Now you can step on that floor board full-force and she does not stir. Often times, Debbi's bed, "Mom's bed," was the central meeting place for our family. Now it is quite quiet indeed. Life in the Cape house does go on around her but the heart of our family seems like it is slowly being tugged from our midst.

When he finishes, Dad stares at the computer screen, struck by the gravity of his words and what it means to send them out to the world. His eyes grow wet, and he rests his glasses on the tabletop, dropping his head in his hands. As Dad wipes the tears away with his thumbs, I come to his side and rub his back and shoulders.

I've never comforted my father before. It's a strange role to catch myself in, like the first time someone called me "Mrs.". It hurts to see him cry, but I'm grateful he's let me stay with him. To me, my father has only ever been remote and impenetrable, an emotional vault locked securely from everyone. For all the loneliness it caused, the distance let me liken him to a mythic hero, his mortal side too far away to see. But as he unravels in front of me, it feels like I'm meeting my real father for the first time, sad and scared and broken, just like the rest of us.

I like him better this way.

Chapter Eight

Just as the sun peeks over the sill of our bedroom window, Ezra starts yakking with the toy elephant in his crib. I doze beside Ben, snoring lightly next to me, until the inevitable groan of the crib frame as Ezra sits up. His familiar grunt informs me that he's awake, and I am officially on duty. With limbs stiff as steel rods, I peel myself from the bed and shamble over to his crib.

"Morning, Buddy," I croak. He smiles at me with his four pearly teeth, the blonde fuzz on his head glowing in the sunlight like a halo. "You're lucky you're gorgeous, kid. I wouldn't get out of bed for anyone else."

Ezra reaches his arms to me, and I carry him to the rocking chair for our morning nurse. As he latches, I close my eyes, anticipating the sweet hormone crescendo of my milk letting down. But it doesn't come. Ezra pulls happily from my breast, but doesn't swallow. Loosening his lips with my finger, I the nipple from his mouth and squeeze. Nothing.

I squeeze again, running my thumb down the flesh to coax out a drop or two. No luck.

I shouldn't be surprised. My breasts have gradually deflated over the past few weeks, the swell of hormones growing weaker and weaker each day. I told myself it was just a temporary dip, but deep down I knew that stress was killing my milk supply. Ezra latches again, but it's no use. I've gone dried up.

The highlight of my day for the past eight months has been my son nuzzling up to me in the silence of early morning like we were the only two people in the world. Now I feel like I've been robbed.

Ezra, thankfully, doesn't seem to notice. He simply unlatches, looks up at me and smiles again.

"Come on, Ez," I say, hitching him onto my hip. "Let's go make you a bottle."

Mid-morning, Dad marches into the kitchen and grabs his wallet and keys.

"Where you going?" I ask.

"We're going out."

I look at Ezra. "We, who?"

"Mom and me. We're going to Macy's."

"I'm sorry. What?"

"Mom wants new sheets. She asked me to take her to Macy's so she can pick out what she likes." He's buzzing with happy energy, like a kid about to go on a fishing trip.

"You know she can barely sit up, right?" I say, treading gently.

"That's why we're bringing the wheelchair." *Silly.*

His determined air renders any argument pointless. And when I see Mom smiling at him while he gathers the oxygen tank and morphine pack, it's clear that this trip out is as important to her well-being as any of her medications. But it still makes me nervous.

Dad rolls the wheelchair up to the bed and helps her into it. "Ready, Willie?"

"Let's go," she says.

And they're off, giggling like two teenagers.

A montage of everything that could possibly go wrong plays in my brain: the blood pressure drop in the middle of the linen section, the oxygen tank going bust. The phone rings, and I jump.

"It's Della. Is she awake? I want to come by."

"Umm...actually, she's out right now."

"She's out." Della says the words nice and slow, giving me plenty of time to feel like an idiot.

"Dad took her to Macy's," I say apologetically. It was supposed to be my job to keep things calm around here. "She wanted new sheets..."

Della laughs, loud and deep. "She went to Macy's!"

"Yeah," I say with a weak chuckle.

"You know, all the nurses are talking about your mother. When her name comes up at our meetings, they all shake their heads and say, 'She's still here?' That Debbi's a tough cookie."

"I know. Do you think she'll be okay?"

"Sure," says Della. "What's the worst that could happen?"

I pull open the pantry and cabinets, unsure of what I'm looking for but moving with purpose, like a puppet on strings. In a blink, there are mixing bowls, flour, eggs, sugar, oil and vanilla on the counter, and I'm mixing them together with absent skill. Apparently, I'm baking cookies, and now that I've started, I can't stop. I whip up batch after batch: chocolate chip, oatmeal raisin, peanut butter. They fill the kitchen counters as they cool on sheets of foil.

Erin, her eyes ringed with red, joins me at the counter.

"Can I help?" she asks, like she's begging for a life jacket, and I hand her a bowl of sugar cookie batter. Like a zen meditation, we mold kites and letters and monkeys, giving painstaking attention to the curve of an S, to the bow on a string, like the future balances on their perfect placement. As we work, I sneak looks at her, trying to read her thoughts. Erin has withdrawn into a pensive silence after two shut-door conversations with Mom in 24 hours. Years later, I will ask her what they were about, and she will say, "I can't talk about it," with a finality that walls off the question forever. Alex said the same thing to Dena when Mom called him in for a conversation of their own. I found my sister on the steps with her neck stretched toward Mom's bedroom, eyes narrowed like she was trying to see through the door.

"What are you doing?" I asked.

"Shhh…" Dena whispered. "Mom's talking to Alex."

"About what?"

"I have no idea. That's what I'm trying to hear."

We both listened for a minute, but Mom's room was quiet as a monastery.

"I was in there before," said Dena, "and she was rocking me, saying, 'My baby, my baby…' over and over, crying her eyes out. Then she asked me to get Alex, so I brought him in and waited to hear what she wanted. But she pointed to me and said, 'You. Out.'"

I chuckled. "What do you think she's saying?"

"I have no idea," my sister said, "but I'm going to find out."

As Erin and I seal the last batch of cookies into Tupperware, the Jeep pulls into the driveway.

I run out to help Mom from the car, gasping at the gunmetal gray of her skin. She wobbles against my arm and throws up on the front lawn. I glare at Dad, who smiles like everything is peachy.

"Are you okay, Ma?"

She hands me her bag. "800 thread count."

When Mom is settled back in bed, Della arrives with a playful smirk on her face. "How was your little outing?"

"I liked feeling the wind in my face," Mom says.

"She threw up on the lawn," I report.

Della shrugs. "So what? A trip out is worth a little vomit."

Della's forgiving attitude thins the anger some, but not completely. She looks Mom over, then herds us out for a report: "The morphine drip seems to be working for her; kept her in good enough shape for a trip." Della grins at Dad. "No major changes otherwise. She's hit another plateau."

Fury flares up in me all over again, so fierce I have to walk away from both of them. Though I'm glad Mom isn't declining so quickly, at this moment, I wish she would just hurry up and get it over with already. I'm tired of the waiting place. Everyone grates on me; an innocuous comment of my sister's makes me so livid I can't catch my breath; every word out of my husband's mouth is an invitation to attack him. Inquiries after Mom are incensing, because no one really wants to hear about her chemical cocktails or the fall she had in the bathroom, after which Dad had to pick her up, bare-assed, from the floor. They want my pat answer: "She's doing the best she can." I hate when people ask what they can do, because there's nothing, unless they know how to cure cancer. I'm done being gracious and positive; I want to hit something until it bleeds.

Then comes this humdinger of a phone call.

"How *is* she?" says one of Mom's old friends in a sympathetic drone.

"She's doing the best she can."

"Ugh, God, I feel so *guilty* I wasn't in touch with her more. It's so *terrible* that I missed out on all that time with her. Is there anything I can *do*?"

"Yup. You can screw off and take your guilty conscience with you."

Okay, I didn't actually say that, but Dear God, I was close.

Perhaps more than anyone, it's Mom who is pissing me off the most. As I make Shabbos dinner with Ezra on my hip, Dad and Dena suddenly burst in from outside and dash to Mom's room, tracking black mulch from the hydrangea beds.

I chase after them. "What's the matter?"

"She took herself to the bathroom and passed out," Dena calls over her shoulder. "I saw it through the window."

The two of them run into my parents' bathroom and reappear, moments later, holding up my mother.

"Dammit, Mom," I mutter as they help her into bed. "Is it so hard to ask for help?"

She's fine, not even a bruise, and wide awake now. She sits against the pillows, watching me vacuum up the mulch as my mood darkens by the second.

"I'm sorry I can't help you," she says, over and over.

After the fifth time, I hold my palms up like a traffic cop. "Stop saying you're sorry, okay? It only makes it worse."

"Rea, why don't you take a nap?"

She knows me way too well.

I walk to her bed in defeat and rest my face on her belly. Her hands weave into my hair.

"I can't," I say, my voice muffled by her shirt. "There's too much to do. I have to finish cooking. Shabbos is in an hour..."

"God, I know how you feel. Can't someone else do it?"

"Who? Dena and Dad are doing the mulch. Ben's getting your prescription. I'm the only one left."

"Someone always comes through in the end. You'll see."

As the sun begins to set, Noah and Sammy magically appear and take over the last-minute details. I guess Mom was right. But my frustration hasn't abated, so I throw it at Ben, who comes downstairs to ask if I need help.

Lifting Ezra from his high chair, I stare daggers at my husband. "Nice of you to ask now, twenty minutes before Shabbos."

"At least I asked," he snaps.

Sammy and Noah silently put the salad together, looking everywhere but at us. Ben takes the baby from me and stalks out of the room.

Great.

I steal ten minutes for a shower. Turning the water as hot as I can stand, I let it pound against my shoulders, which drop in exhaustion. These past few weeks have pushed the outer limits of my strength and sanity like a marathon run entirely uphill, with no plateaus to catch my breath. And the worst part: it's only going to get harder from here.

My bedroom door is locked. It's never locked.

"Can you let me in, please?"

Ben's muted grumbling grows louder as he nears the door. He pops it open, then turns his back to me. As I get dressed, the room is thick with silence.

"There's something bothering me," he says. "Should we talk about it now or later?"

"Tell me now."

"You just treated me like an idiot in front of your brother. You made it sound like I don't help at all. I just got Mom's prescription. I take care of the baby. I'm there for you whenever you need me."

I know he's right, and the guilt makes my back seize up. Ben has been more than available through all this, firm and steady for both me and Dena, who leans on him when Alex isn't here. While I pinball between Ezra, Mom, and the phone, he has never once complained about feeling neglected. The night he arrived home from his week away, we had barely kissed hello when Mom called to me with a fever.

"Go," he said without hesitation, and came down a few minutes later to help.

I push the words I don't want to say through the thin passageway of my throat: "I'm sorry."

Ben doesn't answer. He's still angry at me, but I have no time to wheedle him out of it; I have to light Shabbos candles before sundown.

My dreams replay a recent conversation I had with Mom.

I always felt like a spectator watching my own life, she says in a faraway voice. *Then, one day, I caught Daddy looking at me, smiling, and I thought to myself, "This is probably how he'll want to remember me." It was like the first time I knew I was really alive. Two weeks later, I got diagnosed.*

I've had that "bystander" feeling before, surrounded by strangers at a party, walking through an airport terminal, staring out a bus window at the barren, pink landscape of New Mexico. The moment always seemed a prelude to the "real life" waiting somewhere beyond. But Mom's declaration jolts me into consciousness, a final puzzle piece clicking in: There is nothing to wait for. This is it.

I'll tell you something, I say. *I always knew I would never see you get old.*

When I wake, my limbs are dense and heavy, and there's a fog behind my eyes I can't clear. Ben takes Ezra, and sleep pulls me back down. I'm aware that my entire family is downstairs, that my mother is dying slowly in her bedroom, but I am an island floating far away. It takes two hours for me to find the energy to join them, and to bear the weight of my son in my arms.

All of Mom's belongings are tagged now, so we know who gets what. Her iphone goes to Noah, because he's the only one who doesn't have one yet. Of course, his first download is an app that makes the phone fart when you touch the screen. He lays beside Mom all morning, farting his phone at her. Sammy and Erin coo to Ezra, who bats his eyelashes at them like a professional flirt. Erin bounces him on her knees, and he squeals with joy.

Dena adores Ezra, but she's been avoiding him because he keeps throwing up on her. This weekend alone, he's sent her twice to the shower.

"Does he only do this to me?" she asked, incredulous, when he projectile vomited on her shirt.

I smiled sweetly at her. "You inspire him."

She plops down on the couch next to Erin and pulls the baby into her lap.

"What's up, Ez?" she says.

He squawks back his greeting, mouth open wide, and pukes all over her jeans.

"Dude!" she says. "I just washed these!"

After changing upstairs, Dena comes back in her pajamas, dragging a full laundry basket. She gives Ezra a fake scowl as she passes by his exersaucer. He burps at her, and a tiny drop of vomit dribbles down his chin.

Mom has been delirious all day, carrying on conversations with people only she can see. She reaches out and twists her wrist like she's plucking an apple from a tree, then brings her hand to her mouth and bites. Later, she places something invisible in Noah's hand. He looks at his empty palm, then at Gabe.

"Throw it away," Gabe says.

Noah shrugs and tips his hand over the garbage can.

"It could be the drugs," Della says, referring to the Scopolamine patches we're trying for nausea. "We'll cut everything except the morphine and the Haldol. In twelve hours, we should see a difference. If we don't, this may be how she stays."

"How long can she go on like this?" asks Dad.

"A human body can go without food and water for ten days. If she doesn't improve, she may only have a couple of weeks left."

Mom sits up with her eyes closed. "Kathleen and Joann are much more creative with the lesson plans. None of that garbage shit…"

Despite ourselves, Dad and I chuckle as a breeze sweeps in from outside, carrying in the first warm day of the year.

"If this is it, I want her to go this way," I tell Sammy, who comes to sit with me on Mom's bed. "She's not in pain. She doesn't even know where she is. Is that bad?"

"I know what you mean," Sammy says. "Every time I get a call that my mom's in the hospital I think to myself, 'I hope this is it.' Then it isn't and I'm sad that it isn't and then I feel guilty."

Mom can't stand by herself; it takes three people to get her to the bathroom and back. I run upstairs to grab waterproof mattress pads, which I remember, coming back down, that Mom bought for Ezra. The cruelty of it stops me in the middle stairwell.

In an alternate world where all is fair, Mom would be on the beach right now, walking up the sand in her bathing suit, leading with her hips, her feet turned slightly outward, dragging a beach chair and a book. At the perfect spot, she'd settle into her seat with a low groan, tip her face to the sun, and sigh.

"It's a mechaya," she'd say.

This gives me life.

But Mom is not on the beach. She's floating elsewhere as her body betrays her, life bleeding from her with each passing second.

She will never see the ocean again.

I don't even know that I'm crying until I feel Ben on the step behind me, gathering me into his arms.

After dinner and bath time, I carry the baby into Mom's room for our good-night routine. Through the windows, clouds of mauve float through a lavender sky. Mom lays on the bed with her eyes closed, whispering to herself. As soon as he sees her, Ezra starts jabbering. Her eyes pop open, and she looks right at him.

"Hi, beautiful," she says.

Then her eyes sink closed and she drifts away.

When Mom finally comes to, she looks around like a wide-eyed little girl. She eventually has the energy to sit up in bed and chat with us, and send Dad to Captain Frosty's to fetch her some ice cream and french fries. The request is hardly out of her mouth before Dad runs out, leaving a silhouette of smoke in the shape of his body. Looks like it was the drugs after all.

But when Della comes by to check on Mom, she sits Dad and I down in the living room. "It's starting to get close. She has that look."

Della gives us a small, cream-colored pamphlet: *The Journey's End*, which highlights signs to look for as death approaches. "We give this to the family when things start getting serious."

"She was lucid today, though," Dad says. "We might have more time."

"I'd say you've got a couple of weeks at the most," says Della. "Middle of May the latest."

Later on, I overhear Dad on the phone with Dena. "She's doing better; she was lucid for a while this morning. Looks like we've got some more time."

"That's not what Della said," I say, unable to help myself. "You're giving her the wrong impression!"

Dad cuts off mid-sentence and thrusts the phone at me. "If you're so sure when Mom is going to die, why don't you tell her?"

I take the phone gingerly, senses dulled by confrontation. "She-she was lucid today," I tell my sister, "but I took the pamphlet as a sign that we've only got a few weeks left."

"Fine," says Dena. "I'm moving in on Friday."

After I hang up, I creep over to Dad. "Are you mad at me?" I ask, hating the inner third grader who can't function unless everyone likes me.

"Not at all," he says with heartbreaking coldness. "You have your impressions, and I have mine."

The irony of that statement is striking, considering what Alex told me over the weekend. Dena and I were laying across the couch, feet in each other's laps, while Alex chatted with us from one of the island stools.

"What's Dad doing?" Dena said, at the sound of typing from my parents' bedroom. "I never know what he's doing..."

"Probably building a bomb," I said.

"No, he's not," said Alex, with his slight Ukrainian lilt. "He's figuring out when people are going to die."

I was so shocked, I actually sat up. "What did you say?"

"That's what he does. He figures out when people are going to die."

I didn't understand. What did my father's endless hours at the computer have to do with people dying? What was he, God?

Patiently, Alex (who, incidentally also has a shadowy job involving "weapons") explained: "Your dad works with life insurance policies. He writes the programs that speculate return on investment based on the life expectancies of the insured. Basically, he figures out when people are going to die so other people make money."

It was nightmarishly sinister, reducing a human life into an algorithm in pursuit of the mighty dollar. But then I realized how perfect a job it was for my father, who could replace people with numbers. But now that the number has reverted back to its human form - in this case, his wife's - his brain can't compute it.

The result is a painful migraine, which sends Dad crawling into bed just a few hours after our tense exchange. Mom calls for Ben to get her two wet washcloths, and, curled in semi-fetal position, tries to shift herself over with her one working arm. Grunting slightly with the effort, she struggles across the ocean of their bed to reach her husband, then drapes one of the washcloths across his forehead. She lays the other on her own, pressing her body against her husband's back, and the two of them fall asleep.

Later on, when she's awake but hazy, I bring Ezra in to say goodnight.

I lay my head on her belly. "Mommy…"

"It's okay, Honey," she says, stroking my hair. "Just let it all go..."

I eye the giant bottle of Ativan she's been taking for anxiety. "Seriously?"

She nods placidly. "I have to worry about me now. I spent my whole life worrying about everyone else..." Her eyes tear up. "I just have one thing to ask you, okay?"

"Okay."

"You are going to be losing a mother, but this man over here" - she points to my father, still asleep next to her - "he's going to be losing his wife. He's going to tell you he's fine and he's going to push you away. Don't you let him. Don't let him push you away."

I look down at my hands, so dry that the skin on my knuckles is cracked and bleeding. Mom's hands are as soft as ever, though the flesh has melted away. Now, I can see the veins and capillaries running beneath her skin like a subway map.

"Is that all I should know?" I say, hoping for some parting wisdom I can dip into after she's gone.

"You'll figure out the rest of it," she says. "I don't worry about you anymore."

But I don't want to figure it out, I could shout at her. *I want you here to help me!*

I feel an urge to push all the furniture against the doors and nail planks across the windows to shut death out. I want to distract God with something shiny and smuggle Mom to South America. But there's nothing I can do to stop what's coming. Not one thing. My powerlessness is so staggering, the unfairness of it all so incensing, I could eat an entire sheet cake, drink myself unconscious, or smoke enough pot to send smoke signals out the top of my head. Instead, I bake my rage and sadness into oatmeal raisin cookies and brownies as rich and dense as bricks. Then I start cleaning, vacuuming up every last dust mote, wiping down countertops, organizing shelves and clearing away clutter. When the floors are gleaming, I can breathe again, comforted by the illusion of order amidst chaos. Then I spend three hours on Facebook.

Dad, meanwhile, escapes into his power tools. From the garage comes the whirr of his power saw, the smell of sawdust and hot, sliced wood. He wields his tape measure with authority, his face knitted in concentration as he aligns corners just so.

"Are you building something?" I ask.

"Just taking a break," he says. "Sawdust therapy."

He sounds like me, losing myself in mindless activity just to keep from scalping someone.

Before turning in, I look in on Mom, who sits with her legs dangling over the side of the bed, hunched over a notebook.

"What are you up to?"

"Writing down my meds," she says in a strange, dreamy voice.

I look over the top of the page as she writes, "Ativan," scribbling an "r" where the "v" should be. I wait for her to erase and correct it, but she moves on, blind to her mistake. She makes a similar switch writing "Vancomycin," the final letters dropping into the line beneath like a wilting flower. Halfway through the word, "Tylenol," she stops, peers up at me, then looks back at the pencil, which makes a few incomprehensible markings that trail downward like a worrisome EKG.

"Let me," I say, gently sliding the notebook from her hands. I record the meds, surprisingly few today, and the times she took them, without erasing what Mom has written.

Mom rests her head against my chest, and I kiss the top of her head, smelling her skin and honey lip balm.

"Do me a favor…" she murmurs.

"Hmmm?"

"Put sand and shells in with me."

"Okay."

"Re?"

"Yeah, Ma?"

"It's going to go fast now."

"Guess what?" Mom says, steering the car through icy rain.

"Hmmm?"

"We're going to Israel for Passover!" Her eyebrows rise as she waits for my excited reaction. But when I hear the word "Israel", all I think of is empty desert, cartoon men with swords, and the likelihood that I will have to walk a lot.

"Whyyyyy-uh?", I say, pushing my head back against the passenger seat.

Her face falls. "It's Gabe's bar-mitzvah! Dad wants to take him there to put on tefillin for the first time."

"Is there anything to do there?"

"There's everything to do! We're going to the Dead Sea and the Wall and Masada..."

"Like the mountain?"

"Yup."

"You're going to make me climb a mountain?" I point to my body, all 225 pounds of it, to remind her who she's talking to.

"You can do it," she says. "And there's more good news."

"Let me guess: we're going spelunking."

"Alisa is going to have Seder with us!"

Now I'm excited. Alisa Flatow is the smiley, popular, big sister I always wanted but never got. She's the picture of everything cool: wild black curls, bright leggings under her skirts, and big glasses over brown eyes. Our families have been friends since I was in preschool, and for years I watched her from afar, zipping off to youth group weekends and sleepovers with a duffel bag slung over her shoulder. I used to imagine being just like her when I got to high school. It didn't quite work out that way. This year, Alisa is studying in Israel before leaving for college, which for her will probably be twice as fun as high school seemed to be.

"Is she gonna stay at the hotel with us?" I ask, trying not to sound too interested.

"I think so. We'll have to arrange for an extra bed."

I'm happy for about four seconds before I remember that all of this will be taking place 6,000 miles away, where I'll be forced to wear shorts in public.

"But why Israel?" *I whine. "For my bat-mitzvah we went to the Radisson. Why should Gabe get a big, fat trip just because he's a boy?"*

"Don't even start. You wanted a big party."

"So?"

"So, you got your party, and Gabe is going to Israel."

I play with the lock button on my door, making the tab click noisily up and down a dozen times in a row. Mom starts humming, which means I'm annoying her.

"You know, there are bombs there," I say.

"There are bombs here, too," Mom replies, turning into the parking lot of the orthodontist's office. "Probably a lot more."

"What if someone blows us up?"

She turns the key sharply in the ignition. "No one is going to blow us up, Rea. We are going to Israel because it's Gabe's bar-mitzvah and when you're Jewish, that's where you go."

"Jews go to Florida, too," I say. "Maybe you could drop me off there."

Mom gives me a long look, like she's debating if it's worth answering me. I guess it's not, because she gets out of the car without another word.

The waiting room in Dr. O'Brien's office is packed and noisy, with two kids banging away on the Pac-Man console at the far end. Seeing Mom, the receptionist waves us right through. Dr O'Brien - Dr. O, everyone calls him - races up to us, and my heart gives a little flutter. It's not that he's so handsome; he's well past forty, his reddish hair is thinning and you can barely see the whites around his eyes. But Dr. O is one of the few men I know who always pays attention to me.

"Those eyes! Like Liz Taylor!" he says, cupping my chin. "Where did she get those eyes?"

He says that at every appointment, but I grin anyway.

"And you..." He leans in to kiss Mom's cheek. "You look fantastic."

"Thanks," Mom says, running a hand through her hair, which smells like shampoo and the heat of a blowdryer.

I feel my thin bubble of confidence pop. I know it's not just me that Dr. O fusses over; he flits across his office from female to female like a bee in a garden, pollinating the assistants, his patients, and their mothers with compliments. But with Mom, he's different. He zeroes in on her like a missile and doesn't leave her side. Dr. O leads us to one of the side rooms, sitting across from her as I slide into the slick dentist's chair.

"How's it going, kiddo?" he says. "Feeling good?"

"Mm-hmm," I reply, running my tongue along my braces.

With a robotic hum, the chair tilts backward and my eyes get heavy, as they always do in the dentist's chair. Over my head, Mom and Dr. O banter back and forth, a volley I follow in a half-sleep state. There are snatches about books and the best way to get out of the city. Now that his divorce is final, Dr. O has moved from the suburbs to an apartment on the Upper East Side.

"A bachelor pad," Mom teases.

He laughs. "Something like that."

I hear Dr. O ask after Dad, then listen for Mom's usual reply: "Who the hell knows? I barely see him."

"Working?"

"Yeah. Or out with one of his rabbi friends. He won't drive on Saturdays, so he's not going to synagogue with us anymore. I take the kids by myself, and everyone asks where he is. He's got his own life now."

Even in my hazy state, I feel the familiar prick of guilt hearing these things about my father, then the flash of anger at Mom for telling everyone in the world about us.

But Dr. O doesn't seem troubled by it. His voice gets low, and I feel him shift a little closer to her. "That was the hardest part for me: living with someone and feeling a million miles away."

Something about the way he's talking pulls me fully awake, but I keep my eyes closed.

"Well, you didn't have kids," Mom replies. "Makes things a lot less complicated."

"Maybe. Maybe not."

Mom's comment floats over me like a dark cloud. What does she mean about kids making things complicated? Do we make things complicated for her? Is she only with Dad because of us?

I let my eyes flutter open.

"She's awake!" says Dr. O. "Braces are looking good, Liz. Last hundred yards 'til you get them off in March."

"Right before we leave for Israel!" Mom says in sing-song, another lame attempt to get me excited.

"You're going to Israel?" Dr. O says.

"My parents think we're in need of culture," I say, knowing it will make Dr. O laugh. When you make people laugh, they see you, and they forget about the things you don't want them to see.

"You don't want to go?"

"She doesn't want to do anything but argue with her mother," Mom says. "Right, Reez?"

I wrinkle my nose at her.

"You be nice to your mom," says Dr. O in fake seriousness. "She's a good lady."

On our way out, Dr. O pulls a book from his briefcase. "It helped me a lot," he says, handing it to Mom. "Maybe you'll like it."

As we walk to the car, I try to get a glimpse of the cover. "What is that?"

She holds it up so I can see: The Bridges of Madison County.

"What's it about?"

"I read it already," Mom says, tossing it into the backseat. "It's about a housewife who has an affair while her husband is away."

I'm not sure if it's what she said, or the nonchalant way she said it, that makes me so uneasy. "Why would Dr. O give you a book about a housewife who has an affair?"

She shrugs. "I guess he thought I would like it."

"Why? Does he want you to have an affair with him?"

Mom bursts out laughing. "Rea! I'm not having an affair!"

"Why'd you take the book, then? Why didn't you just tell him you're married and you're not interested?"

"He just got divorced," she says. "He probably feels alone right now."

"Come on, Mom! He likes you!"

"He likes everyone! He probably has ten copies of that book in his office." She reaches for my hand. "Listen, Cookie. No one's having an *affair. I would never do that to your father. Dr. O is just...he's lonely. People do things when they're lonely."*

I can see she's telling the truth, but not all of it. Mom may protest that she's being kind to a lonely man, and she is, but I see the pink in her cheeks and the smile she's biting back. She likes his attention.

We ride the rest of the way home in silence.

As we get out of the car, I grab the book from the backseat and run my fingers along the raised cover image: a hazy watercolor of a covered bridge. It's a stupid picture, with its soft pastels and picturesque scenery, like a fake cover for the contraband book you're hiding inside.

"Did you like it?" I ask.

"The book?" She looks at it for a second. "Nah. I thought it was stupid."

A few days later, I have a dream that I'm in the locker room before gym class, while all the pretty girls get changed. Leah Mandel daintily removes her clogs and bell bottoms, then pulls a ribbed turtleneck over her head. Her body is taut and golden, a plane of smooth lines and budding curves.

"Ugh," she says, patting her belly. "I feel so gross. I got my period."

The other girls cluck in sympathy.

"I've got mine, too," says Emma Lantzman, pulling a scrunchie around her frizzy brown curls. "I feel like I always have it."

All of them take turns, standing in their underwear, complaining about their cramps and headaches and PMS like they're in a Midol commercial. I say nothing, holding my track pants in front of me so they won't see the rippling flesh of my thighs or my belly hanging over them.

"What about you, Rea?" says Laurie. "Do you get your period?"

"No," I say. "My body is broken."

Then I wake up.

I can't shake the shame left over from my dream, because what I said is true: I'm 14 and I haven't gotten my period yet. Most of the girls in my class have it already (at least, they say they do), and I'm starting to worry that I'm too fat to period. Delaying getting dressed for school, I sit on the edge of my bed in my underwear, absently picking at a scab on my knee. I catch it under my nail and it peels off, forming a smooth red dome of blood. There's a pleasure in disturbing it with my finger, watching the blood release down my leg and drip into my palm. Holding up my reddened fingerprints, I'm struck with an idea.

I reach for the maxi pad I have in my dresser drawer and wipe my fingers on it, then dip for more blood and wipe again. There are only a few short, reddish stripes, but they stand out sharply against the white cotton.

I run downstairs to Mom's room, where she's sitting in bed with a book, her glasses perched on her nose.

Mom! I got my period!" I say, holding up the pad.

She beams. "Mazel Tov!"

"Thanks!"

"You know how to use the pad and everything?"

"Yeah, you showed me already."

"Great. I'm so happy for you, Honey!" she says, then goes back to her book.

That was disappointing.

By the time I get upstairs, I feel empty and even more broken than before. It occurs to me: What happens next month when I'm supposed to get my period again? What about this month? Am I going to leech my scab for the next five to seven days? Sheepish, I go back down to Mom's room.

"Mom?"

"Hmmm?" she says, her eyes still on the page.

"I didn't get my period."

She looks up at me. "What do you mean?"

"I picked my scab and wiped the blood on the pad so you would think I got it."

She looks at the pad still in my hand, then back at me. "Why did you lie?"

Why did you? I think, but I don't say it.

I scream at her instead. "You don't know anything! You think you know everything, but you don't!"

I march out of the room and slam the door behind me.

I don't know if Dad ever found out about "The Bridges of Madison County", but on the day I'm supposed to get my braces off, he takes me instead of Mom. There's a quiet fire in my belly as we walk into the office. What will Dr. O say when he sees Dad? What will Dad say?

In the end, neither of them says much. Dr. O's pink skin goes white when he sees Dad, and he stammers as he reaches to shake Dad's hand. Dad takes it and nods without looking at him. I sit wide awake through the whole appointment, listening to the scrape of Dr. O's tools against my teeth.

"You look great, Liz," Dr. O says as we head out. "Best of luck."

"Doesn't he know your name?" Dad says.

I shrug. "I guess he forgot."

We land in Tel Aviv in the middle of the night. The palm trees are silhouettes, and the cab drivers are brusque voices with no faces. Even the restaurant in our hotel is dark, each table lit only by a muted overhead lamp. I order a Coke - "Water will give you diarrhea," Mom warns - and swallow the entire glass in one long gulp.

I study the menu, finding nothing familiar. "What's 'Shakshuka'?"

"Eggs in tomato sauce," Mom says. "It's delicious."

"Puke," I mutter, stuffing a pita in my mouth. "There's no Taco Bell in Israel?"

After a rough night's sleep, our marathon of sightseeing begins. We go to Caesarea, King Herod's port city, which looks like it was transported out of Ancient Rome. There's an amphitheater, and rows and rows of columns and arches. Mom reads from the guidebook, giddy with excitement, while I look around for a snack bar. On the way to the Judean Desert, we visit a string of museums, memorials and archaeological sites. Then we're off to Masada.

I don't know if it was Mom's or Dad's idea for us to wake up before the sun in order to climb a 1,300-foot rock plateau, but I hate them both for it. Sweat and dust cement together between my fat rolls and my inner thighs are chafed raw. My lungs burn like I've been breathing ammonia. My shoelaces stretch tight against my swollen feet. As I hike the snaking upward path, my bones creak loudly enough for the dozens of tourists passing me to hear. I stare venom into their backpacks as they grow smaller ahead, like hares to my tortoise.

Dad doubles back to me, red-faced and puffing. "How's it going?"

"Not dead yet," I snarl.

We reach the top as dawn breaks. It takes me a good five minutes to catch my breath, by which time Mom is already in teacher mode, reading extra-loudly from her guidebook: "'When the Jews revolted against the Romans in 66 CE, a team of rebels took the Roman garrison of Masada. Jewish zealots and their families fleeing from Jerusalem joined them on the fortress after the destruction of the temple in 70 CE. They held out there for three years, raiding and harassing the Romans, who built ramparts and catapults below.'" A few people, hearing Mom's booming teacher voice, assume she is a tour guide and join our group.

As she continues reading, we walk along the top of the plateau, passing the remains of old bathhouses, storehouses, and a Mikvah, the Jewish ritual bath. I can see the Judean desert beyond, the waves of sand rising and falling, and the Dead Sea in the distance. In my mind, I rebuild the decaying rubble into a small city of Jewish rebels going about their daily business, while hundreds of feet below, the Roman armies build a ramp up the side of the mountain, trying to destroy them.

The sky is light now as we enter the ruins of a synagogue. A frame of walls stands around us, half-crumbled, like a Lego project abandoned halfway through. Noah, Dena, Mom and I sit on the broken foundation stones as Dad takes out his tallit, *prayer shawl, and* tefillin, *phylacteries, for the morning prayers. Out of habit, I glance around to see who might be staring, but then I remember we're in Israel, where almost everyone is Jewish.*

After Dad wraps his tefillin, *he helps Gabe with his, placing the black wooden box at the crook of Gabe's forehead and fastening it with the attached leather strap. Gabe winds the other strap from his elbow down the forearm, just as Dad instructs him to, tucking the tail around his middle fingers. Once Gabe is set, Dad drapes his* tallis *over his head like a chrysalis, swaying back and forth in prayer. Gabe does the same, but more stiffly.*

I watch them pray, wondering if Gabe really believes he's talking to God. Dad does. But how does he do it three times a day with such concentration, talking and talking to someone Who never answers back?

I take the tourist pamphlet out of Mom's hand and continue reading where she left off:

When the Roman Tenth Legion was close to breaching Masada's walls with their battering rams and catapults, Zealot leader Elazar ben Yair declared that all the Jewish defenders should commit suicide rather than fall into Roman Hands. Led by ben Yair, almost 1000 men, women and children burnt down the fortress and killed each other. The Zealots cast lots and chose ten men to kill the remainder, until the last Jew standing killed himself. Only two women survived, later relating the event to the historian Josephus.

Beside me, Mom gasps. "Look!"

The sun creeps over the edge of the mountain directly behind Dad and Gabe, shining rays from their silhouettes in all directions like they're the center of a star. Mom takes out the video camera to record the light making its way slowly up their bodies, resting for a moment at their heads like a crown before lifting into sky.

At the Dead Sea, we slather our bodies in black mud and I burn my eyes in water too salty to sustain the basest form of life. After that, it's to Jerusalem, which looks like a new city built on top of an old one, with modern apartment buildings crammed against ancient stone houses. From the silence of the desert, Jerusalem is a boombox turned up high. There are shouting voices and car horns blaring, and the sidewalks swarm with people. We've barely put our bags down before Mom and Dad have whisked us to see David's Citadel and the ancient artifacts under the Old City. I'm so bored I consider eating a rock so I'll choke and we can leave.

Finally, we reach the Kotel, the Western Wall, which from the age of five I've been taught to turn toward while praying. This wall, the last remnant of the Temple, is the holiest site in the world for the Jews, who believe it was once God's dwelling place on Earth. Now it's just a lonely wall of white stone, the afterthought of a conversation long over. Men and women split to each side of the dividing wall and approach the enormous stones. Many reach out to touch them, while others bury their faces in prayer books. Some cry. I follow Mom to the women's side, waiting to feel something as we walk up to the Wall. I stare at the creamy rock, touching it gently with my fingertips, and am surprised to find it cold. Hundreds of notes, like wads of chewing gum, are stuffed into the cracks between the stones. I reach into my pocket for the note I wrote before we left for Israel, and reread it:

Please make me thin.

I don't know if God will ever read this, if God is even there, but just in case, I fold up the paper and jam it into the wall.

Back at the hotel, Dad and Mom go to the lobby to arrange a cot for Alisa, who is coming tonight, while the four of us eat pizza and laugh at "Forrest Gump" dubbed in Hebrew. They chose a deep, manly voice to speak over Tom Hanks, making him sound like his chocolates are hand grenades. Dena struts around in a shower cap and Israeli Defense Force fatigues she made Dad buy her at a military museum, calling herself "General Showercap." As she flexes her skinny biceps, we laugh so hard we don't hear Mom and Dad come back in.

"Guys," Mom says. "Shut off the TV."

I turn around to argue, but stop when I see their faces. "What's wrong?"

Dena's arms drop. Gabe flips off the television.

"Alisa isn't coming for Seder," Mom says.

"That's all?" says Noah.

I smack his arm. "Why not?"

"She's dead."

The room gets so quiet I can hear a tinny hum from the lightbulb above me.

"I saw a newspaper at the front desk with a girl's face on the cover," Mom says, staring at the middle distance like she's seeing the paper in front of her. "I kept staring at it, the face was so familiar...It said there was a terror attack on a bus coming up to Jerusalem..."

She shakes her head, unable to go on.

Dad continues for her. "I thought there was a mistake in the article. It couldn't be her. But then the concierge pointed at the paper and said, 'That's Flatow, the girl from New Jersey...'"

"Alisa's dead?!?" Gabe cries. "How can she be dead?"

The word "dead" wraps dark and fearsome around me.

"I know," Mom says. "It doesn't make any sense. She was supposed to be here tonight..."

Dena's shower cap falls out of her hand.

My whole body, even my fingers, start to shake. "I want to go home."

"We can't," says Dad. "It's Seder tonight."

"So after the Seder. Tomorrow. We can go home tomorrow. I don't want to be here anymore."

Mom and Dad look at each other, lost.

"I should call Roz," she says.

We sit in shocked silence while Mom murmurs into the phone in the next room. I eye the grocery bags on the counter in the kitchenette, full of Passover snacks and candies. I want to haul it all to my bed and hide there, but I'm too stunned to move. It feels like I've had a protective skin around me I never knew about until it was ripped off, sharp and quick like a band-aid. Now there's nothing to protect me. At any moment, a wrecking ball could crash through our window. A tidal wave might wash us all away.

When my parents come out of their room, Mom's eyes are red. "Roz and Steve say we should stay. They said Alisa would want us to stay."

I grip onto the arm of the couch. "Why should we stay here? So we can get blown up, too?"

"We're not going to get blown up," Mom says, but she doesn't sound so sure this time.

The Seder is long and sad, as Alisa's chair sits empty at our table. There's none of the usual joking. We simply get through it, eat our dinner, and go back upstairs. All night, I jump at every footstep in the hallway, every car horn from the street. I close my eyes and think of our quiet neighborhood in New Jersey, where there are big houses with green lawns and nice cars in the driveways. Nothing bad ever happens to anyone there. At the sound of a siren, I shoot up in bed and curl against the wall, the blanket covering everything but my face.

In the morning, Gabe, Noah, Dena and I park ourselves in front of the television and stay there all day.

"Don't you want to go out and do something?" Mom asks half-heartedly.

We don't answer.

We find an American news station broadcasting live from Oklahoma City, where someone has bombed a federal building and killed hundreds of people. Over and over they flash images of the building's charred skeleton, dusty bodies on stretchers, crying families. We watch it for hours, shaking our heads like it's an offer we can refuse. The wreckage replays in my dreams, along with Alisa's face on the front page of the *newspaper. Her smiling expression twists in horror as she's suddenly on the seat of a bus, a yellow-eyed man before her with an explosive strapped to his chest. Alisa's mouth opens, and the beginning of a sound escapes from her throat before she's swallowed by a swell of fire.*

In the middle of the night, I creep out to the living room of our suite, where Dad is studying one of his books at the table. He doesn't notice me until I slide into the chair across from him.

"I can't sleep."

"Why?" he says, though he knows why.

"Why did this happen?"

"Ask Hashem. He runs the world."

"You really believe there's a God up there" - I jab my finger at the ceiling - "controlling everything?"

"Yeah, I do."

"Then why would He want to hurt people? It's sick. It's like He just wants to punish us."

"Maybe it's not a punishment," Dad says. "Could be there's a deeper reason."

"So what's the reason?"

"I don't know."

I roll my eyes. "Well, that's just stupid."

For some reason, this makes him smile. He sits back and pushes his yarmulke back from his forehead. "Imagine you're looking at the back of a tapestry," he says. "There are strings hanging down all over the place, the stitching going this way and that. There's no order, no direction. That's this world. Everything's a mess, nothing makes any sense. Bad things happen all the time. But if you walk around to the front of the tapestry, you'll see that the mess comes together into a beautiful design." His finger traces the Hebrew script on the page in front of him. "There's a Master Artist making this tapestry. He knows the whole design, and from His side, everything looks perfect."

"So what?" I say. "It's okay, then, that Alisa's dead, because it's all part of God's 'design'?"

"It's not okay. It's terrible. But we have to trust that Hashem knows better than we do."

This exasperates me. "How can you trust a God that creates Nazis and earthquakes and AIDS? That's like walking around with a 'Kick Me' sign on your back!"

"But He created all the good things, too: love, family. It's easier to trust a God like that."

I try to imagine it, but it's like pulling on a locked door. Even if Dad's God exists, there's no way I could trust Him. He's already taken too much from me, including my father.

"I'm tired," I say, because it's true, and because this conversation has done nothing but confuse me. All I want is for Dad to hold me and tell me everything is okay, that this whole thing was just an accident of fate, and that nothing bad will ever happen again. Instead he's talking about God, which is the one thing I don't want to talk about.

I float, dazed, through the rest of the trip, sitting up each night eating matzah after matzah spread thick with cream cheese and grape jelly. I jump at every loud noise and stick close to my parents through a thousand art galleries and boring old synagogues. Soon we'll be home, I tell myself. Soon we'll be home.

Boarding the plane back to the States, I speed up the beltway like I'm running from a burning building. As soon as we're in the air, I'll be safe. I can go back to my life on the other side of the world and forget that this trip ever happened.

The plane eases onto the runway, and I feel my body start to relax.

"We'll be back one day," Mom says.

Ha, *I think.* Not in a million years.

As Israel shrinks to a speck outside my window, I fall asleep for the first time in a week.

Chapter Nine

A couple of years ago, Mom called us all to the Cape House for Thanksgiving.

"Bring jeans and a white shirt," she said.

This was code for: *Clean up nice. We're having pictures taken.*

Jeans and white shirts have been our family-picture uniform from the time we were kids. At the end of each summer, Mom would scrub us pink, comb our hair and take us to the Jan Press Studio, where Gabe, Noah, Dena and I would stand barefoot on a white canvas backdrop and climb all over each other. Jan would fish for smiles by calling, "fuzzy pickles!" through his thick mustache. When we ignored him, he resorted to profanity. It was the only time in our lives we didn't get in trouble for screaming, "ASSHOLE!" at the top of our lungs.

That Thanksgiving was the first time Mom and Dad posed with us. Wound up by memories of our sessions at Jan Press, it took precisely four seconds for trouble to start. There were crossed eyes, surprise piggy back rides, farts. The photographer, a prim Bostonian, regarded us with mild alarm yet managed to get some beautiful shots. One in particular stood out; it was of Mom, seated on the edge of the sofa in the living room, the sun casting a glow through the windows behind her. Her shoulder-length hair glints red, and her eyes are a luminous green. Mom's smile, always slightly crooked, is relaxed and genuine. She's in her happy place, at the Cape House, with all of her children nearby.

This is the picture Dad has blown up to poster size and shipped to him overnight. When it arrives, he unrolls it on the dining room table.

"*That's* Mom," I say.

"That's morbid," says Dena.

"You'd rather a picture of her the way she looks now?" I point toward the room where Mom lays sleeping, sallow and ashen, her short hair sticking up at all ends.

Mom's been asleep for 22 hours now, and the nurses have given us firm directions not to disturb her under any circumstances. On the blog, Dad refers to the house as a "No Wake Zone", a nautical term from his Navy days: *Nationwide, any vessel operating in a zone posted as "No Wake" must operate at the minimum speed that allows the operator to maintain steering and make headway.* I suppose Mom is making some headway, though none of us like where she's going. We're all hoping a gale-force wind will blow her off course, back home to us.

"She wants us to remember her like this," I say, tapping the poster.

"I'm going to get a frame and hang it here," Dad says, pointing to an empty wall next to the doorway to their room.

"We'll go with you," I say, hitching Ezra up on my hip. Dad might need a second opinion; as someone who has made no major wardrobe changes since 1980, I wouldn't call him a paragon of taste.

At the frame store around the corner, a stylish girl in black leggings attends to us while her pug, whose collar says, "Adonis", pokes around our legs. Ezra's eyes follow the dog's every move.

The salesgirl gushes over the baby. "You're so sweet!"

"Thanks," I reply. "We'll keep him."

Dad and I pore over the racks of frames, trying and rejecting a few different options.   "I want silver," Dad says, "but something that looks a little older, kind of banged-up."

"A distressed finish," the salesgirls says.

"Right, that."

Dad's clumsiness reminds me of the time, years ago, when he took me to buy clothes after Mom quit taking me shopping. It was hard enough to find something that would fit me, she said, let doing it when I acted like a turbo-bitch. Dad took me to Delia's, a trendy store that specialized in pleather. This was his first mistake, as their clothes only fit people with no internal organs. He wandered aimlessly through the racks, stroking the corner of a shiny jacket, examining the underside of a tutu skirt, looking like someone trying to hit a nail with an egg yolk. Holding up a pair of skinny black pants, he said, "These are nice."

I sneered. "Like, as a bracelet?"

As he returned them to the rack, a salesgirl in a t-shirt dress crept over. "Can I help you find something?"

"Yeah," he said, pointing his thumb toward me. "You have anything for *her*?"

I almost hung myself with a sequined belt in one of the dressing rooms.

Dad comes across a distressed frame with red undertones. "This would be good with Mom's hair."

"It would," I say in surprise.

We lay it over Mom's picture, and indeed, it does bring out her red highlights. But Dad isn't satisfied. "What if we...?"

He reaches for another, more modern, frame and stacks it inside the first. The effect is remarkable. There's a completion to the image that wasn't there before, and the elaborate frames lend distinction to the woman in the picture. Even the store owner, a lithe man with a beak nose, leaves the older couple he's helping to admire Dad's creation.

"I would never have thought to put those together," he says.

"Well, you see here how the angle here is sharper?" Dad runs his finger along the corner of the modern frame. "It functions as a contrast to the other one."

"I see..." the framer says, studying the image. "She's beautiful."

"Yes," says Dad. "She is."

The framer rings us up himself. I nearly choke when I hear the price, but Dad doesn't blink.

Our drive home is quiet. Ezra sleeps in the back of the car while I watch the familiar strip of budding trees and old houses pass by.

Out of the blue, Dad says, "Did you know I once went to a shrink about Mom's spending?"

I'm stunned by both the randomness of this admission and the admission itself. "What do you mean?"

"The credit cards. She was spending more than I could pay back. I'd tell her to stop, but she didn't care. Once, she got pissed at me about something and put $13,000 on American Express."

"*What?*"

He laughs. "I know! How am I supposed to pay a $13,000 American Express bill? I didn't know what to do. I'd ask her, 'Why'd you have to buy a couch now? Why couldn't you wait until I get my bonus?' And she'd say, 'No, no, no, you don't understand.'"

I understand. Mom wanted what she wanted when she wanted it. Once an idea was in her head, a fleet of navy ships couldn't have stopped her.

"So I went to the shrink," Dad says, "and the shrink says, 'You have to take control. You don't have to do it her way. You're allowed to say no.'"

Picturing a therapist giving my bewildered father a pep-talk is sweetly sad/funny, like Lucy playing headshrinker to Charlie Brown. His need for backup is understandable, though; going head to head with Mom is not for the weak of heart.

"When Dena had her gallbladder attack, the two of us sat in the waiting room of the hospital and I told her I was taking the credit cards away."

"What did she do?"

"She was *mad*."

I shake my head in wonder. "You really took them away?"

"Yup. Except the American Express. She wouldn't give it up."

We laugh.

"The whole thing was crazy," Dad says. "Listen, it counts for one half of one percent of our whole relationship. But money is one of the things that can get under the skin of a marriage."

I mull over this new knowledge the rest of the drive home. A door has been opened into my parents' relationship I'm not sure I should have access to; it feels like walking in on them having sex. But there's also a twisted comfort in seeing my mother's dark side, with which I can so deeply relate: the petulance, the selfishness, the use of my father's mistakes to excuse her bad behavior. She threw tantrums, made messes and expected Dad to clean them up. It shrinks her, in my mind, down to human size.

If they ever find the a gene that determines addiction, I can guarantee you it's as plentiful as leaves on my family tree. My great-grandfather was an alcoholic, and his wife, his supplier, brewing bathtubs full of gin during the Prohibition. There are pill-heads, sex addicts, workaholics, gamblers, and, of course, food addicts - including my grandmother, who, walking into her own anniversary party, detoured into the synagogue kitchen to steal an eclair. My mother paddled around the lake of food and exercise, but compulsive shopping was where she made waves. She would fill her closet and ours with bags of new clothes almost weekly, or buy some major piece of furniture (or three) every few months, then redo the room to go with it. It wasn't about owning these things, but the high of acquiring them. Because soon after her big, fat purchase, sometimes within days, she'd be itchy again, trying to soothe herself with some new project or event or trip or drama. She runs on the same faulty motor I do, which bleeds as it consumes, requiring constant filling in order to function. I always thought I was worse than she was because I wore my sickness for the world to see. But sometimes, the invisible addictions are even more insidious, like foundational rot you don't know is there until the whole house collapses.

But for all the damage Mom's addiction has done, Dad's right at her side the minute we get home. "Hey Willie, you want to go for a walk?"

She's weak and her lips are dry, but she manages a tired smile in his direction.

Dad dresses her in a shirt and sweater and a down coat too warm for the spring weather, then guides her wheelchair down the front steps. Holding Ezra in the doorway, I watch them roll slowly up the road. Dad's muffled voice carries back to us as he shows Mom the new buds on her beloved hydrangea bushes, moving the wheelchair closer so she can see them. They are a world away from the couple who fought over credit cards in a hospital waiting room.

"Mostly it is loss that teaches us about the worth of things," Schopenhauer said. It's true not just of our possessions, but in our stumblings in loving each other. One of death's good qualities is the callus it forms over our memories, reducing pain aged over decades into a tiny, barely discernible pinprick. Our histories look different through the prism of loss, the ups and downs blending into one long, love-colored memory. Who did what to whom is no longer relevant; what matters is that we were there, together, when it happened.

Death has done its work for my parents. The incidentals of forty years together have been stripped away, leaving only the essential: a walk beneath a canopy of trees, the sky a minuet in blue, Spring opening before them like a brand-new world.

Chapter Ten

I wake to the sharp scent of baby pee. The Diaper Genie, our smell-proof diaper bin, has been full for a good three weeks now, and we've taken to piling the loaded diapers on top and on the floor around it. There is now a mini-mountain of infant waste fermenting in the corner of our bedroom, which I was able to ignore until this morning, when the uric-acid-soaked air could singe the hairs in my nose.

I blame Mom for this.

When we went shopping for baby gear, I chose the basic model of Diaper Genie, the Diaper Genie I: functional, compact, and convenient, with refill bags available in every local drugstore. Mom, however, insisted on the Diaper Genie *II*, the newer, flashier, and more expensive model, whose negligible improvements consisted of a blue stripe and maybe a quarter of an inch off the circumference. I didn't fight her on it because she was paying, and because I didn't think the grand scheme of my life would be much influenced by one model of Diaper Genie over another.

Ha.

What they don't tell you about the Diaper Genie II is that, unlike the Diaper Genie I, there is only one store in America where sucker parents can purchase refills: Babies R' Us. The inconvenience and stupidity of this confirms that the designers of the Diaper Genie II don't only not have babies, they also hate babies, and their parents, too. Had we bought the Diaper Genie I, I could have snuck out to the Rite-Aid down the street and picked up a refill (and possibly a salt scrub, because I deserve it), and been home in less than ten minutes. But because we have been condemned to the Hades of the Diaper Genie II, I now have to *take the baby out* for a morning-long trip to Hyannis, 20 minutes away.

There's a song we sing on Passover called "*Chad Gadya*", which is basically the bloody, Jewish version of "I Know an Old Lady Who Swallowed a Fly." The epic tale begins with a goat that gets eaten by a cat, which is bitten by a dog, which suffers a beating by a stick, and so forth until the end, when the angel of death kills a butcher. (Kids *love* it.) It takes about half an hour to sing, because after each new plot development, you have to go back and re-sing everything that already happened. For this reason, any slow, tedious process is referred to, in Jewish jargon, as "A Whole *Chad Gadya*." This, for me, is the perfect description for going anywhere with a baby. First, you get the baby dressed (forget about you; the cruddy sweatshirt you've been wearing for three days will do just fine). Then you pack for the road: bottle, burp cloths, diapers, wipes, change of clothes - better make it two - pacifier and emergency toys. Smart people keep their diaper bag pre-packed, but the laws of my world dictate that even if I do, one vital thing will always be missing, and I will have to spend 30 minutes searching for it. Then there's feeding the baby, which can swallow up the good part of an hour. So about three hours after you decide to go out, you and baby are ready to roll.

Then he pukes all over both of you.

Back in for a quick change (in really bad cases, a shower) and finally, you and your travel companion are in the car. By the time you arrive at your destination, your energy reserves are depleted, but dammit, you're on a mission now.

If you've timed it right, Baby might be asleep, which is as close to being out by yourself as you will get for the next, oh, eighteen years. If he is awake, you'd better pray he's in a good mood, because no one likes a baby that's wailing like a siren while they're trying to shop in peace. They will stare ice picks at you like it's your fault, that you are a failure as a mother, and if you don't use your magical powers to shut that kid up they WILL call child services on you. But, of course, your baby is an angel and would never do anything to humiliate you in public.

They will, however, crap their pants. Every time. You won't know right away because they're sneaky about it, and because your attention is devoted to finding the aisle where they keep the stupid designer Diaper Genie II refills. But then, somewhere around the strollers, you get slapped with The Scent, nasty yet semi-pleasant, because it's your kid's. You can try to ignore it, but if someone gets too close, you can bet they'll wrinkle their nose at you like you're the one who's packing.

Time for a diaper change.

If you're lucky, there's a family-friendly bathroom with a changing table, but America likes to punish mothers, so there probably isn't. You may have to get cozy with a sketchy bathroom floor you pray has been mopped at least once in your baby's lifetime. It may occur to you that you've had to go to the bathroom since you got dressed the first time, but you can just forget about that.

By now, you and Baby are both wrecked, so you grab what you need and check out without incident - unless, of course, Baby decides to puke again. Then you'll have to wipe off your dripping debit card on the butt of your jeans and hope the magnetic strip still works. You stumble home with vomit in your hair, reeking like a dirty diaper, and hating everything that's not your bed.

Diaper Genie II. Good call, Mom.

Dena moves home with a duffel bag, her guitar, and her laptop, on which she spends hours playing "The Sims."

"Whatcha doin'?" I ask, passing by her room with Ezra.

She leans back in her chair and stretches. "Planning my virtual wedding. Not doing my homework."

"I thought you were getting an extension."

"Nope."

"What the hell? Your mom is dying! They couldn't give you an extra week?"

"I didn't tell them."

"Why?"

"I don't need anyone feeling bad for me. I don't want them thinking I'm using Mom as an excuse."

"Better they feel bad for you than you fail!"

Dena tips her head back in annoyance. "Who *cares* if I fail? Does it even matter?"

"Ummm, yes?" Ezra makes a fist around my hair and pulls. "Ow! Dude!"

"Take care of your kid," my sister says. "I got this."

Shabbos comes again, and this time Mom is too weak to join us for dinner.

"She can't even lift her finger," Gabe discloses, then starts to cry.

Gabe has been the quietest through all of this, his composed exterior my proof that things weren't really so bad. His tears do the opposite, washing the film from my eyes and bringing everything one step closer to real.

The time comes for my parents to bless us, and we file slowly into their room so Mom can reach us from her bed. I lean down at her side, feeling my parents' hands cover my head, as they have every Friday night of my life:

May God make you like Sarah, Rebecca, Rachel and Leah...

May God illuminate his countenance upon you and be gracious to you...

May God turn his countenance to you and grant you peace.

You don't usually know when something is happening for the last time. You breeze through a final phone call, give half your attention to the last book your child will ever ask you to read. It's not until later that you realize that was it. It's tragic, but it's also kind, because the pain of a "last time" cuts much deeper when you know it will never happen again, and you're forced to watch it flow past like water through your hands. A primal sob erupts from me like a mournful surrender, wrenched from somewhere deep. Resting my face on Mom's belly, I give into the pain, vaguely aware of my entire family watching and crying behind me. I'm more present than I've ever been, feeling the vibration in my chest, the wetness of each tear, while the observer within me bears witness: *This is grief.*

"I love you," Mom says. Her words are slurred, but I hear it.

Gabe and Dena come forward, weeping, for their blessings, followed by Ben and Erin.

Dad stands at the foot of the bed and recites *"Eishet Chayil,"* pushing through tears.

Her husband's heart relies on her, and he shall lack no fortune…
Her children rise and praise her, her husband, he lauds her…
Let her be praised at the gates by her very own deeds…

He shuts his prayer book and calls out to her. "I love you, Willie! You're my *Eishet Chayil…*"

Then he breaks down.

From some hidden reserve of strength, Mom cries, "I'm so proud of all of you!"

As we all cry together, the doorbell rings.

"*Now?*" Gabe asks, and we laugh.

"It's Ralph," Dad says. "Mom's physical therapist. He told me he was coming."

Dena slips out to open the door, and we hear her greet Ralph in hushed tones. The floor creaks beneath them as she leads him to Mom's room, where we all chuckle in awkward greeting, unable to hide our tears. Ralph, with his compact jockey's physique, glides in and smiles at all of us, comfortable in the presence of grief.

"My bear's keeping you company," he says to Mom, stroking the teddy bear around her neck.

She smiles. "I named him after you."

"I brought you a present," he says, reaching into the bag over his shoulder. He produces a fleece blanket and a framed photograph of all the therapists from his firm. Each of them have signed it, sending Mom their best wishes.

"Is that a PT thing?" Ben whispers to Dena.

"No," she says. "That's a Mom thing."

Ralph talks quietly with Mom for a few minutes until she falls asleep, then we all sit down for dinner. Our talk is animated but quiet.

"My mom died of cancer fifteen years ago," Ralph says. "I know what you guys are going through. It's hell."

We nod in agreement.

He continues, "I was almost finished with PT school when she died. I had a moment when I could have screwed up my whole life. I could have used it as an excuse to quit everything. But she made me promise to finish."

There's no possible way that my mother could have told him to come at precisely this moment, when Dena is teetering, but it's very possible that Mom may have seen this coming months ago. Ralph looks directly at Dena, who shifts forward in her seat, sensing something at work through him.

When dinner is finished, Ralph excuses himself to sleep, as he'll be leaving first thing in the morning.

"That's it?" I ask, handing him a towel and blanket. "You drove all this way to spend ten minutes with someone you met three months ago?"

He shrugs. "I love her."

I'm no longer surprised by declarations like these, just as I wasn't surprised by the call I got yesterday from a high school friend living in Beijing. I hadn't heard from Rob in years, and he hadn't seen my mother in almost a decade. But he called the minute he heard.

"Remember how I would come over all the time, just to say hi?" he asked.

I did indeed. Rob would walk in without knocking, fill a bag with Cheerios, kiss my mother, and leave.

He laughed at the memory. "Your house was 35 minutes out of my way, but it didn't matter. I'd even come by when you weren't there, just to see her."

Then there's the email we got from one of Mom's nurses in New York:

As a cancer nurse, one would think that I would be used to patients filtering in and out of my life like routine clockwork. And I guess in some ways, they do. Every once in awhile, however, I meet a patient or a family that sticks with me. Your family has done just that. Believe it or not, I read your blog every day. It's my morning ritual: I read CNN, I

166

watch the news, check my email, and then I read your blog. You are so brave and your words are so inspirational. I admire you for continuing to write the blog, even after so much has changed. Sometimes, I find myself laughing at your funny stories and other times, I find myself so very sad for what you are going through.

When this journey started, I did not have a doubt in my mind that Debbi would beat this, that she was one of the people that HAD to be okay. I guess I had that thought process because I realized that I saw a lot of my own mother, and my own story, in Debbi and your family. Debbi, you have become more than just a patient I took care of a few times; you have become someone I feel like I know in my personal life and care so deeply about...

When I was still living at home, I used to visit Mom's class to watch her with the kids. At any given moment, she was picking one of them up, kissing them or tickling them like they were her own, deliberately flouting the district code of "professional distance." The children all flocked to her, begging her for more, more, more. It didn't stop out of her classroom, either. She was this way with all children, and with everyone she met, including the fellows at a training Mom once attended who dubbed her "The Walking Hug." It was as if she had never learned to guard herself, the way most adults do. At times, her abandon embarrassed me; I wanted to temper her, lest she make people uncomfortable. But she never did. People drank her up as if they were filling a deep, forgotten well. Mom saw how thirsty they were for someone to see and appreciate them, and they opened to her like flowers to the rain. It was like a miracle, in a world where the most dangerous thing a person can do is reveal their heart. But, as Theodore Roethke says, "Those who are willing to be vulnerable move among mysteries."

Ralph leaves after breakfast and a whispered goodbye to Mom, who is in a heavy sleep. Dena walks him to his car, where they speak in confidence for a few minutes before he drives away.

"Want to go for a walk with us?" I ask when she's back inside.

"Sorry," she says, and heads upstairs. "I've got homework."

Chapter Eleven

I surprise Dad in the kitchen, where he's learning Talmud, by holding Ezra up to his face and bellowing, "HAPPY BIRTHDAY!"

He smiles. "Thanks."

"55! Big Stuff!"

"Yeah," he says, reaching under his glasses to rub his eyes. "I feel like I'm 80."

"Rough night?"

"The tremors were really bad. They woke her out of her sleep. The nurses told me to double the Ativan, so I did, but I was nervous; she's so sensitive to the meds. I stayed up most of the night to make sure she was breathing okay."

I've noticed, too, that Mom's tremors are getting worse. Yesterday, she was drinking a bottle of Propel, and her arm jerked so sharply that the drink flew out in an arc across the bedspread. When I asked Della if it was the Morphine, she said, "Hard to say. I think the dose is too low for that. It's probably the disease progressing."

"Is that normal?"

"There is no normal. There are signs, but everyone does it differently. Your mom, especially." Della smiled at that. "You never know what to expect with her."

Dad rubs his eyes again.

"You should go rest," I say. "We're having a surprise party for you later, with ice cream cake."

"Aye-aye, Captain," Dad says with a salute, and shuffles off to his room.

Around mid-morning, Mom stirs. Her eyes are glassy and translucent, but I can see her in there. I want steal all her lucid time for myself, but say nothing as everyone drifts in to see her.

"It's Dad's birthday," Dena tells her.

Mom moans softly. "I don't want to die on his birthday."

Dad touches her foot in encouragement. "If you need to go today, Willie, you do that."

But she doesn't. She drifts through the day, half-present, awaking at intervals to talk to us. We stay with her for long, suspended hours, like those spent waiting in an airport terminal for a flight with no set departure time.

"You take care of my daughter," she tells Ben. "You're a good husband and a good father."

"Thank you for loving me like your own son," he says. "Deep down, I always felt it. It was an honor to be loved by you."

I prop Ezra in her lap and she sings "The Itsy Bitsy Spider" to him, making the gestures with shaky hands.

"I wanted to take you to Disney World," she says.

Ezra gives her a gummy smile.

When Mom falls asleep again, Ben takes the baby upstairs. Dena curls next to Mom on the bed while Gabe perches on the stepstool at her side. Noah sprawls on the chaise. Dad rolls back and forth in the wheelchair. Alex sits, straight-backed, in a chair, and I stand by the glass doors to watch the sunset.

Two lanes of clouds float in a sky the color of my grandmother's roses, a golden core that pinks outward, bronzes, then deepens into magenta. For a brief moment, I allow myself to witness the scene I stand in as I do the sky: it's nature taking its course, a season of life passing by with a poetry that's beyond words, the kind that rips you open and puts you back together at the same time.

When Mom wakes again, Dad wraps her in a blue woolen blanket and wheels her to the living room, turning the chair toward the windows. Her eyes stay closed as the sinking sun shines gold on her face. I wonder if she can feel the light or our eyes on her.

"Willie," she says, "I'm going to die."

After dinner, we sing to Dad and present him with a Carvel ice cream cake.

"Mmm…" says Noah. "Tastes like birthday."

Talk around the table meanders from Dad's gift (a two-volume "Fundamentals of Maimonides") to a discussion of horoscopes.

"It says here," Gabe says, reading from the local paper, "that Sagittarians love to travel and hate commitment."

"True," I say, thinking of the year I spent riding trains through Europe, and the charge I get in rail stations and airports. "But I'm also married with a kid and I never leave my house. Explain that."

"It also says you're contradictory."

"*You're* contradictory. And you smell."

Gabe blows a raspberry at me. "What's Mom again?"

"Aquarius," Dena says.

"'Aquarians have magnetic and attractive personalities,'" Gabe reads. "'They can be exuberant, lively and exhibitionist.'"

"Wow, they're *way* off," Noah says.

We all laugh.

"Did we decide where we're sitting shiva?" Dena asks, making everyone go quiet.

"Here," says Dad. "We'll be here the whole week."

"What are we not supposed to do?" says Noah.

I mentally flip through the Maurice Lamm book. "We can't shower for the whole week, or cook for ourselves, or work. Then for the year, we don't cut our hair or go to parties, concerts, movies. There's more, but I can't remember."

"I'm not going to cut my hair," Dena announces.

"Oh yeah?" Dad says.

"It's not a big deal. It's not like I'm saying *Kaddish* every day."

Women are exempt from time-bound commandments, such as reciting the *Kaddish* with a *minyan* three times a day. I'm glad I don't have to; it's beyond inconvenient to have to find a quorum of ten men to pray with every morning, noon, and night, and your comings and goings are chained to that obligation for eleven long months. But I suppose this is the point. By reciting *Kaddish* three times a day, a mourner is forced to acknowledge their grief, to express their faith, and to allow their community to comfort them.

I didn't know what the *Kaddish* was until I was ten, although by then I'd heard it enough times to recite the entire prayer by heart. One Shabbos morning, I led the final songs of the morning service, then began reciting the *Kaddish* along with a handful of people scattered around the congregation. I was no more than three words in when I felt a hand on my shoulder, which belonged to one of the elderly men who sat up front.

"Don't say it," he whispered in a heavy Eastern-European accent. "It's not for you."

I was embarrassed and outraged that he'd done that to me in front of everyone, until my father explained why: "You only say *Kaddish* if someone in your family has died. It's not good to say it if you don't have to."

From that moment, the *Kaddish* took on a chilling quality, with its slippery Aramaic and droning cadence of an incantation. Though the words are a praise to God, they seem to beckon to death.

"I think I'm going to say it," Gabe says.

Dad jumps in. "It's tough. You need a *minyan* three times a day, even if you're on the road. If it's too much, there are people you can hire..."

Gabe holds up a hand, overwhelmed. "We'll see, Dad. We'll see."

As Noah scoops the last of the ice cream and cookie crumbles onto his plate, we tease him about the extra cake Mom bought each year so he wouldn't polish off the original.

"Didn't she even have 'Noah's Cake' written on it?" asks Dena.

"It wasn't my fault," Noah protests. "Rea ate it, too, and blamed it on me!"

I grin at him. "You were a good alibi."

From Dad's end of the table comes a light snore. He's fallen asleep.

"What a party pooper," jokes Gabe.

"He was up with her last night," I report.

Dena puts a hand on his arm and shakes it lightly. "Dad. Dad!"

His eyes flutter open.

"Go to bed."

He nods and rises from the table. "Thank you everyone for the birthday party. And this..." He holds up his gift. "I'll see you in the morning."

As the door to my parents' room closes, Dena shakes her head. "He looks terrible. I'm worried about him."

"Now's not the time to worry," says Noah, tapping his fork against his plate. "It's after. Mom's always looked after him. I don't think he's cooked a meal in 40 years. What's going to happen when he's alone?"

I picture him in the dining room of their apartment in New York, magazines and newspapers strewn everywhere, sitting down to a dinner of bagged salad and a can of tuna.

"Maybe we can all go in and have Shabbos dinner with him once a month," Gabe suggests.

"What's he going to do the rest of the time?" I ask.

"He has his life there," Noah says. "He'll go back to work. His friends will invite him for Shabbos."

"But what about the everyday stuff? Laundry, cooking..."

"He'll hire someone."

This doesn't satisfy me. "You know what's going to happen. He'll just go and go and never let himself think about it. He'll just work and come home and fall asleep in front of the TV. He won't even know how sad he is."

Noah traces the rim of his soda can with a fingertip. "We can't babysit him. He's a grown man."

My brother is right, but the cold pragmatism bothers me. I want things to be fair and right, and for everyone to be okay. My brother sees things as they are, not how they should be. That's why he's a lawyer, and I'm a writer.

Gabe looks at my parents' closed door. "Even if we could, I doubt he'd let us."

In the morning, Ben packs up the car for a short trip to New York to see the girls and pick up Dad's Torah from the apartment. We'll need it here while we sit shiva.

"Try and take care of you," he says, and kisses me.

I stand in the driveway long after his car disappears down the street.

Dena, Noah and I take Ezra to visit Jazz, our honorary youngest sibling, who once filled our lives with wild activity and dog hair. The wood floors of our house took a beating from her constant racing, while Jazz took a beating from Mollie, our other golden retriever, who'd swat Jazz away with a lazy paw when she tried to steal Mollie's food. We adopted Jazz when Mollie was ten, hoping an infusion of youthful energy would extend the old girl's life. It worked: Mollie lived four more years, if only to see what Jazz would do next. The two of them together were like that old cartoon with the small, hyperactive dog who yaps and runs circles around the big, silent one: "Hey, Mollie, you want to play ball? Let's play ball! Huh, huh, Mollie? You wanna? You WANNA?"

Smack.

Jazz was always Mom's baby, even more so after we left for college. She ate better than we ever did. She even got her own bed in my mother's room. Where Mom went, Jazz went, riding in the backseat of the Jeep with her head out the window and ears flapping in the wind. But her puppy energy couldn't be contained in a two-bedroom apartment, and within a week of my parents' move to the city, Jazz was climbing the walls. Our friend Terry, whose farm is a short drive from the Cape House, offered to adopt her. Now she runs free on five acres, terrorizing rodents with Terry's golden, Russ.

As we approach the entrance to Terry's Farm, a peace settles about my shoulders. Out my window are aisles of baby apple trees, a lush vegetable patch where the dogs nose for bugs, and a simple wooden house on top of a hill. I exhale and think, *Paradise was a garden.*

Terry, a sixty-something hippie with leathery skin and long, yellow-white hair, lumbers up the hill from the chicken coops, wiping dirt-covered hands on his t-shirt. As he approaches, the writing on his shirt gets clearer: *Follow the Eagle's Way*. He wraps each of us in a rib-cracking hug.

"Welcome, welcome. Take a seat," he says, gesturing to wooden benches carved with lotus flowers.

Before we can sit, Jazz launches herself up Noah's torso.

"Hey, Jazzy!" he says, laughing.

I scratch her behind the ear. "I can't believe she still remembers us."

"Of course she does!" Terry says in his radio deejay voice. "Dogs have no concept of time. Two years for you is a week for her."

At the sight of Jazz, Ezra practically jumps out of my arms.

"You want to see the doggie?" I say, and place him on all fours in the tall grass. Jazz creeps over and pushes her nose right up against Ezra's. The two of them stare at each other for a long moment, then Jazz snuffs in greeting and gives his face a lick. Ezra's mind is blown. He watches Jazz and Russ wrestle, shifting back and forth on his hands and knees like he's trying to hurl himself forward.

"He'll be crawling soon," Terry says.

"Any day now."

We sip iced tea made from nettles that grow from behind Terry's house, feeling the sun and the breeze and talking about Mom.

"Yesterday, her eyes opened really big and she said, 'He's holding me'," says Dena.

"Wonderful," Terry says, radiating pleasure. "She'll have a good death."

Noah grimaces. "Is there such a thing?"

"You bet. The Buddha says that a good death is the stamp of a good life. And your mom had a good life. She knew what this whole trip was about. She was good to people, she told the truth, and she found her God. She'll leave here in peace and land gently on the other side."

I wait for Noah to roll his eyes at Terry's spiritual hoo-ha, but he doesn't.

"She's so young, though," I say. "There were so many things she wanted to do..."

Terry grins at that. "Who ever said we're here to do what we want?"

I swallow that down with the iced tea, which tastes like grass.

"How's your dad?"

My brother, my sister and I all exchange a glance.

"He keeps trying to fix it," says Dena. "This morning, he kept offering Mom sips of water. She said no, so he cut the straw shorter and shorter, like that was going to make her drink. It was bugging her, so we finally kicked him out of the room. He's been in the garage with his power tools since then."

Terry looks us all, sage-like, in the eyes. "Have compassion for him. He's losing more than a wife."

When we get home, Della is creeping out of Mom's room. "She just needs to rest now," she whispers.

I look over her shoulder at Mom. "She's been in the same position for eight hours. Shouldn't we move her or something?"

"Leave her be. Your mother has work to do."

In the middle of the night, Dad's cry echoes up the stairs: "DENA!"

I bolt upright in bed, fearing that the worst has happened, and throw on my robe. My sister meets me at the steps, her face white with fear, and we both charge down.

"Move it!" Dena says, my short steps blocking her long ones.

I shift over and give her the lead to Mom's room, where we find her sitting on the floor, murmuring to herself, while Dad, Gabe and Noah stand over her like a lost child they don't know what to do with.

"Dad!" Dena says, breathless. "Why were you screaming like that? You scared the shit out of us!"

"Sorry," he replies, self-conscious. "She just used the commode" - he points to Mom's rolling toilet - "and now we can't get her back on the bed."

Noah and Gabe make a dismal attempt to lift her again. Noah hooks his arms under Mom's armpits while Gabe hauls her up by the waist, both of them grunting. They get her maybe two inches off the ground before slumping down in defeat.

"She's heavy," Gabe says.

"Everyone move back," says Dena with mild impatience. She pushes past the boys and crouches down to Mom, speaking softly and calmly.

Mom's eyes are wide open and darting everywhere, like a dog tracking a squirrel, but her body visibly relaxes. Dena beckons Dad over, places Mom's arms around his neck, then pulls her upright from the waist. The fluid motion makes my mother look weightless.

"Call an ambulance," Mom says, agitated. "Hurry…Sit me, sit me, sit me…"

Dena gently reassures her that everything is okay, and in less than a minute, Mom is settled back in bed.

"That was impressive," I say, squeezing my sister's arm.

All the activity has shaken some awareness back into Mom. "Write this story," she says.

"What story, Ma?" says Gabe.

"*This* one." Her eyes shoot to me. "Rea, you write it. How Dad and Dena had to lift my fat ass to get me back on the bed."

Our laughter makes her wince.

"Who are you?" she says, looking at Noah.

"I'm Noah. I'm your son."

She scans the room. "Where's Ben?"

"He's in New York," I say. "With the girls."

"Who's with the baby?"

"I am. He's upstairs, sleeping."

She shakes her head with impatience. "You didn't answer the question. Who's with the baby?'

"I am, Mom. Ben's in New York."

"BEN!" she yells, eyes to the ceiling, like he can hear her through the floor. "THANK YOU! Good Yontif, Yois!"

We laugh again, stealing guilty looks at each other.

"You want water, Ma?" Dena says. "Your mouth is so dry…"

Dena holds the straw up to Mom's white, crusty lips. She tries to drink, but the water makes her choke. "No water. Gabe…"

"Yeah, Mom?"

"What company do you work for?"

He tells her.

"I want to write them a note…Tell them how talented you are…"

"What should the note say?" asks Dad.

"That he used to wear his Superman t-shirt and jump from bed to bed and yell, 'SUPERMAN! Master of the Ernieberts!'" She grasps onto Gabe's hand like she's afraid he'll run away.

Mom shows no sign of fatigue, and we all want to be here while she's still with us. Slowly, like we're trying not to scare off a skittish animal, we climb into the bed and arrange ourselves around her.

"How's your pain, Ma?" I ask. "You want some meds?"

She shakes her head. "I want to say a *bracha*" - a blessing - "The *Shema*."

The six-word Shema is the central prayer of Judaism: *Hear O Israel, the Lord our God, the Lord is One*. It is one of the first prayers we learn as children, and it is meant to be our last words before we die. Righteous people have shouted this prayer as they were tortured, others have recited it in deathbed repentance. After the Holocaust, one rabbi traveled to orphanages all over Europe in search of Jewish children still in hiding. When he was told there were no Jews, he would sing the Shema out loud, and each time, a chorus of tiny voices would echo it back to him.

Mom sings the ancient melody: "*Shema Yisrael, Adonai Eloheinu, Adonai Echad.*"

We are silent.

"I want to say it again."

This time, we sing it with her. "*Shema Yisrael, Adonai Eloheinu, Adonai Echad.*"

I've recited these words thousands of times in places much holier than this one, but never have they been loaded with the awe and anticipation I feel now.

She says, "I want to sing a song. Yankee Doodle."

We sing a laughing rendition, followed by another childhood favorite, "Chester, Have You Heard About Harry?" After "Five Green and Speckled Frogs", Dad suggests we sing something by Raffi. "What about that one... Joshua Giraffe?"

"No, no," Mom says, shaking her head firmly. "It scares Gabe."

She's right; the song terrified my brother when he was little.

Mom starts singing oldies: The Beatles, Carole King. During our mangled harmonies of "California Dreamin'", Noah starts to cry. Then we sing some more, enjoying this stolen time together, like it used to be.

Even Dad is relaxed and smiling. I could almost forget that we're sitting on our mother's deathbed.

After an hour with us, Mom starts to fade.

Dad sighs. "We should let her rest."

We climb off the bed, solemn and silent, moving slowly to stretch this time as long as we can.

"Is this it?" Mom asks me.

I stroke her hair like I'm calming a child. "I don't know."

"Say goodnight," Dad says.

As I lean down to kiss her cool forehead, she whispers, "You write this, okay?"

"Okay, Mom. I will."

"Razel!"

Startled, I look up from the book in my lap and into the cold gray eyes of Rabbi Cantor, my Bible teacher. "Yeah?"

"Are you with us, Razel?" He deliberately uses my Hebrew name, which he knows I detest. On the first day of class I told him I refuse to be called anything that sounds like medieval weaponry ("Unsheath thy razel, young pippin!"), but he has insisted on doing so just to torture me. It's the same reason he makes me sit front-and-center, my desk cozied right up against his, so he can pester me with questions about...what was the question?

"And it was after this," the Rabbi reads sharply from the text, "that David asked of God, saying, 'Shall I go up into one of the cities of Judah?' And the Lord said to him, 'Go up.' Said David, 'Where shall I go up?' And He said, 'To Hevron.'" Rabbi Cantor places his book gently on the desk. "Why would God send David to Hebron?"

"Umm...because he left his ass there?"

Rabbi Cantor narrows his eyes, instantly silencing the wave of snickers behind me. "A witty response, Razel, but incorrect. Can anyone assist her? What is the significance of Hevron?"

Audra Goldman's hand shoots into the air. "It's where Abraham, Isaac and Jacob are buried."

The Rabbi allows himself a small smile at her. "Precisely."

I have to shut my eyes to keep from rolling them. Of course Audra Goldman knows the answer. She always knows the answer, with her color-coded notes written so neatly they look typed. They've taunted me all year long from the next desk over, as Audra, student council president, honors student, and head cheerleader, dutifully records every word out of Rabbi Cantor's mouth like an overcaffeinated secretary.

Audra has been perfect for as long as I've known her. Her father is one of the big guns in our synagogue, so she gets to sit up on the stage between her parents every Shabbos like a princess gazing down upon her minions. She's always been small; when we were younger, she had to drink shakes to make her gain weight. But somewhere around eighth grade, the flesh melted from her bones and sinews rose out of her skin like one of those 3-D topography maps. No one ever said out loud that Audra stopped eating, but you only have to look at the bobble head and grasshopper body to know. There's the pulse vibrating against her yellow temple, the veins straining against her neck as she takes little bird sips from her water bottle. Her lips pinch dryly around her mouth like an old woman's. With her eyes closed, you would swear she's dead.

Ever the overachiever, Audra is by far the rexiest of the anorexics in this school, but she's far from the only one. Jenny Marcus went to the hospital last year after she didn't eat for four days and fainted during gym. Samantha Melnick's parents caught her spitting food into napkins and stuffing them in the back of her closet (which, in my opinion, defeats the whole purpose). People feel bad for anorexics because they're so "sick", especially when they're stuck in wheelchairs and breathing with oxygen tanks. We obese, on the other hand, are moral quadriplegics. When we end up in wheelchairs, it's because we brought it on ourselves.

A few months ago, Mom and I went away to the country's foremost diet and fitness institution, which I called "The Celebrity Fat Farm" in honor of the famous fatsos whose photos lined the hallways. There were only civilians when we were there, though: a nurse from Virginia with wallet pictures of her poodle; an Iranian prince with a bodyguard and chunky gold rings on each finger; a former roadie for INXS whose mullet was as prevalent as the 100 extra pounds around his middle. Mom's personal favorite was Liz, a twenty-something pillhead whose parents had cut her off for being too fat, information that incited Mom to adopt her before you could say, "Twix." The two of them giggled through lunch, had long talks on the rec room couch, and even played hooky from lecture one afternoon to walk around the campus of the local university. Mom was in her element with a broken soul she could fix, but it didn't last long; within two weeks, Liz was gone. She'd been sleeping with the roadie and relapsed on Vicodin when he broke up with her.

Then were was Fern. You couldn't miss Fern; she was 400 pounds, easy. I couldn't stop looking at her, my eyes drawn by the same combination of fear and curiosity one has driving by a burning car on the side of the highway. Fern's eyes were almost completely obscured by the flesh of her face. Hinged forward at the waist, her torso dripped down in swaying pendulums of fat. Her legs barely held her; a cane kept her upright when she tried to walk. She wore tents of fabric stained with food and oil spots, and a sour, cheesy smell rose from between her fat rolls, where she couldn't reach to clean herself. Most of her hair had fallen out; the little she had left formed an oily gray cloud over her creamy scalp. I was terrified of Fern, which is why I was brutal to her. Whenever Fern spoke, I would waylay her with sarcastic comments or outright ignore her. Sometimes, I made jokes at her expense.

That's right. I was a fat girl making fun of a fat woman at a fat farm.

When my mother forced me to apologize, Fern asked, "Have I done something to you?"

"No."

"Then why do you have a problem with me?"

"I don't," I said, eyeing her feet, which looked like marshmallows stuffed into Birkenstocks. I still had dainty feet, despite the 250 pounds on the rest of me.

"You think we're different, don't you? You think you could never end up like this."

Actually, it was the opposite that I was afraid of.

"Let me tell you something," said Fern. "We're no different, you and me. I've just lived a lot longer than you."

I think of what Fern said whenever I look at Audra Goldman, who has somehow figured out how override her hunger indefinitely. I don't care if she looks like the Crypt Keeper; I would sell my soul to Audra Goldman in exchange for her Karen Carpenter superpowers. I tried to stop eating once, and I couldn't even make it to lunch. In fact, I found myself with my head in the fridge, with no actual memory of walking downstairs to the kitchen and shoving half a dozen bagels into my digestive tract, one after the other, until even my chest was full. It was like I was possessed.

I tried to explain this to the professionals at the fitness center, who for $10,000 had this to offer: eat less, exercise more.

"But what if there's a chocolate cake that's talking to me from downstairs and I can't not eat it?" I asked.

The white lab coat did not know what to make of this. "Just don't eat it," she said, like it was the most obvious thing in the world.

"But what if I can't not eat it?"

"You just don't."

By this time, the smell of dinner wafting in through the vent had disabled any social grace I had left. I snapped. "But what if you don't have a choice?!?"

Everyone stared, except Fern, who nodded vigorously.

"Well, of course you have a choice," the lab coat replied. "Everyone has a choice. That's why we're here. We're learning how to make better choices." Then she turned back to the whiteboard, on which she wrote the word "MODERATION."

That was the moment I realized I was screwed for life. These were supposed to be the experts with the magic pill that would stop me from eating - or, better, to eat what I want and still lose weight. Nothing before this had worked, not the parade of diets, the shakes, the fasts. Even the promise of a trip to Paris to buy a new wardrobe couldn't keep me out of the kitchen. This was my last shot. And it had failed.

There is no magic pill for me.

Which means that one day, I will end up like Fern.

Little by little, it's happening. I'm like Violet Beauregarde, swelling and swelling into a giant, round berry and helpless to stop it. The numbers keep rising; I'm at 250 now, and 300 is within view. The only two emotions I have left are shame that I'm so very broken, and terror that someone will find out. They blacken me from the inside. I start using my humor as a weapon, laughing at the world before it can laugh at me. I cast myself in the role of "Tough Girl", and play it 24 hours a day, showing everyone how much I don't care, that they can't hurt me. I stop trying in school and shoot fire at anyone who pushes me too hard, from the seventh-grade teacher I made cry to the prayer group leader I blessed with a tropical disease. Even poor Mr. Silva, the stringy nebbish who runs the choir, got hit with it. The man begged me, begged me, with his hand gripping my shoulder, to stop disrupting our practices. There was some mumbling about dedication, reaching my potential, and putting the needs of the group before my own. It wasn't bad, actually.

When he was done, I said, "Mr. Silva?"

His eyes went wide, his thoughts shining through them bright as neon: I've made contact. *"Yes, Rea?"*

"You're touching me."

Mr. Silva's eyes shot to his hand, still resting on my shoulder, and recoiled like he'd been burned.

The smart teachers have learned to hand me my detention slip at the beginning of class, so I'll disappear to the library where I can read in peace, or to play piano in the empty auditorium. The rest of them just steer clear, except Rabbi Cantor. He's a stubborn one. He pushes and pushes at me like a prospector digging for gold, refusing to let me budge from my seat, even to go to the bathroom. He wants to be The One That Reached Me. It's so pathetic it's almost cute. You'd think after 100 years of teaching, he'd know when to give up, but there he sits each afternoon, four feet away from me with his stooped shoulders and beige pants pulled up to his armpits, a yarmulke resting atop a helmet of tight, gray curls. He peers at me over his beak nose, making me feel like my thoughts are playing on speaker. It gives me the willies.

"At this point, David's about to be made king," he says. "But there's a split between the Jewish people; half of them want to crown someone else. It's dangerous for him to go in their direction, so God sends David to Hebron to hide out and pray for unity at the Cave of Machpelah, the Tomb of the Patriarchs. This is classic Jewish history, by the way. We finally make some headway and then ruin it by fighting with each other. You know the old joke: in a town with two Jews, there are three synagogues." He chuckles while the rest of us listen for crickets.

Not for the first time, I wonder what sin I must have committed against my parents that condemned me to spend my days cracking my head against a dusty, archaic language, dissecting bible characters and mapping places that only exist in pieces underground. I must have poisoned their dog in a former life.

"Jewish infighting, more than any outside enemy, has always been our biggest downfall," says Rabbi Cantor, his hands gently caressing the tops of the pages. "Cain and Abel, Jacob and Esau. You know, the sages say that the Second Temple was destroyed because of Sinat Chinam, *baseless hatred between Jews. This isn't theory; it's historical fact. At the time of the destruction, the different factions of Jews, the Pharisees, Sadducees, and the Zealots, were trapped together within the walls of Jerusalem. If they had been united, they would have had a shot at beating the Romans. But they blew it. The Pharisees and the Sadducees wanted to make peace with the Romans, but the Zealots were so thirsty for war that they burned the stockpiles of food so the others would have no choice but to fight. Instead, they all starved and were forced to surrender. So, indeed, it was* Sinat Chinam *that destroyed the Temple."*

I think of Masada, and the story of the refugees who fled there from Jerusalem after the fall of the Temple. The two events connect in my mind like dots along a timeline.

Then I think of the rest of our Israel trip.

"So what do we learn from this? Razel?"

Dear Lord, he called on me again.

"I don't know," I say, adding an edge to my voice so he'll knock it off. "When in Rome...?"

He points at me like I've done something right, diluting my joke by taking it seriously. "That's one option: do as the Romans do, blend in with the crowd. It's tempting. Rome was a powerful empire. Joining them would have given the Jews protection and opportunity. All they had to do was give up being Jewish."

"Sounds like a good deal to me," I say.

"Perhaps. But imagine you're a Jew, immersed in Jewish history and tradition from the moment of birth. Every choice you've ever made, from what you wear to whom you marry, has been influenced by the fact that you're Jewish. You've never worked on Shabbat, never eaten non-kosher. The only reality you know is a Jewish one."

I picture my father dancing with his black-hatted friends.

"Now imagine you give that up to join a society that tells you that everything you once believed is wrong. The life you knew before?" He snaps his fingers. "Gone. Tell me, Razel: who are you then?"

Before I can answer him, the bell rings.

As always, I'm the first out the door.

Two weeks later I'm sitting on one of the hard wooden benches of the school's auditorium, waiting for a last-minute assembly to begin. The buzz of talk is loud enough that I have to yell slightly for my best friend, Sophie, to hear me in the next seat.

"Can I have?" I ask, pointing to her bag of Chips Ahoy.

"You told me not to," she replies. "Direct quote: 'No matter what I say...'"

I force a laugh. "I was joking. Didn't you know I was joking?"

184

Sophie looks at me skeptically through her glasses. "You didn't sound like you were joking."

"Well, I was. So can I?"

"But you said..."

"I KNOW WHAT I SAID!" I snap, loudly enough to cause the girls in the row in front of us to turn around. Sophie shifts back slightly.

"I know what I said," I repeat, gentler this time, "but I changed my mind. Can I have a cookie, please?"

Sophie gives me one of her half-amused, half-worried looks as pulls down the hem of her Grateful Dead shirt. "Okay," she says. "But don't get mad at me after."

"I won't, I won't," I reply, shoving the cookie in my mouth. I almost moan out loud as it dissolves. Pointing to the empty stage, I ask, "Do we know what this is about?"

"Nope. Maybe student council elections?"

"Puke." I pull a copy of "Bridget Jones's Diary" from my backpack. "Tell me after what they said."

As Bridget obsesses about Daniel Cleaver, I vaguely hear the room quiet, the whoosh-whoosh of our principal's pantyhose as she walks across the stage, then a scattering of applause. Another woman's voice breaks the quiet, but I don't hear a word she says.

About a minute in, Sophie leans over to me. "Maybe you want to listen to this."

"Hmmm?" I look up. On the stage is a woman in a black pantsuit and matching heels. She has the "Rachel from Friends" haircut. With highlights.

"She's blonde," I scoff, and look back at my book.

"From the time I was young," the woman says, "I was always scared I was too fat."

The word "fat" rings out across the room like a gunshot, forcing my head up. I keep my eyes forward, praying that no one will look at me, the token fat girl. No one does, but a few people shift in their seats. Something about the word "fat" sets people's butts on fire.

"I was a dancer and an athlete," she continues. "There was a lot of pressure to be thin from my coaches, my parents, and my trainer. They said if I gained weight, I'd amount to nothing."

This makes me an amoeba.

She goes on, "It never occurred to me to question what they said; I just did what I was told. I was constantly afraid of getting fat. I felt guilty any time I ate anything, but I had to eat a lot to keep up my energy. So I started running. Five miles in the morning, five more miles at night. Anything to keep the numbers low."

I tried running once on my parents' treadmill, but I put the speed too high and flew off the conveyor belt.

"Then I broke my tailbone," the woman says, placing her manicured hands on the podium, " and I couldn't run anymore. I couldn't compete anymore. I had to come up with another way to stay thin."

I lean forward in my seat.

"I actually got the idea when I had the stomach flu. I couldn't keep anything down, not even water. When I got better, I had lost five pounds. So I decided to stick with it. Anytime I ate anything, I would force myself to vomit. I could eat as much as I wanted and lose weight, as long as I purged right afterward."

My whole body goes still. Through the skylight above, a ray of sunshine breaks through the clouds and streams down warm on my shoulder.

"I did that for twenty years. It was my secret. I thought I was the only person in the world who binged and purged. But I wasn't. Thousands of men and women..."

She goes on, but I don't hear her, as the words she said a minute ago trumpet in my brain:

Eat what you want and lose weight.

EAT WHAT YOU WANT AND LOSE WEIGHT.

Every one of my nerve endings is lit up and buzzing like a winning slot machine. I feel like springing from my seat and dancing across the backs of the seats like Gene Kelly in "Singin' in the Rain." At the same time, a calm settles over me, a release, like I'm giving into sleep.

It's all going to be okay now. I've found it.

I've found my magic pill.

I keep my discovery close to me like a secret treasure and wait for the right moment to use it. It comes during Spanish class. I walk in just after the second bell, holding a bag of mini-cookies from the vending machine.

"Ah, Mercedes, Bienvenidos, *" says Mrs. Sugarman, followed by her standard, Bronx-accented greeting: "Ya late and ya rude." She points a bright red fingernail toward the garbage.* "Chicle en la basura. *"*

I throw out my gum and take a seat.

As Mrs. Sugarman drills us in subjunctive verbs, I sneak cookies from underneath my desk, reveling in the feel of them turning to paste in my mouth. At first, I take one or two cookies at a time, but soon enough I'm shoveling them in by the handful. If Mrs. Sugarman notices, she doesn't say anything. In less than two minutes, the bag is empty. I lick the last of the cookie paste from my teeth and cheeks, feeling it settle like a weight in my stomach.

I put my hand up. "¿Señora, puedo ir al baño?"

She raises one eyebrow, sending the blue shadow on her lids stretching upward. "Rápidamente."

The bathroom is blessedly empty. I slip into the handicapped stall to give myself space, the lock cold and heavy as I slide it across the door. The toilet stands white and solitary in the corner of the stall like a wallflower waiting for a dance partner. Bracing an arm against the seat, I peer into the bowl, the water inside it as still as glass. I stick my fingers down the tight, slick tunnel of my throat and wiggle them. My stomach lurches. I wiggle them again, and the food starts traveling upward.

I'm not prepared for the hot, acid rush that comes out of me, nor the blinding pressure behind my eyes and nose. I've thrown up before, when I was sick, but it never felt like I was being turned inside out. I like it. I like the feeling of my body taking over and spasming out everything I've eaten. I like the burn in my throat and the tearing feeling in my head that erases all thought. I like that it hurts. When I'm done, there's a delicious emptiness in my body, like everything ugly inside me has been cast out, and now I'm pure and fixed. I can start all over again.

I'm exhausted now, but manage to get to the sink to wash my face and hands. My skin is splotchy, and my eyes are bright red. It looks like I've been crying, or smoking weed. Breathing into my palm, I catch a faintly sour smell. Maybe Sophie has gum. I slip back into class with my eyes down, stealing a look at the clock.

I was gone for four minutes.

Wearing only a towel, I look down at the open book on my bathroom counter: "Making Faces" by the makeup guru Kevyn Aucoin. Every picture is of a celebrity made up to look like a different celebrity: Drew Barrymore smolders as Marilyn Monroe; Demi Moore is an angelic Clara Bow; Gwyneth Paltrow broods as James Dean. Every night, I reproduce one of the images on my own face, taking extra care to get each contour exactly right. I give my face the same attention in the morning, making sure my makeup is perfect, my hair is perfect, and that I look stylish, no matter what I'm wearing. (Accessories: the fat girl's secret weapon.) It's my painted-on armor, a flawless finish meant to draw the eye away from the rest of me.

Tonight, I'm copying Gina Gershon as Sofia Loren. With a steady hand, I cat my eyes in black smoke, making my irises jump out in blue. I pile on a thick layer of mascara and black pencil in my lower lids. Extra bronzer gives the illusion of cheekbones and a single chin. I paint my lips blood red, taking extra care in the divot of my upper lip, the one identical to my mother's. Then I stare at myself in the mirror for a long time, pretending I'm on a red carpet with thousands of people screaming my name. I'm transformed into someone beautiful and adored.

The door from Dena's room pops open and my sister saunters in.

"I'm in here!" I snap, pulling up my towel.

Her eleven-year-old mouth falls open. "Whoa. What's with your face?"

"What's with your *face?"*

"You look like someone punched you."

I roll my eyes. Sometimes I think Dena was born just to annoy me. "It's Sofia Loren!"

This doesn't impress her. "Whatever. I have to pee."

"Ugh, fine. Let me just wash it off."

I scrub at my skin with hot water, silently wishing that Dena would move to a foster home and I'd get the bathroom to myself. Streams of black run down my hands and into the sink.

"Come on," *says Dena.*

When I look up again, dark rings have formed under my eyes, but the liner has stayed intact. "Heroin chic," I say to my reflection.
"What's that?"
"You wouldn't get it," I reply, and slam the door.

Over the next few months, I fall into a rhythm: eat, purge, repeat, two, five, eight times a day. My stomach muscles tighten in readiness the second I put anything in my mouth. I become a master at quick exits and covering my tracks. The numbers on the scale mostly hover around 240 because I'm still eating too much to lose weight. But I haven't gained, either, and that's enough. I've given up the dream of ever being thin, but at least I won't get any fatter than this.

Now that I can have what I want, I want it all and more. And once I've had it, I need get it out as quickly as possible. The need to be empty is as powerful as the need to be full, leading me around like a puppy on a leash. My friends talk to me, but I'm not listening. I nod as if I'm part of the conversation, but none of it registers. My attention is on what's in their lunches, what's left in mine, what's in the vending machine, how much money I have to scrounge together, and how quickly I can get the food in and out of me with no one noticing.

"Where are you going?" Sophie asks as I pack up my bag.
"Library," I lie smoothly. "I'll meet you in Bio."
"We have Cantor now. You can't skip it."
She's right; no one skips Cantor's class. But there's no way I can sit through it with a belly full of Doritos that are metabolizing into fat cells with each passing second. If Cantor calls on me, I might snarl at him like a rabid dog.
"Whatever," I say. "You'll give me your notes."
Sophie gives me one of her worried looks then goes upstairs. I wait until her black converse are out of view before heading to the bathroom.

The next afternoon, I lay on one of the hard wooden benches in the auditorium, reading a romance novel Mom just finished and passed on to me with her review: "Same old shit." I can guess from the first page what's going to happen, but I tolerate it because this author is known for writing good sex scenes. These are the parts I read and re-read, all stirred up, while studying every line like a textbook: this is what it feels like when he does this, they like it when you do that. It's the closest thing I've ever gotten to sex and possibly ever will.

I thought I had a shot at losing my virginity last year, when my friend Ethan hooked me up with a date for the prom. I'd assumed that none of the boys I actually liked would go with me, so I didn't bother asking them. But Ethan said this guy, TJ, was a perfect fit for me: he had just lost 100 pounds, so he knew what it was like to be fat. He wouldn't be ashamed to have me as his date.

I didn't meet TJ until the night of the prom, but we'd spoken on the phone a couple of times before. He was funny, smart, and did a dead-on Jim Carrey impression. He was like me, using humor as a sleight of hand. As the days to the prom counted down, I wrestled my expectations to keep them from springing out of control. Probably, TJ looked like Christian Bale and would fall in love the instant he saw me. When we had sex after prom, he'd weep and say he'd found his soulmate.

Or it would just be a nice evening out.

On prom night, I paced the foyer of my house in a size-16, baby-pink gown I'd spent a month Weight-Watchering myself into. I was jittery, checking and rechecking my hair and makeup in the hallway mirror. I joked that I looked like "Babe, Pig at the Prom." Mom, trying not to laugh, told me to stop it.

"Wrap?" I asked her, pulling two strips of satin from the back of my dress around my arms. Then I dropped them, revealing my upper limbs in all their cottage cheese glory. "Or no wrap?"

"It doesn't matter," Mom said. "You're beautiful either way."

I rolled my eyes. "You have to say that. You're my mom."

The doorbell rang, and my hands started to shake.

There was TJ, who looked exactly like Christian Bale, if Christian Bale was a six-foot-tall beaver with clown feet. I was disappointed for about a millisecond before I remembered that this was the kind of date a girl like me gets: sloppy, sweaty, and oafish. I should be grateful and not do anything that would make him not like me anymore.

"You look really nice," he said.

I knew he was lying, so I lied back. "So do you."

He gave me a corsage that felt itchy on my wrist, but I didn't take it off. Mom lined us up for pictures, and we fumbled trying to figure out how to stand together. Even in three-inch heels, I didn't reach TJ's armpit. He wrapped his flyswatter hand around my arm, making me go stiff because he was touching my fat, *but I smiled big because Mom was snapping the picture. TJ did his Jim Carrey impression again, then we got into the limo and went to the prom.*

No matter how TJ looked, I was happy and relieved to walk into my junior prom with an actual male date. TJ jumped right onto the dance floor and started cutting up, but I didn't mind. I laughed extra loud to show everyone how funny my date was, how much fun I was having, how I was a normal girl like anyone else having a blast at her junior prom. My friend Joey Feig danced over to us and cut up alongside TJ, which made me laugh for real. Joey had come to prom with Steve Diamond as a joke, even though he has, according to my mother, "the most gorgeous jaw." Joey could have gotten a real date if he'd wanted, but he seemed to be only interested in TJ. In fact, after a while, our circle of three broke into two smaller circles, like a mitotic cell: one circle with Joey and TJ, and another with me. Over the next hour, they danced a goofy sidestep just inches from each other, while all my dreams of casting off my maidenhead went down in flames.

The bell rings to signal the end of the day, and I fold down the corner of the page. As I sit up to pack my things, I hear a sharp voice echo across the room:

"Razel!"

It's Rabbi Cantor, standing at the door. He does not look happy to see me.

Oh, crap, *I think, remembering that I cut his class yesterday. I approach him tentatively, like I'm walking toward an electric chair, steeling myself against the tirade I know is coming. Meanwhile, my mind composes a list of viable excuses:* Stomach bug? Extra credit project? Dead Grandmother? That one is technically true...

But as I get closer, his face wipes my mind blank. His eyes are wet and round and sad, like someone has just broken his heart.

"You didn't come to class," he says.

"Me?" I say, not because I didn't hear him, but because I can't comprehend that I'm the cause of this kind of anguish.

"Don't you know what you're missing?" His voice breaks on the last word.

Oh, my God. He might actually cry.

I've never seen this kind of emotion in an adult, not even my mother. It feels too big for me. "I-I'm sorry."

He dips his head. "I am, too."

I stare dumbly at him, not sure if I should hug him or burst into tears myself.

"I'll see you in class, Razel," the rabbi says, and shuffles off, his orthopedic shoes squeaking against the floor.

On the ride home, I replay the conversation in my head, feeling more and more unsettled. Why couldn't he have just been angry? Angry I can work with. When they're angry, I can act like I don't care, which makes them even angrier and then I win. But sad and pathetic? It knocked me down before the match even started. Maybe Rabbi Cantor knew that would happen, so he went for a sneak attack instead of direct combat...No. He was genuinely upset. I could see it is his eyes, the defeated slump of his shoulders, and the white line around his lips as he squeezed them together. What did it matter to him if I showed up or not? And why, when I didn't, did he act like someone had just died?

But what bothered me the most was that question: "Don't you know what you're missing?" It was like he'd offered me his prized possession and I'd spit on it. How could someone fall apart like that over a few ancient books? I don't see anyone from the English department boo-hooing over The Iliad. Rabbi Cantor was more than sad; it was like I'd slapped him in the soul. This thing is real *to him, like it is for those penguins in Brooklyn my Dad hangs out with. But Rabbi Cantor is educated, articulate. He's not brainwashed or confined to some Jewish enclave. Yet he loves being Jewish as much as they do; it's obvious. For a split second, I consider that there might be something to all these books, all these traditions, all this history they're shoving down my throat, something deep enough to move a grown man to tears.*

This unsettles me even more.

When I get home, there's a stack of pizza boxes in the kitchen: dinner. I hear everyone in Mom's room, along with the music and sonorous voices of ESPN. Must be a Devil's game tonight. I drop my backpack and head straight for the pizza box, polishing off slice after slice until the unsettledness goes away and all I can feel is full.

I stop into Mom's room to tell her I'm home.

"You're green," she says, sitting at the head of the bed, while Gabe, Noah, and Dena lay on their stomachs at the foot with plates of pizza in front of them.

"Headache."

"Come here." She puts a cool palm to my forehead. "You sick?"

"I got nauseous in carpool. I had to sit backwards in the station wagon."

"Go rest," she says, then yells at the TV. "Come ON, Sykora! MOVE YOUR ASS!!!!"

While their shouts reverberate from downstairs, I lean over my bathroom toilet, jam my fingers down my throat, and brace myself for the wave. But halfway up my throat, the food catches. I try to coax it up, but it's stuck. I push my fingers deeper, almost to the back knuckle, trying to move the blockage, but I can't reach it. And I can't breathe.

So this is choking. I try to grunt a signal for help, but no sounds comes out. I grip onto the sides of the toilet bowl in terror, yet I'm oddly calm, hearing a muffled version of the game, the announcers' voices, and my brothers' cheers as if I'm underwater, drifting far away.

This is it. I'm going to die. They're going to find me here, slumped over the toilet, covered with pizza vomit.

That might actually be worse than dying.

I start to get dizzy.

Please, God, *I think.* Please don't let me die like this. I promise, I'll never do it again.

Just like that, the food dislodges, shooting up and out of me like it's spring-loaded. As my stomach spasms, I slide to the floor, weak with relief. I rest my head on the cool white tile, trying to recover my breath. My vision is hazy and my body, jelly. A headache forms above my right eye, throbbing in time with my heartbeat.

All at once, the quiet of the bathroom is shaken by a swell of cheering from below. "GOOOOOOOAAAAALLLLLL!!!!!"

My family's clapping vibrates through the floor, along with the music from the television. The noise jostles me, shaking up the energy I need to crawl out of the bathroom and into my bed, where sleep comes instantly.

When I wake, the house is dark and silent, and I'm starving. The stairs creak beneath me as I walk down to the kitchen, where the numbers on the oven clock shine an eerie green in the darkness: 2:31 a.m.

I open the fridge and squint into the bright light, feeling around until my hand falls on a package of yogurt. Perfect. I flip on the lights over the sink and leave the rest of the kitchen in semi-darkness, mood lighting for a romantic dinner with myself. But as I slide onto a stool at the island, I hear the door to Mom's room open, followed by her familiar step across the wood floors.

Dinner for two, it seems.

Mom enters the kitchen, thighs swishing under the pink seashell nightshirt she bought on the Cape last summer. Her lower legs stretch down in thick blocks that don't taper into ankles but feed directly into her feet, facing outward, almost penguin-like, as she walks. Her hips are wide and her butt sticks out, shifting the shirt up and down. Mom is not delicate or small, but she's not fat, even though she thinks so. She just takes space. Mom rubs her eyes to show me how just-asleep she was, but her hair is smooth and there's an indent on her nose from her reading glasses. She's been waiting for me to wake up.

"Oh, good, you found something," she says in whisper-talk, heading to the other side of the island, where her hands rest against the marble in active "Mom" stance, ready to serve and help and do. It doesn't matter that it's the middle of the night and I've already served myself. "You were out cold; I didn't want to wake you. You feeling better?"

I tip my head back and forth to indicate that I'm so-so, even though I'm fine. I might as well milk it if there's a chance I can stay home from school tomorrow. "I just wanted to eat something before I went back to bed."

"There's fruit, too, if you want."

"This is fine."

She watches me dip my spoon into the yogurt. "So you want to tell me what's going on?"

A tingle goes up my back. She knows.

I stay casual. "With what?"

"Rea," She gives me her best don't-bullshit-me look. "I know what you're doing."

"You sound like a detective," I scoff, then slide the spoon into in my mouth.

She's not fooled. "It has to stop. Now."

I look over her shoulder at my reflection in the window, a lumpy black mass against the wallpaper Mom put up last week, light yellow with bulbous pink and purple hydrangeas. It's quaint and country, perfect for our house in Cape Cod, but not for the contemporary, black-and-white kitchen we're sitting in. Her style must be changing again. I bet she'll redo the whole house soon, like she did a few summers ago when I went away to camp. I came home to find my bedroom's white walls sponge-painted pink, and the ceiling a glossy palette of sea green.

"It's pink!" she said with flourish as I stepped into the room. "Your favorite color!"

She was so sure of it, the way she is about everything, that I assumed it was true.

"Look at me. Rea!"

I force my eyes onto her face.

"It could kill you."

There's a mixture of panic and rage churning in my belly. Meanwhile, the rest of me sinks into relief that it's not a secret anymore, that she's finally swooped in to save me. But I won't give this up. I can't. Not when I finally have this thing under control.

"You have no idea what you're talking about," I snap. *"How could you even know?"*

"I'm your mother. I know everything. And you share a bathroom with your sister."

That brat. *"Dena told you?"*

"She heard you and it scared the crap out of her. She didn't want you to know. She's afraid you'll be mad at her."

"Well, I am. I'm never speaking to her again."

"She was trying to help you!"

"I don't want help!" Yes, I do. But no one can help me.

"There's a clinic in Verona," Mom says. *"There are therapists there who know about this."*

"So?"

"I made an appointment for you. For tomorrow."

"I'm not going."

"You are, if I have to drag you there myself."

"It won't help," I say, recalling the white lab coats. "Just give me a few months. I just want to get under 200. Then I'll stop."

"This isn't negotiable."

The panic spreads across my back and shoulders like a spill. "If you make me stop, I'll hate you forever."

"Go ahead."

"You don't know what you're doing!"

"I'm saving your life, Rea!"

"Don't bother!" I laugh mirthlessly. "Why can't you just leave me alone?"

Mom smiles at that. "Because it's my job to fight for you. I'll fight for you until I die."

"I know that!" I cry, then drop my face into my hands and give in to sobbing.

Chapter Twelve

I hear Mom's voice from her room and follow it, hoping to catch her in a lucid moment. Dena sits on the bed, watching Mom talk with people only she can see.

"I'm going to tell you a story," Mom says, her eyes wide and distant. "It's the story about how Debbi died." Her gaze locks on mine. "I see four ladies. They're taking me on Sarah's boat."

Dena and I smile at each other, comforted by the image of our mother drifting peacefully under the care of whom we can only guess are the four matriarchs: Sarah, Rebecca, Rachel and Leah.

It's amazing how quickly we've all adapted to this new normal, one in which our mother floats between worlds, speaking a dream language none of us understands. She's here, but she's not with us, though seeing her awake makes me hopeful she'll suddenly snap back to her old self. I keep thinking this is just a reaction to the morphine, something that will eventually reverse itself and reveal her again. But it isn't. This is her, dying. It's peaceful around her, though. Quiet.

Then her family comes, and it all goes to hell.

When Mom requested that we ask her father to come, we hesitated. It was already too much for her to have company when she was with it; in her current state, who knows what could happen? It was possible she didn't even know what she was asking for, or that she might not recognize her father. But she asked again, and then again.

"I want to see him," she insisted.

There was no saying no.

When my grandfather arrives with Lewis and Esther, they bring a storm in with them. It shocks all of us, whom for the past few weeks have known only the slow-moving world contained in this house. Lewis's hard hugs and slaps on the back are assaults on our systems, as is the sound of his booming voice off the high ceilings. Esther chases the baby, trying to lure him with high-pitched gibberish, but Ezra clings to me. He, too, can't seem to handle her maelstrom of energy. When Esther tries to gab with me, I avoid her eyes.

The moment my grandfather enters the house, Dad takes him to Mom's room. Zadie leans hard on his cane, weariness personified.

Dad opens the door. "Willie," he calls gently. "Look who's here..."

"I want to see him," I hear Mom say.

Dad helps Zadie into the room and shuts the door softly.

At first, all is still. My brothers, my sister, my husband and sisters-in-law sit taut in the living room, waiting for something, but unsure of what. It comes one minute later: a strange, guttural wailing from behind Mom's door.

"What is that?" Dena murmurs, sliding forward on her stool like she's ready to spring.

"I WANT THEM!" we hear Mom cry. "BRING THEM!"

The door to their room swings open and Dad sticks his head out.

"She wants you," he says, nodding toward us.

Gabe, Noah, Dena and I stand. The in-laws know instinctively to stay put and watch the action from the cheap seats.

Entering Mom's room, I almost run out at the sight of her face. She looks haunted. Her eyes stare at the middle distance like a blind woman's, while tears stream down her face. She rocks and waves her arms, agitated, as if she's building the momentum to launch herself at her father, who sits, terrified, on a stool beside the bed.

"They're here, Willie." Dad says, then slips out, speed-dialing the VNA on his phone.

Mom's eyes move slightly toward the sound of us filing in.

"You see them?" she says, pointing at us. "This is my legacy! These beautiful babies! I raised them, these beautiful babies! It wasn't me...It wasn't me..." She drifts, then snaps back, looking directly at her father. "You never helped them! *YOU NEVER HELPED!*"

My grandfather, though taller than Dad, seems to shrink. He shakes his head, eyes wide and afraid. He tries to speak but nothing comes out. My eyes dart from Mom to Zadie and back, unsure of what to do. Mom is out of control, but I want her to get what she needs from her father. I search his face for a spark of understanding. Does he know what she's talking about? Does *she* know what she's talking about? From the sobs jerking her chest upward and the wild movement of her body, I'm almost positive she does. But if she wants remorse, she won't get it. My grandfather gapes at her, looking like a wrecking ball is demolishing his insides. Meanwhile, Mom waves frantically at him, screaming, like she's caught in an undertow that would kill anyone who tried to save her.

Finally, he says, "I will help."

"Promise me! Promise me you'll help them!" Mom's sobs make the whole bed shake.

"I-I promise."

Dad rushes back in. "Everyone needs to leave. Now. We need to get her calmed down."

Overwhelmed, we walk out in silence while Dad whispers soothingly to Mom, pressing his body to hers like he's trying to warm her.

As we walk into the living room, Lewis storms out the front door. Taking Ezra from Erin, I look out the window to see my uncle pacing in the driveway, pointing angrily at the house as he shouts at my grandfather. Esther follows but stands apart, studying the shrubbery on the side of the road with extra concentration.

"What's his problem?" I ask Gabe, who's watching nearby.

"I think he thinks we kicked them out."

When Dad steps out of the bedroom, Gabe says, "Dad, you didn't mean for them to leave, did you?"

"Of course not. I just meant we needed to take a break."

"Fine," Gabe says, regarding my uncle warily. "I'll go talk to him."

"I'll go with you," says Dena.

My brother and sister go to the front yard, where Lewis explodes at them. His words are muffled, but his volume carries all the way back to the house. Gabe comes in looking disgusted, with a hand pressed to his jaw.

"What happened?" I ask.

Gabe shakes his head. "I tried to tell him it was a misunderstanding and that they should stay, but he just kept swearing at me. Just went *off*, saying how selfish we all are, how I never called him when Bubbie died. He kept talking and talking and refused to listen to anything I said. Finally I told him to fuck off, and he punched me."

"He *what*?!?"

"God, what a shitshow," Noah says under his breath.

After Dad gets Mom calmed down, he invites Zadie to try speaking to her again.

"Talk about her childhood," he suggests, mildly pleading. "Tell her she was loved."

But by the time Zadie gets to her, she's fallen asleep.

Lewis herds Zadie to the car, Esther trailing behind, and they peel out of the driveway less than half an hour after they arrived. Then they're gone, like an earthquake that fells an entire city in a matter of seconds.

For a long time, we all sit together, silent and shellshocked. Then Dad starts talking.

"I know how hard this is," he says. "Your mother is being ripped away from you. I know what that is. But at least she isn't being torn from you, like mine was."

He starts to cry.

Dena, Ben and I look tentatively at each other, unsure of what to do. So we listen.

"My father wasn't a good man," Dad continues. "All the other boys thought he was great: he coached the sports teams and was on the news, but they didn't know. He would get tickets for the press box at the baseball game, find a seat for me in the stands and leave me there. He shit all over my mother, cheating, then left her for a girl who was about three years older than me.

"But my mother was strong, and she worked hard. One of her three jobs was an overnight shift on the weekends, admitting at a hospital. She was under so much pressure, raising three boys alone, but she was always easygoing, always trying to help people. She was creative, like Mom, especially with music; whenever there was a talent show, she would put an act together for us. Sometimes, my mom would bring kosher chicken home from Baltimore, but back then you had to pluck it yourself, so she'd fill the top of a Jiffy container with alcohol and light it to loosen the skin and get the feathers out. Her father was a chicken farmer, so she knew all about that. Her parents and all her siblings lived around the farm, up in Millis. She wanted to move back after the divorce, to be near them. She probably would have, too, if things had been different…

"It's funny. She and Mom were very different, but in many ways they were the same. My mom didn't like Debbi, because one night, while she was working at the hospital, Debbi came to stay at my house with another couple during a youth convention. We fell asleep in the same room, and my mother found us there when she got home in the morning. She thought Debbi wasn't a good girl, and not good for me. She wouldn't let me invite her to my brother's bar-mitzvah. But I was really serious about Mom; after that night she slept over, I was pulling out of my driveway and I suddenly slammed on the brakes. It just hit me: *I'm gonna marry her.*

"At my brother's bar-mitzvah, I told my mother I wanted to talk to her about Debbi, but she didn't want to then. She said, 'We'll talk about it at Thanksgiving.' I said fine, but it was tense. I was upset. I left to go back to the Academy.

"At school, I had a weird dream. I was sitting at lunch in the mess hall, and there was an announcement over the loudspeaker: '*Midshipman Buckler, you have a telephone call at the M.O.D's office.*' You didn't really get calls like that unless it was an emergency. So I went to the office, and it was my father on the phone, telling me my mother was dead. It was weird. And the detail..." He shakes his head at the memory.

"The very next day at lunch," he says, "there's an announcement over the loudspeaker: *'Midshipman Buckler, you have a telephone call at the M.O.D.'s office.'* I ran like hell. It was my father; all he could say was that my brothers were injured badly. When I asked him what happened to my mother, he didn't say anything. But I already knew."

He breaks down again, wiping tears from his face. "I know it's hard for you. But you get to say goodbye. It's not ending for you with a phone call. So, in a lot of ways, you're lucky."

Dad goes on for hours, telling us about the night of his mother's memorial service, when he and Mom made their pact to always take care of each other. His years at the United States Merchant Marine Academy, where he would tamper with the time stamp machine to steal extra hours with Mom. How the two of them tried to elope at 18 to Providence, but couldn't find a justice of the peace to marry them at 11 o'clock at night. Going to Greece while he was in the Navy, getting drunk on Ouzo and nearly falling off a building. Their wedding, on an August afternoon so hot, Mom almost fainted. Moving to upstate New York for Dad's doctoral program, where the snows would cover the front door of their house. Working with some of the first computers when they took up an entire room and needed punch cards to operate. Appearing with Mom on a news show in Pittsburgh to talk about infertility, in the days when the topic was still taboo. While they waited in the green room, Mom spent twenty minutes chatting with Lynn Swann, star of the Pittsburgh Steelers, with no clue who he was. Each of our births. Getting into the freezing bathtub with me when I ran teething fevers. Pre-dawn hockey practices with Gabe and Noah and hash browns from McDonald's afterward. The Meadowlands fair with Dena. Seeing the Devils win the Stanley Cup. Meeting Rabbi Itzik. The pain of drifting away from Mom, but refusing to split up his family the way his father had.

"I made a calendar when Dena was in eighth grade," he says, "that counted every day until she graduated. If I got tempted to leave, I would look at the remaining days and remember what it was like after my father left. Once a week, he came to take us out to dinner, completely disrupting our schedule. I hated it. I didn't want to do the same thing to you, or have to run back and forth trying to see you. I used the calendar to remind myself that I could at least guts it out until the countdown ended. By the time it did, leaving your mother was the last thing I wanted."

None of us move, so rapt are we by the fact that he's *talking* to us. I've heard almost every story before, but I've only ever heard them from Mom's perspective. Dad spins them differently, grounds Mom's exaggerations, fills in blanks we didn't even know were there. It's like watching the camera shift focus from Mom at the foreground to Dad in the background, a surprise twist that ties the whole story together. It's well past dark when he winds down, spent, eyes glassy, yarmulke slightly askew. He says goodnight, giving each of us a kiss on the head, and retreats to his room.

For a while, no one speaks. Then, quietly, thoughtfully, we each get up and excuse ourselves upstairs.

"That just happened, right?" I ask Ben as we slide into bed.

"I think so," Ben replies, lost in thought.

I lay awake for a long time, listening to my husband and baby's breaths falling into rhythm then slipping out of sync again. I replay my father's story, wondering why he chose tonight of all nights to tell it. *Mah Nishtana?* Was he trying to comfort us? Himself? Was he fearful of one day standing in Zadie's shoes, failing to convince his children that he did, indeed, love them? Or maybe it was simpler than that. The probability that he would have all of us together again, in the same room, without distractions, was slim. Perhaps his calculations determined that there would be no better time than now.

But more importantly, will this ever happen again? Or was it a one-time phenomenon, sudden and unexplained? Maybe that it happened once is enough, like seeing an Aurora or the Great Wall of China. But I'd like to think that my father has made some kind of beginning, unlocking a door he'll open wider with time.

I picture Mom's half-smile and shrug when presented with a question that had no answer.

"We shall see," she would say.

Indeed.

Since her family's visit, Mom has been battling demons. She cries, screams, and accuses us of trying to hurt her. *The Journey's End* calls this stage "Terminal Restlessness", a profound change of mood as the end of life approaches. It's partly the result of waste buildup as the systems shut down and throw off the body's chemical balance. The dying start hallucinating, having psychotic episodes, fighting off caregivers like domesticated animals gone savage. Dad's getting it the worst; Mom screams at him through the night that he doesn't understand, that he doesn't help her, that he's always lying. He looks like he's been microwaved.

"It's hell on the family," Della assures us, "but it makes them more willing to let go in the end."

She said we were looking at 24 to 48 hours, but that was five days ago.

This morning, Mom's yelling is loud and clear on the other side of the house: "I'M NOT GOING IN MY DIAPER!"

When I run in, she's edging off the bed toward the commode, the diaper half-unfastened and hanging off her body. She looks like an enormous toddler, mid-tantrum. Noah blocks her way with his hands up and knees bent, goalie stance, but from the desperate look on Mom's face, I wouldn't put it past her to fight him. Enya sings soothingly in the background (Della's suggestion), an odd accompaniment to the standoff taking place. Trying not to see the wiry pubic hairs poking above the diaper, I climb onto the bed and put my face up close to Mom's.

"Mom," I say in my teacher voice, "It's time to lay down."

My mother's faraway eyes give me the chills. She reminds me of someone with autism, locked in a world no one else can see.

"Not you, too, Rea," she says, like I've betrayed her. "You gotta help me. Re, help me…"

Noah's eyes are open so wide I see the whites all around his irises, mirroring my terror and helplessness. It makes me think of a movie I saw once with Ben, a romance in which the male lover dies. His death took place in a clean, stark-white room, saturated with light to look heavenly and tranquil. His beloved, also clad in white, cried prettily at his side. The dying man said something loving and profound, then closed his eyes like a child going down for a nap. At the time, I cried, having no clue what death actually looks like. Now, trying to maneuver my deranged mother into her bed, I could laugh out loud.

Death is a pitiful mess. There's nothing clean or white or tranquil about it. There's waste and blood and fluid and crusted flesh and the smell of rot that sneaks in early. There are commodes, adult diapers and catheters. Pills and patches and syringes and ports. Wheelchairs and medical equipment with long wires you trip over constantly. Piles and piles of laundry. Marathon hours of waiting that somehow exhaust you more than an actual marathon ever could. The exhaustion infiltrates every cell, until your husband says you look like you've been hit by a house. Crying is an afterthought. As for the dying, words of wisdom are no guarantee. They may scream nonsense at you and refuse to let you help them. They say things that don't comfort, but haunt, like when Mom begged Gabe to kill her.

I'm not sure how much more any of us can take. Everyone is jumpy and on edge, a thick tension stewing in the air around us. It crackles especially around Dad and Dena, who are at odds about the best way to handle Mom. The house echoes with their slamming doors.

And yet we push on. We prepare to sit shiva, forming a long queue for the laundry we won't be able to do during the week of mourning. We get haircuts, buy clothes to wear to the funeral, and stock up on food we'll need around the house. These tasks are the only clear-cut directions I have right now, so I grab ahold of them gratefully, like a buoy on a churning sea. Preparing for Shiva makes me feel like I got the one-up on death, snatching away its power of surprise. But that won't stop it from coming.

I start to think about seeing Mom dead. Della says it will be shocking, expected or not. What will I do? Faint? Scream? Run?

What will Dad do?

I can't imagine, seeing that he's already starting to collapse. This afternoon, while I feed Ezra, a howl comes from Mom's room, high-pitched and gasping, like someone having an asthma attack. Erin and I run to find Mom resting peacefully, while Dad weeps at her side. His face is bright pink, his hair in disarray. He's taken off his glasses to make way for tears.

"You can't leave me, Willie, please, I'm begging you...I'm so scared. I don't want to be alone. You're my only friend, Willie. I don't want to be without you..."

My body goes numb, an instinctive cushion against seeing my father reduced to this.

Abruptly, Dad gets up and walks right by us as if we're not there, exiting the house through the front door. He's gone for an hour, and when he comes back, his shoes are sandy. I follow him to Mom's room and watch from the door as he sits beside her and takes her hand. She's awake now, turning herself toward him with the little strength she has. The back of her hospital gown rides up her neck, revealing the slit we cut to get the gown over her head more easily.

"I was just at the beach," Dad says. "You can see the bridge today, and the tower in Provincetown. I looked out at the water, Willie, and I prayed to God that you would be able to see it through my eyes. I screamed to Hashem to take you now or to return you to us in good health. No more of this."

Mom murmurs, her eyes half-open, "It feels like a game..."

"You're right. And I'm the loser. The kids are losers."

"Help me..."

"I'm trying, Willie," he says. "But I'm not doing a good job."

Chapter Thirteen

"I need you to do me a favor," Gabe says while I stir up a batch of banana muffins.

"Okay."

"Can you please stop making bad-for-you food? I feel all the simple sugars doing things to my body."

Noah pipes up from the couch. "But she likes baking."

"Fine," I say. "Let me just finish these."

The house fills with the scent of baking bananas and cinnamon. Every so often, someone passes through the kitchen, sniffing at the air like a bloodhound. When I pull the muffins from the oven, everyone magically appears, swarming in on the tin like fruit flies. They eat reverently, sensuously, with eyes closed. Gabe watches.

"Those look like rockin' muffins," he says.

"*Mplhmghf*," says Noah.

Gabe eyes the last one on the plate, perfect, golden, and crowned with steam, then holds it up to his face like he and the muffin are in a pistols-at-dawn showdown. Gabe loses. He bites deeply, chews slowly. Then he swallows, shaking his head in shame.

Ezra, meanwhile, has still not crawled, but he loves to mess with us by pretending he's about to. At first, just Ben, Dena and I were looking out for it, but now everyone is taking bets on when it's going to happen, and who's going to see it first. Ezra lifts himself onto hands and knees, sending us scrambling around the island to get a good look. He shimmies a bit, his diaper crinkling.

"Come on, Ezra!" Gabe says. "DO IT!"

Ezra plops down onto his belly to a chorus of groans.

"Oh, man!"

"Dude, you were so close!"

Ezra has become a mascot of sorts, a happy sunspot amidst the darkness filling the Cape House. Even the more baby-wary of our crew gravitate to him like a fireplace in a cold room, absently stroking his cheek or ruffling his hair as they pass. Erin grabs him for an impromptu dance. Sammy pulls him into her lap to read to him. Noah does the same. Gabe bounces around to a Sesame Street album to make the baby laugh (I laugh harder). And they've all started signing to Ezra, using the flashcards I bought to teach him. Gabe sticks his pointer and middle finger downward for "G"; Noah makes an "N" by hooking his pointer and middle fingers over his thumb. Dena and I, for our own entertainment, practice the signs for animals. She likes "Alligator", clamping her hands together like a chomping mouth. My favorite is "cow", which I make by forming a "Y" with my hand—thumb and pinkie up, middle three down— putting thumb to temple, and tilting the pinkie forward, like a cow flicking a fly off of its ear.

Dad paces into the kitchen with surprising energy. "What's everybody's plan today? Can we do dinner or lunch together?"

"I was going to make salmon later," Dena says.

"So, dinner?"

We nod in agreement.

"What if we do like a big dinner?" says Dad. "Gabe can make his chili and Erin can do guacamole or something…"

"Multicultural. I like it," I say.

Noah chimes in, eyes on his computer. "You know it's Cinco de Mayo today."

"Omigosh!" I say, building on Dad's momentum. "We need to have a party!"

"Are we Mexican?" Gabe says.

I shake my head firmly. "Irrelevant."

Everyone gets swept up in the excitement.

"Can we wear hats?"

"Can there be a piñata?"

"Margaritas!"

"Cuervo!"

"We should hang the piñata from the ceiling fan," Dad jokes.

I laugh. "Don't tell Mom. She'll get really mad."

Gabe looks at the fan. "Can you do that?"

"The fan can't really handle the weight, but maybe I could come up with something else…" Dad takes a step back to survey the ceiling, a good twenty feet in the air, holding his yarmulke to his head so it doesn't fall off. "Maybe I could build some kind of pulley to suspend the piñata. It just depends on the angle…"

"Dad, what time does the party start?" I ask.

"I say drinks at 5, dinner at 5:30, then maybe a special event? Like a movie?"

"*The Three Amigos*. Obviously." Noah says, eyes still locked on his laptop.

"Fine. You guys get everything, and I'll see you at 5." Dad hands me his American Express card and trots back to his room.

We bat around recipe ideas, then make a huge shopping list that includes everything from salsa to skateboards to a new pet goldfish. We feed off each other, half-hysterical, granting each other permission to forget, just for a little while. The tension in the house starts to deflate. We go on a shopping extravaganza, from Party America to BJ's to Newbury Comics to Stop and Shop to Toys R Us. At each store, we plow through the aisles like contestants on *Supermarket Sweep*.

"Remember when Mom took us with her to Shop Rite?" Gabe asks me with a grin.

I grin back, recalling the afternoon Mom came into the kitchen, threw her purse on the table and said, "That's it. I'm tired of you guys telling me there's nothing to eat around here. You are coming with me to the store and you'll choose what you want. If you're still starving, that's too damn bad."

While Mom shopped on the opposite end of the store, Gabe and I rode our cart like a sleigh through the aisles. We'd shout at random, "Go long!" then toss something, an avocado, a salami, or in one case, a box of Pastina that exploded when it hit the floor and sent tiny stars flying in all directions. As Mom shopped, she tracked our whereabouts by the announcements over the loudspeaker: "Cleanup in aisle 4...Cleanup in aisle 10...Cleanup in aisle 16..."

We fill our carts with sombreros, ponchos, an inflatable beer cooler, a majestic burro piñata, and more food than we could eat in a week. By noon, our bags have crowded the kitchen, and we spend the rest of the day preparing for the party. Everyone makes one dish: Sammy puts together Mom's layered bean dip, Gabe cooks his chili, Dena takes care of the salmon, I sautee veggies and fry bananas, and Erin whips up the best guacamole I have ever tasted in my life. The house smells spicy and rings with laughter.

In the middle of the action, Dena smiles. "This would be a good day for her to go. Then we could have a Cinco de Mayo party every year."

"It feels weird, though," Gabe confesses, "having a party while she's dying in the next room."

"I think she'd want us to," I say. "It would make her happy to see us together like this."

As promised, Dad hangs the piñata from a length of PVC pipe with a broom stuck through it, held aloft on a stepladder. We cover the dining room table with a festive print tablecloth and sparkly confetti in the shape of sombreros and jalapeño peppers. Everyone eats with relish, passing stories and jibes around the table. The door to Mom's room stays open.

Dad sets his fork down. "I just want to say that this is a really special thing you guys did, working together and helping each other. Mom and I are proud of you."

Mom and I. I wonder if he can still speak for the both of them, when she's not really here anymore.

But she is, I realize, as Noah, to our laughter and applause, tosses a piece of avocado across the table and into Gabe's mouth. I survey my the rest of family, Dad chatting physics with Alex, Dena with Ezra on

210

her hip, trying to tease guacamole into his mouth. Erin and Gabe making faces at each other, and Sammy leaning over the back of Noah's seat, necklacing her arms around him. And my husband, reaching under the table for my hand.

She made this.

"To Mom," Ben says, raising his beer bottle.

"To Mom," we echo, clinking our glasses together.

"I don't know about you guys," Gabe says, off a long pull from his beer, "but I'm ready to beat the shit out of that piñata."

"Fast Eddie fell in the moat last night," Jake says, dragging deeply on a Gauloises.

I stop chewing my toast and Nutella. "Shut up."

"I swear. He was so wasted, I had to walk him home from The Vink. The whole way back, he was going on and on about how his Dad is Lord of the Dance."

"His Dad is Michael Flatley?"

Jake raises an eyebrow. "You a fan?"

"That's classified information."

He chuckles, smoke seeping through his wide, square teeth. "Anyway, I'm like, 'Whatever, dude, fine, your dad is Lord of the Dance.' Suddenly, Eddie stopped walking and got up in my face: 'What, You don't believe me?' And he started doing that Irish jigging thing."

"Stop it!"

"He's like a foot from the moat, right? So I tried to grab him, but I wasn't fast enough. Boom: Eddie's in the water, covered in moss and goose turds and God knows what else."

"That's amazing." I savor the dark pleasure of laughing at Ed Welsh, AKA Fast Eddie Douchebag, who has distinguished himself among our group of student travelers by getting drunk every night and doing something ridiculous. When he's sober, he's not a bad guy, intelligent, mildly handsome, nervous in a sweet way. But when Ed drinks, he becomes someone else. His eyes turn dark, like whoever lives there is no longer home. At the Vink, our Dutch town's local bar, I tease Eddie with extra gusto, highlighting his foolishness and establishing myself on the safe end of the joke.

"So, listen," Jake says. "Come with me to Germany this weekend."

"We're Jewish," I say reflexively, as the word "Germany" conjures images of children's shoes, piles of corpses in mass graves, a little boy with arms skyward and an SS gun at his back. That last image, which I saw in a textbook in fourth grade, gave me nightmares through my teens. Though less gruesome than others I would see over the years, there was something disturbing about the timing of the shot, the camera shutter closing on the living boy, leaving me to imagine the dead one he would become seconds later.

"So what?" Jake replies, tapping his thumb and pinkie against his thigh to a beat only he can hear. "National Socialism went bust like 60 years ago. And there's an Indian Avatar there who sees people."

"Like dead people?"

Jake bursts out laughing. An avatar, he explains, is the human embodiment of a Hindu god. They have the power to see into people's souls, infuse them with deep spiritual knowledge, and, if one has refined oneself sufficiently, grant instant enlightenment.

I picture a raisin-faced swami shooting laser beams from his eyes. "How do they know he's a god?"

"She," Jake corrects me. "It's a woman. I forget her name, Jasvinder something. When she was six, she could heal people with her dreams."

"Impressive. What's she doing in Germany?"

"She's married to a German guy. He does her P.R."

"Avatars can get married?" Somehow this knocks her down a few spiritual rungs. "Shouldn't she be abstaining from worldly pleasures or something?"

"That's monks," Jake says, flicking ash off his cigarette. "Guess the rules are different for Avatars. Meadow saw her last week and said it was awesome. We should go."

I'm hesitant, but intrigued. I've been on a search for enlightenment (or something) since a Halloween party last year, when I was struck with a strange epiphany. I was dressed like a geisha that night, kimono draped strategically to hide my stomach, my face painted an exotic powder-white that drew second and third glances. My date was a six-foot-tall, African-American drag queen named Mahogany Brown who entertained the crowds in Copley Square by doing cartwheels and belting Celine Dion. I don't know what it was about the evening: the crisp air of Autumn, which always makes me feel wistful and melancholy; the surprise of my own reflection, unrecognizable in the shop windows of Boylston Street; the Celine Dion; or the mason jars of Sangria I guzzled, one after the other, when I arrived at my friend Vanessa's apartment. Whatever it was, my mood was pensive. Instead of socializing, I watched from the kitchen as the other party guests swirled around each other, trying to get as intoxicated as possible, to do something worth noticing, and maybe get laid.

From nowhere, a thought bubbled up:

There's got to be more to it than this.

I didn't know what I meant by that, but the thought wouldn't go away, even when I was sober. It was like a toddler had grabbed my hand, yelling at full volume, and pulled me out of my current conversation. It led me to the bookstore, where I bought titles like The Four Agreements, The Dalai Lama's Art of Happiness, The Alchemist *and* The I Ching. *It dragged me to classes on Eastern religions, meditation, and Tai chi. And it took me to Boston's Museum of Fine Arts, where I spent afternoons in the Japanese Temple Room with a giant statue of Buddha, trying to glean something from his stony silence. (And, just maybe, fill myself with enough spiritual wisdom to kill the itch for food. Alas, holding a copy of* The Power of Now *in one hand still left the other hand free to dip a four-foot baguette in boursin cheese.) Inevitably, I would leave the Buddha's side with more questions than I'd come with, then wander into the gallery of impressionists to the famous mural of Paul Gauguin. His scattered sequence of browns and blues depicting life from birth to death fascinated me, and I studied it like a map. There was the baby asleep on a rock, the two confidants glowing pink in the background, the bare-breasted beauty luxuriating in her youth beside a bitter, brown crone. A bright blue idol presided. In the top left corner, like a narration, Gauguin had painted the mural's title, which put my own thoughts on canvas:*

D'où venons-nous?

Que sommes-nous?

Où allons-nous?

Where do we come from?

What are we?

Where are we going?

I fed my head to the point of bursting, hoping to strike a deep chord that would make me hum with wholeness and purpose and awe. I strained my eyes staring at sunsets and cityscapes and the wind rippling through trees, willing inspiration, hope, or anything, to move me. But there was no breaching the wall between me and the rest of the world, or from feeling like a mystery appliance, relegated to a high, dusty shelf, that could whir to life if only it was plugged in. And there was no quieting the incessant, terrorizing stream of thought that has hijacked my mind since I moved away from home: The world is too big...I don't know the rules...Anything could happen...I have no protection. *It's even worse now that I'm in Europe, thousands of miles from anything familiar. I had hoped this new place might make me brave, a change of scenery that rewrites the story. But just a week ago, walking down the Champs Elysees, a free-floating panic gripped me so fiercely I had to abandon my friends for the safety of the hotel room to sedate myself with room service.*

There was this one night, though, after reading the Dalai Lama, when I parked myself on my bed and resolved to sit in meditation until something happened. At first, frame after frame of thought shot past at rapid-fire. My back hurt. The sheets bothered my legs. I was antsy and wanted to go eat something. But I forced myself to stay there. Maybe ten minutes in, it occurred to me: I am watching all this like I'm watching a movie, the thoughts, the pain, the itch, which means that I am separate from it. The thoughts are not me. The back pain is not me. The itch is not me. I am something else.

It was like a bomb detonated in my mind, blowing all thought into a silent void. For a sweet moment, all was calm, the stillness dense around me like a forcefield. The gnaw in my spirit was soothed.

Then came a thought: I want to live here. *Instantly, the spell broke and the flow of thoughts rushed back in, washing me out of my sacred lacuna. I was grief-stricken, having discovered something life-changing only to lose it. But I sensed the power of the discovery itself, in knowing the lacuna existed at all. I would see things differently just by having been there.*

I've been trying to get back ever since.

There's one other thing, too, that's drawing me to see this Avatar: Jake, who in three short months has become my best friend. We go to the same college in Boston, but never met until we arrived at a medieval castle in Holland (complete with moat) to travel Europe for one wild semester. At the time, he was fresh from a breakup with my friend Jules, moping around all lovesick and puppy-faced. I learned quickly that this is his way, falling quick and hard for damaged beauties who are hard-wired to hurt him. Jake brings it on himself, of course, driven as he is to fix all things broken in the world. He's on a search, like me, if not for enlightenment, than at least for some meaning behind all the suffering he sees. A staunch socialist, he loses sleep over everything from the genocide in Kosovo to child labor to pesticides. If asked, he can recite the full list of Native American tribes that were displaced as part of Andrew Jackson's Indian Removal Act of 1830. The night George W. Bush was elected, he sat in front of the television with his head in his hands, like someone whose life had just fallen apart.

"He stole the country," he said. "He stole the whole goddamn country..."

Surprisingly, Jake is not a vegetarian, and he smokes like a burning building. A stranger might take in the baggy jeans and patched hoodies, the aggressive hunch and leather bracelets, the "Congress of Cow" and "Rancid" t-shirts and assume that Jake is the combative type. In fact, he is the opposite, sunny and calm, quick to laugh despite the heaviness in his mind. Being genuine, he expects the same from others. The posturings of "sexy girls" hold no interest for him; he likes full-flavored women who stand for something. Sadly for him, these women love their causes (often, themselves) more than they love him.

I know all this because when Jake gets burned in love, I'm the one he tells about it. He looks to me for solace and insight. I parrot some threads of wisdom from my spiritual books, offering advice I've never had the chance to test. In his eyes, I am worldly, experienced, evolved. In reality, I am a scam artist, playing the best friend because I'm too afraid to tell him I'm in love with him.

I tell myself it's enough just to be with him, getting stranded in the rain trying to visit Monet's house, being stricken with a rash from a Dutch mystery flower, eating sweetbreads in Rotterdam without knowing they were innards, and losing hours talking and talking and talking as the European landscape zips past our train window. But then I make him really laugh, and he'll look at me and say, "You know, I really love you," and a tingle spreads up my arms. I long for him to mean it the way I want him to, instead of the platonic way he actually does, cupping my hands around a tiny flame of hope that Jake might be the one who's different, the one who will bypass my outsides and see the real me buried underneath. The possibility sweetens the seconds with him, deepens a brush of the arm or a head resting on a shoulder to sleep, and dilutes the sadness of knowing it's all a game of pretend.

"Alright," I say. "We'll go."

Wherever I land in Europe, from Dublin to Milan, the first thing I do is call my mother.

"Mom! You'll never guess what."

"Hmmm...?"

"I'm in Copenhagen. Denmark. It's crazy, eight out of ten people are the most gorgeous you've ever seen in your life. And get this: they have holes in their money!"

"Rea?"

"Yeah, Ma?"

"It's four in the morning here. Get off my phone."

On the surface, I'm giving Mom a pin to locate me on her mental map of Europe. But really, each call is a reassuring tug on the invisible cord that connects me to her, to the one place in the world I belong. I think of her everywhere: climbing the steep ladder into Anne Frank's annex, seeing the disappointingly puny Mona Lisa at the Louvre, hanging upside down to kiss the Blarney Stone. In a sleepy fishing town on the Italian coast, I watch an impossible sunset rouge the sky and spread a blanket of stars on the water, and all I can do is miss her.

As soon as we get to Bamburg, I find the nearest pay phone.

"I thought the whole place would look like Auschwitz, but Germany is gorgeous," I say, taking in the quaint, cobblestoned town square surrounded by old world shops. The spine of a green mountain range runs beyond the rooftops and slopes into lush, sheep-dotted farmland. "It's like Epcot Germany, where the guys in lederhosen roll around on beer kegs."

"Who are you with?"

"Jake."

"Ohhhhh," Mom says in that ooh-la-la way that both annoys and thrills me.

"It's not like that," I insist, more to myself than to her. "I told you we're just friends."

"Your father and I were friends first."

I'm grateful that eye rolls are silent. "It's different, okay?"

"Why?"

"'Cause you looked like Cher. I look like" - I glance down at my giant ski jacket and monumental thighs bulging underneath - "this."

"The right guy is going to love you for who you are," she says.

"That applies to everyone but fat girls. Fat girls live in the friend zone." Through the cafe window next to the booth, I see Jake sipping from a coffee cup. As if sensing me, Jake looks out, spots my phone booth, and waves. I hold a up finger to tell him I'm almost finished.

"Maybe," says Mom, "you like living in the friend zone."

"Yes, Mom. I'd much rather watch everyone else be happy."

"Well, it is safer."

Her presumption, and its correctness, makes me want to smash the phone booth window. "Right, so I'll just get over my fear of intimacy and suddenly I'll have a million boyfriends."

"Who needs a million? One good one is enough. I'm not saying Jake is the guy for you. I'm just saying you don't even give yourself a chance."

"Why should I, when there is no chance?"

Her sigh reaches me from across the ocean. "So what's your plan there?"

"I don't know, see some castles, eat some food..." I deliberately don't mention the Avatar. It takes a lot to shock my mother - she packed me off to college with a box of condoms and a note: "These need no explanation. Call MOM (note the capitals) for advice!" - but something about seeking enlightenment from a Hindu deity feels verboten. On the train here, I imagined some pickled yenta heading me off at the Avatar's door, slapping the back of my hand, and saying, "That's no place for a Jewish girl." In reality, it's possible that at the word "Avatar", Mom would book a redeye to Berlin to save her hippie daughter from a cult.

"I'm sure you'll have a blast," she says.

After I hang up, Jake and I drop our things at the hostel, then find the address provided by the Avatar's secretary: an imposing white castle overlooking the town from the side of a mountain.

"That's not intimidating," I say.

He whistles in appreciation. "Avatars get sweet real estate."

We walk through the main entrance to a red-carpeted parlor, where a tiny woman with thick glasses sits behind a wooden table.

"Namen?" she says.

Jake and I look at each other in confusion.

"Noms?"

"We're here to see the Avatar?" I say lamely.

She nods like she's cracked a riddle. "Americans. Names, please?"

She finds us on her list and waves us toward a door to her right. "May you be open, and receive..."

Jake and I enter a wide room with creamy walls, dark wooden beams, and a few mounted heads that hearken more to a Nordic hunting lodge than the salon of a castle in rural Germany. A dark, heady mixture of incense and human musk swirls around us, along with the hum of chanting from 100 people seated on the floor: tanned, Australian surfers with dreadlocks, a chocolate-skinned couple in African Dashikis, a ruddy, football-jerseyed Scotsman, baldheaded men and women in marigold robes, and backpackers in the uniform jeans, boots, and hippie-print scarves. At the front of the room hangs a massive red tapestry with a gold "Om" symbol in the center, fat and smooth and satisfying to the eye. Along the rim, pairs of tiny golden elephants stand tail-to-tail. The tapestry leaps into vision against the white walls, demanding recognition as the center of the room. An ornately carved wooden chair sits before it, soon to hold an Avatar.

Near the back of the room, Jake and I find two open cushions, one of which he folds down to in one easy movement. I pray silently that I can maneuver to the floor with a modicum of grace. I sink to one knee and tip over like a teapot, anchoring my hand to ease my butt onto the cushion. The carpet is slippery, though, and my hand skids. The rest of me plops down sideways.

Not my best work.

No one seems to notice, though, not even Jake, who has already closed his eyes. He never quite sits still, his hands drumming against his kneecaps, head pulsing slightly. I leave him to it, shutting my eyes and turning inward. I imagine The Avatar gliding in wearing a bright gold sari, light dripping from her like water, saturating the room with peace. She touches her nose to mine, giggling like a child, and suddenly I'm back in my lacuna, safe, content and there to stay.

There's a shift of energy in the room, 100 people's anticipation intensifying as the minute hand on the clock inches closer to the twelve. As I open my eyes, the chanting heightens. Hands rise toward the air. Backs sway. From some deep recess of memory, my old Torah teachers whisper to me of the grave sin of Avodah Zarah, *idol worship.*

I'm not worshipping anything, *I hiss back.* I'm just looking for a power source.

Just like that, the chanting stops. A dark wooden door at the front of the room softly opens, and a diminutive woman enters. She wears a simple tunic and pants, a zip fleece, and a chenille scarf wrapped thickly around her neck. Her obsidian hair is pulled into a messy ponytail, like she's just woken up from a nap.

This is the Avatar? *I think, searching for a hint of divinity about her.* She's wearing North Face, for God's sake.

The Avatar seats herself in the wooden chair, closes her eyes, and breathes in deeply. Then she sets her shoulders, ready to begin. There's a loaded moment before the first brave soul approaches the Avatar, kneeling at her feet and gazing up. She studies him intently, making no sound. After maybe ten seconds, the man rises and returns to his seat.

"How long are you supposed to look at her for?" I murmur to Jake.

"Until one of you are done, I guess."

I think of my staring contests with Gabe and his absurd Muppet face.

A line forms down the center aisle, snaking slowly toward the Avatar like a vein carrying blood to the heart. A respectful yet awkward hush, the kind that precedes a funeral, falls over the room as person after person kneels down before her in silent supplication. I study their faces when they rise: one frowns like he's just been given bad news; another looks thoughtful; a few smile. I rhythmically rub my hands against my thighs, torn between the conviction that this whole thing is a hoax and the hope that I will see infinity.

It's my turn. I sink to my knees and look up at the Avatar's face.

Her eyes are pools of sadness, shiny with unshed tears, her irises yellowed like the pages of an old book. The brown of her skin is washed out, her clothing drab and muted. It's like she's draining away.

Show me something, *I beg her with my eyes.* Anything.

But even as I ask it, I feel absurd. She's just a person. *A human person.*

She looks and looks at me, her eyes growing heavier.

Do you see something?

It strikes me that The Avatar isn't trying to transmit anything. Maybe it's the opposite: like a spiritual garbage collector, she's looking for mess to remove.

No wonder she's so depleted. The woman is a landfill.

I wait for lightness, for the relief of a burden unloaded, but there is no change. I'm an American plug to her European outlet, with no adapter to connect us.

She blinks, and I know that we're done. I rise and step away.

Thanks for trying, *I think.*

Then her eyes briefly flicker in my direction, a few heads turn toward me, and I realize I've said it out loud.

"Instant enlightenment," Jake says, disgusted, on the bus home from Nijmegen. "Instant coffee, instant breakfast, instant gratification..."

"You're just upset because you didn't feel anything, either." I unwrap a Bounty bar and hold out half to him. "Want?"

He waves it away (to my relief), hands full of coffee and the inevitable cigarette. I still haven't gotten used to the ubiquity of smoking on this continent, in restaurants, bakeries, on public transportation. The minute you light up in America, a chorus of stage coughs insist you keep your cancer to yourself. Here, someone could blow smoke rings on your dinner and you thank them for sharing.

"Whatever," Jake says, "I can't even blame her. Americans are idiots. We need to have everything yesterday. I would cash in on us, too."

"No, you wouldn't."

He smiles at that. "It was weird, though, right? Cultish?"

"A little, but not because of her. I think it was everyone else wanting something from her."

"Idiots," Jake grumbles.

The bus winds through one of the dozen tiny towns between Nijmegen, one of Holland's larger cities, and Well, home of our castle. The tight-packed houses sit so close to the street, I can see into living rooms as we drive by.

"I don't know," I say as we pass a family at dinner. "Maybe I wasn't open enough. 'Be open and receive', right?"

"Nah, it wasn't you. The whole thing was bogus."

"But what if I'd convinced myself it was real and it had an effect?"

"So what do you need an Avatar for, then, if you can do the job yourself?"

Energized by the debate, I turn toward him, my knee angling against his. "Maybe that's the point. Maybe meeting her was just to find out that I have to do the job myself."

"Okay," he says, smiling lazily from one corner of his mouth. "So how do you do it?"

"Hell if I know."

The setting sun leaps across a field and angles in through the window. Jake pulls down the mesh shade to block it.

"What would you have wanted to happen?" I ask.

Jake takes a minute to think. "I would have liked to know how to stop taking everything so seriously."

"Is that possible? Life is pretty serious."

"Yeah, but I make it more serious than it needs to be. What about you?"

For once, I tell the truth: "I would have wanted not to be so scared all the time."

"You're not scared of anything," he scoffs. "You say exactly what you think. You bang on strangers' doors and talk to them in crappy French so we don't have to stand in the rain. You don't try to be like everyone else. You're just...you."

I ache inside. If only you knew.

As if hearing my thoughts, Jake looks me full in the face. "You are the bravest person I know. It's one of the things I love most about you."

For a split second, I consider forming my feelings into words and releasing them to the world, where they could be twisted and trampled and mocked.

You don't even give yourself a chance, *Mom said.*

"Do you ever...?" I begin.

"What?"

Just then, a brunette with a backpack approaches, holding the seat tops to balance herself. She looks like Winona Ryder in Reality Bites, *chicly unwashed and disheveled. She sways gently with the bus, like a willow.*

"May I...cigarette?" she says with an unplaceable accent.

"Sure," he says, handing one to her. "You have a lighter?"

The girl titters and shakes her head. He offers his cigarette, which she uses to light her own, sucking deeply from his burnt end. She hands it back to him, smiling shyly. He smiles back.

"Sank you," she says, and slinks away.

Jake's eyes follow her until she disappears.

We ride a few minutes in silence, then he turns to me. "You were saying something. Before."

"Was I?" I reply. "I don't remember."

Jake and I arrive in Well with the first stars, and find all our friends at The Vink. Everyone shouts stories of their weekend travels over the clink of glass and a Dutch cover of Fleetwood Mac. I beeline for the bar, where I drink nine glasses of wine over the next twenty minutes. The room begins to swim, the music a pleasurable buzz on my skin. Feeling falls away, thought hazes over. I am languid. Surrendered.

Who needs an Avatar?

An inner door clicks open and my thoughts start flowing from me like a pressure release. I start with the pretty boys at the pool table.

"You never look at my face," I say, planting myself in their lines of vision. "You look past me, like I'm not there. Well, I'm right here. Hello? I EXIST."

I urge their girlfriends to read books, leaning in and pointing at them like a football coach: "You are more than a pincushion!"

I admit to my friend Gavin that he has always reminded me of Pauly Shore. I declare to my friend Martin that she's so pretty I wish we were both gay. Then I order grilled cheeses for everyone, laughing so loudly it pierces the room like a foghorn.

As I set down my wine glass, I feel someone stagger up behind me.

"Lookie who it is," I say, giving one of Fast Eddie's flushed cheeks a squeeze. "Our resident alcoholic."

He smiles like the joke is on me. "I know you."

"Yeah, Eddie. I know you, too."

"No," he says, locking his glassy, vacant eyes into mine. "I know you."

A chill shoots through me as I realize what he means. It's the same chill I felt when 400-pound Fern told me the only difference between the two of us was time.

Jake appears at my side. "Hey, hey, what's going on? Are you okay?"

"Blurgle!" I shout. Then I start laughing, on the verge of hysteria.

"Time to go home," Jake says, grabbing my jean jacket from the back of the barstool.

I snatch it from him. "No! I don't go home with strangers."

Jake pulls his head back in question.

"You don't know me," I say.

He laughs warily, unsure if I'm joking or not. "What are you talking about?"

I point at him. "You think you know me, but you don't."

Just like that, I'm crying harder than I ever have in my life.

Martin swallows down the last of her Stella Artois and shifts off the barstool next to mine. "I got this," she says, taking my arm. "Come on, Honey. Walk me home."

The town of Well tips back and forth like a seesaw with every step, making my stomach churn. Gulping cold air, I close my eyes and let Martin lead me back to the castle, travelling in my mind back to the to the Buddha room, craving the calm and stillness. But my imagined self walks past the Buddha, past the painted shoji screens and statues, and into the gallery of impressionists. I know exactly where I'm headed: the Paul Gauguin mural. There's the yellow baby, the brown crone, the blue idol. There are are Gauguin's blasted questions, framed in gold, in his childlike French hand.

Where do we come from?

What are we?

Where are we going?

The answers are beyond the scope of the painting, yet Gauguin, like a dog worrying a bone, can't leave them be. He watches the life cycle turn and turn, waiting for a clue that might reveal the infinite. It seems almost crazy, searching for answers one knows they'll never find. But maybe it's the search itself that comforts, the lesser madness to never asking at all.

The museum guidebook said that Gauguin was an alcoholic who left Paris for Tahiti to live simply among the native people. I think he was on the run. He thought he could abandon his old life and begin again, change the scenery and thus, the story. But when he got to Tahiti, he discovered that he'd brought himself, the nagging questions, and the alcoholism with him.

Gauguin is just like me.

The divide between the painting and the world vanishes, and I step into the canvas like a doorway to another room. Blue trees coil around me like snakes, dropping a gloomy shade. Every figure in the painting turns to watch me as I pass. I keep my eyes down, trying not to trip over hills of sand. The deity, glistening with cobwebs, steps down from her pedestal and walks into the shadows behind her. Instinctively, I know to follow. She leads me through a dark tangle of bushes, so thick they block out the sun. Thorns and brambles scratch at me, and I raise my hands to protect my eyes.

Abruptly, the bushes vanish and we are drenched in sunlight, facing a wide, green field. The sky above us is a perfect blue. Grass reaches my hip, waving slowly and whispering in the breeze. Beyond, there's a verdant mountain, a volcano perhaps, surrounded by a glimmering sea. I must cross this field, traverse that water, climb that mountain, and see the world from its peak. I look to the deity for encouragement, but she is gone, and the dark tableau I just passed through has disappeared. I am to go on by myself.

I start forward, but the grass winds around my legs, pulling me down like an anchor. I try to extract them, uprooting the grass, but more and more of it grabs at me the farther I go. Halfway through the field, I am covered to the waist, immobile. I stretch my torso, summoning a strength I don't have. Must get to the water...Must reach that mountain... *But the more I struggle, the more tired I become. The pull of the grass calms me like a compression vest, as does the hiss of the breeze. My muscles go slack, no fight left; all I can do is surrender. I let my body sink down as the grass mummifies me in its sweet, chlorophyllic embrace. It bracelets my wrists, sleeves my arms, blankets my shoulders, twines into my hair.*

It dips into my ears, fills my nostrils. Then it covers my eyes, and all goes black.

I awaken on the floor of my room in the castle, smelling of vomit and cigarettes, my head resting on a pile of dirty laundry. The room is silent, my roommates already gone off to class. But I am not alone. From the moment of consciousness, the fear is right there next to me, breathing an amused greeting into my ear:

"Nice try."

Chapter Fourteen

Della arrives in a showstopping outfit: a red, sequined top, matching flats, and a slew of ropy gold necklaces shimmering on her bosom. She looks like she's on her way to Mohegan Sun, not visiting a dying woman.

"Della!" Dad says, popping up from his seat at the island. "Good morning!"

"What's that?" Della asks, pointing up at the piñata. We opted not to break it, just in case it made too much noise and disturbed Mom, who has calmed again. Instead, we cut a hole in the top and left it there, like a giant, burro-shaped candy bowl. "You guys have a party?"

"Cinco de Mayo," Dad says, reaching into the piñata for a Special Dark.

"Good. You needed that."

"Can I get you something? Cookie? Coffee?" Dad speaks in a booming voice with big gestures, overshooting the role of "gracious host." Having never mastered the social skill, he mimicks what he's seen Mom do, only he can't quite calibrate himself.

"Not a thing. I just wanted to check on the kids before I go in to see Debbi." Della looks to me, feeding Ezra, and Noah, whose nose is in a law textbook. "Where's everyone else?"

"Out there," I say, pointing to the patio, where Dena, Gabe and Erin are potting impatiens to put by Mom's window.

Della shakes her head in wonder. "You guys are amazing. I've seen so many families who spend these last days fighting with each other, screaming at each other, bringing up baggage that's twenty, thirty years old. It's a nightmare for everyone, us included. You've all been so helpful to each other and kind to your Mom. She'd be proud of you." She turns to Dad. "So how's our girl?"

"Well," he says, looking sheepish, "We had a little incident this morning."

That's putting it mildly. Dena called a family meeting this morning, marching into Mom's room and insisting that Dad could leave her side for five minutes to join the rest of us. What she had to say was meant for Dad especially: we need to keep a calm energy around Mom, like the nurses said, and not crowd her too much. While she spoke, Dad perched on the edge of a kitchen stool, knee bent against the leg like he'd have to push off at any moment. Suddenly, there was a THUD from my parents' room, the sound of a body hitting the floor, followed by a cry for help.

Dad shot out of his seat. "SEE?" he cried, running toward his room. Noah and Gabe followed. "Now look what happened!"

With some secret reserve of strength, Mom had eased herself off the high bed to go to the bathroom. She made it about five steps before the morphine pack attached to her port pulled her backward and she fell, smacking her head on the floor.

"Sounds like it's time for a hospital bed," Della says after looking Mom over. Except for a small goose egg she seems to be fine, thanks to a bolus shot of morphine and a squirt of Ativan.

"What for?" I ask.

"Safer. It'll keep her contained." Della pulls out her phone. "I think we need a new commode, too."

Dad, still shaken by Mom's fall, puts up no fight. "Thank you, Della. You're the best. What would we do without you?"

He says this to every VNA staff member, even Amy, the Home Health Aide who comes to bathe Mom and change the sheets, every time they're here. These women have become the lamplighters on his darkened street; Dad would be lost without them, and he knows it. On the blog, he raves about their dedication and patience, how loving they are not just with Mom, but with all of us. And he's right. Just two months ago, Mom was being treated at the best cancer hospital in the world, but that place is no contender for this small but intrepid crew of nurses. These ladies know what the hell they're doing. They have time and attention to give her. Their response time is faster. They get it *done.*

I was thinking this morning, Dad writes, *that the answer to the United States health care system might be visiting nurses. I think the government should use a good chunk of the bailout money to recruit, educate, and train a crop of graduating high school seniors... Spare no expense in making sure that they are thorough in their knowledge....Differentiate the nurses based on their interests, and when they have finished their practicals, let them work in the field at full pay for five years before they move on to the private sector, free of school loans.*

By expanding the VNA system, these trained nurse-practitioners could treat many patients that otherwise would have gone to the hospital. The bills that I get from --- are staggering, yet during an 11-day stay in March, [they were] not able to rid Debbi of her infection. Moving Debbi to Cape Cod, a visit to her physician here, and a follow-up at the Cape House by the VNA nurses knocked it right out...Compared to the bills for the 11 days at ---, the charges for the home care are a fraction of the hospital charges...Let's stop wasting money on health care and start building an effective system that is many times more efficient than the current system. That it costs less is only a part of the true savings.

What Dad says intrigues me, so I decide to poke around about it on the internet while Ezra naps. It turns out that while Dad's is a solid idea, it's not original. Back in the 1800's, Queen Victoria shelled out £70,000 to start the District Nurse Service, which trained nurses and then assigned them to districts around England, particularly poorer areas where access to quality health care was limited. The American government has never funded district nurses, which is why nurse and activist Lillian Wald founded the Visiting Nurse Services of New York in the 1880's, to assist immigrant families on the Lower East Side. (Wald, a real spitfire, also established the Women's Trade Union League, helped abolish child labor, and convinced the New York Board of Education to provide resources for children with learning disabilities, feed them hot lunches, and hire full-time school nurses. We like her.) The women of the VNSNY were the first public nurses in America, teaching patients about health and hygiene, providing care for illnesses, and tending to births and deaths. The organization expanded throughout the five boros and eventually nationwide, becoming what is known today as the VNA.

What both groups of nurses had in common was that most of their work was in patients' homes, where, until a century ago, most births and deaths took place. It wasn't until the 1920's, when hospitals began affiliating with respected universities and medical schools, that a privileged clientele began seeking treatment outside their homes. In the 1950's, shiny new health insurance policies began covering hospital expenses, setting home-based care on the decline. Today, less than 0.5% of medical care is given at home.

The question, though, is whether a hospital's standard of care is actually better than care offered at home. In some cases, the answer is an obvious yes. It's impractical to get an X-ray at home, for example, when the equipment and technicians are at the hospital. The safest setting for surgery is, without a doubt, an OR or outpatient clinic. But what about the dying? Is the hospital truly the best place to end your life?

Well, it's certainly not the cheapest. Last year, Medicare shelled out $50 billion just for doctor and hospital bills during the last two months of patients' lives, an amount that exceeds the budget of the Department of Education and that of the Department of Homeland Security. According to the National Association of Home Care and Hospice, it costs Medicare nearly $2,000 per day for a typical hospital stay (it can be up to $10,000 in the ICU) and $559 per day for a typical nursing home stay. Home care, meanwhile, costs a daily average of $44. I'm no math genius like my father, but the difference seems obvious, even to me.

But in my humble, nonprofessional opinion, the most valuable benefit of home care for the dying is the *quality* of care. It all comes down to turf, I think. In a hospital, you're on their turf, with their rules, which means you're at their mercy. And if their resources, time, and patience are limited, the probability of a good death shrinks significantly. If you're lucky to have dedicated nurses, like Mom did, you might get a few perks: an extra blanket, extended visiting hours. But there's only so much a nurse can give when there are 50 other call buttons to answer. At home, though, the dying are *at home*, surrounded by their families, their memories, and their own antibodies. They're not anonymous. They have your full attention. And they are free to die how they wish, which I believe is the greatest respect you can give another person. Our nurses know this, which is why they're here every day, guiding us forward like sherpas through extreme mountain passes.

"How do you do this?" I ask Della. "How do you care for these people and get close to their families when you know what's going to happen to them? Doesn't it break your heart?"

She grins at me. "Nah, I love it. It's like the OB nurses, only the other way around: they like them coming in, I like them going out."

I get a similar response when I ask another nurse, Leslie, the same question. She was an aspiring dancer when, at 21, she quit to care for her dying grandfather. "It was an incredible experience," she says. "I was hooked."

I never imagined that helping people die could be something you get "hooked" on, but this seems to be the pattern with the superwomen who care for my mother. They are called to what they do; it feeds their souls the way teaching did Mom's. Maybe that's what gives them the strength to stare death in the face while the rest of us pretend it doesn't exist.

Della's mention of OB nurses is one of many comparisons I've heard made between birth and death. Both are processes that take as long as they take, only one is an entrance and one is an exit. One could even say that they are, in fact, the head and tail end of the same process. From the Jewish perspective, it's even trippier: birth is the exit and death, the re-entry. From that angle, Death loses its macabre sheen and takes a place alongside every other normal, human function. It's not death itself that is fearsome, but the pain that precedes it, the loss that follows it, the unknowable mystery behind it.

The hospital bed arrives. Sammy and I sit with Mom while Dad, Ben and Gabe move out furniture and put the bed together. Mom is jumpy, sensing change. Sammy and I talk to her to keep her calm. She keeps moving over to Dad's side of the bed, closer and closer to the sliding door, like she's trying to get out.

They manage to set everything up and move Mom without her freaking out, but I almost hope she does so they can't put her in the bed. The thing eats up a third of the room, looming heavy and gray, the raised sidebars like two rows of teeth around an open mouth. This hospital bed is a deathbed, and once Mom gets in it, it's *her* deathbed. I want her to stay in her own bed, where we can all pretend she's still herself and might recover. A hospital bed is the next, irreversible step away.

It hits Dad, too. As soon as Mom is settled, he leaves the house. I assume he goes for a walk, but Ben informs me later that Dad never got farther than the front stoop.

"He just stood outside alone, crying," he says. "It was the saddest thing I've ever seen." My husband's eyes well up, and I open my arms to him. Dena comes over, munching on a Krackel she snatched from the piñata.

"Don't cry," she says, holding one out to him. "Eat chocolate."

After dinner, while Dad keeps his vigil at Mom's side, the rest of us lay around on the couches, reading jokes off of candy wrappers. Each joke is worse than the one before, but they make us laugh so hard we cry.

"Hey," says Gabe, trying to catch his breath. "Why did the cactus cross the road?"

"Why?"

"Because he was stuck to the back of the chicken!"

Tears roll down our faces.

Chapter Fifteen

Ezra's crying pulls me out of sleep at one in the morning. This is the third night in a row that my son has decided to wake up at some ungodly hour, only to rally us again for 6 a.m. reveille. Ben and I are incoherent with exhaustion, so much so that my husband doesn't even stir at the noise. Bleary-eyed, I slide off the bed.

"Shh-shhh-shhhh," I whisper, tiptoeing through a line of moonlight that bisects the floor. "Mommy's coming…"

Ezra's wailing stops the minute I pick him up, and his chubby arm wraps around my neck. As I rock and whisper to him, his tight little muscles relax and his head grows heavy on my shoulder.

"Sometimes, they just need to make sure you're there," Mom told me when Ezra was a newborn. It made me think of my seventh birthday, when Mom came to school with ice cream cupcakes. I'd been expecting her all day, my body tense with anticipation and the usual anxiety. When I finally saw her walking into school, my whole body unknotted. *My mom is here,* I thought. *It's all okay now.*

It's amazing (and frightening) that Ezra feels that way about me. I have no idea what I'm doing most of the time. Of the great span of information in this universe, I probably know only a fraction more than he does. But that's the gift of childhood: a few good years in a world where all is safe and fair, secure in the protection of our omnipotent parents. It's a shame that time will dismantle the illusion, that Ezra will slowly discover that I'm human and, thus, unequipped to protect him forever. The comfort he gets from me now will eventually become an inside job. It may feel like a betrayal in the beginning, but perhaps one day it will be a relief to know that I don't have all the answers, either.

We rock in silence for a few minutes until I'm sure the baby is asleep, then I lay him down and slide back into bed. In what seems like seconds, Ezra is awake again, rattling happily on the crib rungs as the morning sun streams in. I could laugh and cry and smother someone with my pillow.

"Got up with him yesterday," Ben murmurs.

"I got up last night..."

Ben flings a petulant arm over his shoulder. "I can't..."

"Dying mom card."

"*Fine*," Ben says, kicking off the covers.

Two hours later, Ben and Ezra return with a mug of tea for Mommy and a thick purple envelope. "Happy Mother's Day!" Ben cries.

Mother's Day. My first as a mother, and my last with Mom. A day that will be both treasured and blighted for the rest of my life.

I cover the ache with a big smile, rip open the envelope, and read the cutesy card with "Ezra's" signature.

"Thanks, Buddy!" I say, reaching for the baby. I kiss him everywhere.

I thank Ben, but can't quite look at him. The distance between us is widening, thanks to our exhaustion and short tempers. Mostly, though, it's because I keep snapping at him. He finally lost it on me yesterday, when Ezra was overtired and refused to eat.

"I'm tired of being your punching bag," he said, echoing Mom's old words. "You're turning into a crazy person, baking muffins all day and treating me like garbage. Every day I try to figure out what I've done wrong, but you don't tell me. If you've taken on too much, then say so.

You don't have to cook dinner for everyone. If you want, I'll come down and do it. You're not a weaker person because you can't do something."

"There's no one else to hold things together," I said.

"Hold *what* together? You can't stop her from dying!" He took a breath. "I get that there's a lot going on and your family needs you. But I'm your husband. I come first. Your son comes first."

I didn't know how to explain that for me, it's not so simple. That it's not just obligation that is keeping me cooking and cleaning and helping and doing, but terror of the void that will be left if I don't. Tess told me that in the wake of loss, much of life looks different than before. But I don't want things to be different. I want to stay certain of everything, for my world to remain cemented in stone. But I'm not, and it isn't. Everything I knew for certain is disappearing before me like smoke into the air. I had no words to convey to Ben the terrifying prospect of finding myself in a life I don't recognize, with no clue where I belong.

"I'm just trying to survive this," I said.

"Well," said Ben, settling Ezra, "so are we."

On my way downstairs, I brace myself before going in to see Mom. After a week without eating, she looks like a prisoner in a concentration camp, the flesh along her temples and cheekbones melted away in a painful contrast to the image of her hanging in the dining room. The hospital bed throws me, too, imprisoning my mother behind the rails. Mom grips onto them like she's trying to climb out. Even if she had the strength to do it, there's no way she can stand on her own anymore.

"You look beautiful today," I say, stroking a brush across her scalp. She stirs at my touch. "You know it's Mother's Day? Mother's Day for you *and* me…"

"Re…" she says, pulling weakly at the rails. "Out…Out…"

Her words sadly parallel those she would say as a child, hat in hand, begging her mother for release from the prison of her house.

Mom launches into a coughing fit, a deep, hacking sound that rattles through the house.

"It's normal," says Della, appearing in the doorway. "Fluid buildup in the lungs."

"One of the signs?"

She nods. "I'm going to try the catheter again."

Mom is sleeping more and more, which makes diapering complicated, but inserting a catheter is apparently just as tricky. Della's last three attempts failed.

"You sure?"

"We'll get it," she says.

Outside the door, I hear Della speak soothingly, then Mom grunt in resistance. If she's still trying to escape the bed, Mom won't be friendly to someone sticking a tube between her legs. After ten minutes, Della comes out looking flushed, but calm.

"Got it," she says.

"How's she looking? Worse?" I'm feeding her the answer, hoping she'll tell me that death is imminent.

Della smiles. "I never would have predicted it."

My disappointment must show, because she says, "I see how worn out you're getting."

"I just want it to be over. Is that terrible?"

"It's normal," she says, squeezing my wrist. "The waiting is so hard. And you're trying to take care of everyone. You have to take care of yourself, too."

"I don't know how."

"Most people don't," she says. "They think they're supposed to push through until they collapse. We have a Reiki practitioner who volunteers her time. How about I call her for you?"

"Okay."

Within 90 seconds, an appointment is made for tomorrow morning.

"You'll love it," Della says. "In the meantime, get some sleep."

Ezra is hyped up and refuses to nap, which puts me on edge. I'm out of flour so I can't bake, and going on the internet is making me squirrely.

"We're going out," I tell Erin, who comes in with Abby, her mother's dog, who has come to stay with us for a few days to improve morale. No one is more excited about this than Ezra. The minute she arrived, Abby walked right up to the baby, who had sprung to all fours, and licked him. Since then, his life's aspiration is to climb on her back.

"Where?" Erin says.

"I don't know. Just out."

"Sounds good to me."

We load Ezra into the car and we're off, opening the windows to let in the warm air and sunshine. I instantly relax as the familiar salt smell whooshes into the car. So does Ezra, who falls asleep as soon as we hit the main road. As Erin and I talk books - I just finished *A Confederacy of Dunces* on her recommendation - she pops Jelly Bellys into her mouth.

"Every time I try a red one, I think it'll be cherry," she says, frowning. "But it never is. It's always cinnamon."

"So expect cinnamon and then it will be cherry."

"Okay." She pulls another red jelly bean from the box and looks at it with intention before popping it into her mouth. "Nope. Cinnamon."

"Guess you didn't expect hard enough."

As we pass a lush, rolling golf green, I tell Erin of the day when Gabe, a devoted golfer, made the mistake of inviting Dena, Noah and me to play with him. With access to golf carts, Noah and I were much more interested in racing each other and chasing geese than beating the par. At one point, I turned so sharply that Dena flew off the cart, while Gabe cradled his head in his hands. At the ninth hole, Gabe set up his ball and sent us a hundred feet ahead to the women's tee.

"Be careful," he said. "I don't want to hit you."

"Your aim isn't that good," Noah called back, setting his ball down.

Gabe teed off, and within seconds, something whizzed past my nose and hit Noah in the thigh: *THWOK!* Noah screamed like a soprano and grabbed his leg. The damage was bad: a deep purple welt in the shape of a golf ball.

To this day, Gabe swears it was an accident.

Erin and I are crying from laughter when my phone rings.

"We need Depends," Dena says.

"Well, hellooo, Dena, I'm fine, thank you. How are you?"

"The kind with the straps. Not the pull-up kind."

"What times we live in, with such variety in disposable adult undergarments!"

"You're an idiot. Bring them back soon."

At CVS, Erin, Ezra and I scavenge the shelves until we find the exact Depends that Dena requested. Erin slides them under one arm, then grabs a jumbo box of tampons for herself.

Leaving the aisle, we almost collide with a man who looks like Lurch from the Addams Family. We crane our necks to look up at him, and he eyes Erin's cargo with visible discomfort.

"There's a lot going on here," she says.

We start giggling as he walks by us, and don't stop until we run into him again at the register. This time, he pretends not to see us, which makes us laugh even harder. On the way out, we pass a man wearing zebra-striped MC hammer pants, and we double over with our arms around each other, like a couple of drunks.

"I can't walk…" I say, holding onto my side. "I can't…."

I lean against the brick wall outside the store until I'm calm. Next to me, I notice a stand of flowers and balloons and an easel with a message in chalk: "Just in time for Mother's Day!"

"Should we get her something?" I ask, pointing to the flowers.

Erin studies them. "I don't know."

"Me neither," I say. "Let's go home."

The next morning, the doorbell rings at 10 on the dot: Reiki time. I expect a patchouli-scented, mood-ringed hippie wiccan, but instead open the door to a tailored lady in head-to-toe beige. She tells me, with a sweet Southern drawl, that her name is Mackie.

I lead Mackie into the house, past Mom's open door, through the dining room, under the pinata, and into the kitchen, where Dad is eating breakfast. He waves as we pass, with a courteous nod to Mackie. Yesterday, when I mentioned the word "Reiki", he screwed up his face like he'd eaten something rotten. "Not for me," he said.

My siblings' reactions were fairly similar, which means I get Mackie to myself.

"Can we use the shul?" I ask him.

"Go for it," Dad says with a mouth full of Grape Nuts.

Mackie settles me in the white leather chair, the same one I sat on when Mom told me she was coming here, and stands behind it, placing her hands on my head. Her touch is light and calming. My heartbeat slows, my muscles relax. I close my eyes.

Mackie explains that in healing work, she is a channel. "I'm not the source of energy, but I can summon certain things to send into you. What do you need?"

I breathe in the question. "I need strength. I need so much strength right now. I feel like I have none left."

I hear Mackie inhale, and her hands grow heavy on my head. My body follows, soothed by the sensation of being touched. Mackie's touch is different than Ezra's, which seeks food and comfort, or Ben's, his language for connection. This is a touch that asks nothing from me except to feel it. We sit in silence for a time, and I picture my organs all working together, floating leisurely in the murky cavern of my body like a lava lamp. I envision the chinese fingertrap of my spine, forming an escape hatch between each vertebra for spinal nerves and arteries to reach the rest of my body. When I learned the structure of the human form, the intricate dance between brain and tissue, the marvel of engineering left me awestruck. It was all too perfectly designed to be an accident of evolution; the human blueprint was clearly drawn by a Divine hand.

When Mackie lifts her hands, I feel both energized and ready for a nap.

"How are things with your husband?" she says.

"Why do you ask?"

"Just a sense."

I feel a twinge of tightness in my shoulder. "It's not comfortable right now."

"Transition isn't comfortable," Mackie says, giving my shoulder a squeeze. "But it's temporary. You'll see. The bond you share with him will be stronger than ever."

Mackie collects her things and asks the way to Mom's room. "I've scheduled some time for her."

"But she's...You can't heal her."

"The return to non-physical is the ultimate healing," Mackie says. "I can help with that, too."

I lay out a dinner of chicken and potatoes which we all eat together, except Dad, who stays by Mom around the clock and hasn't been eating much of anything. Ezra is extra adorable at dinner, picking up his sippy cup with both hands and edging it toward his mouth. It's fascinating to watch him learn to be a person, to master skills I take for granted: pick up cup, open mouth, insert. Most of the water ends up on his shirt, but that's beside the point.

In the middle of the meal, Della arrives, and we immediately send her into Mom's room: "Dad needs you more than we do."

When Della comes out, she slides into an empty seat, refusing an offer of a plate.

"Your mother is actively dying now," she says.

Although this isn't news, it's painful to hear it said so plainly.

"Gabe and I tried to help her today," Noah says, "but she kicked us out. She doesn't want us in there anymore."

"She's protecting you," Della says. "She doesn't want you to see her die."

"What about Dad?" Noah asks.

"He's her protector. They have to go through the last stretch alone."

After Ben takes the baby to bed, the house clears. Dena and Alex go to a concert, Noah and Sammy get ice cream, and Gabe spends the evening with Erin and her family. Dad goes to pray in the little *shul*, so I grab a moment of alone time with Mom. She sleeps on as I pull a chair up to the hospital bed. I stare at her face, willing her to wake up and talk to me, but she doesn't. I take her hand, expecting an instinctive squeeze back. There's no response.

It suddenly hits me that Mom will never get better. We will never have another one of our talks. She will never throw her head back and laugh, or smile like she knows the secret of life. She will never say, "I love you" again. The woman in the picture is gone.

I lay my forehead on her hand and cry. A warm hand touches my back.

"Hi," Ben says.

I sniff. "Hi."

He pulls a chair up beside me.

"I should have said I was sorry," I say. "It's not your fault. I'm just scared out of my mind."

"Of what?"

"What if everything changes? What if I'm completely different after this?"

"Everything is *supposed* to change, and you're *supposed* to be different. That's one of the good parts of all this."

"But what if I outgrow us?"

The corner of his mouth tips up. "Nah. You're my person. That doesn't change. You're stuck with me." He leans toward the hospital bed. "You hear that, Ma? She's stuck with me!"

I laugh through my tears and lean into him. "This hurts so much..."

"That's good," he whispers. "That means you got a great blessing."

I look out on the gloomy winter drizzle over the Boston common and wonder if today is the day I will kill myself. It goes like this most days. Once or twice, I've gone so far as to pour an entire bottle of aspirin into my hand, but always, it is the image of Mom's brokenhearted face that stops me from taking them. Well, that, and the fact that I'm too chicken to actually end my life. There is no place more tortured than the limbo between not wanting to live and being too afraid to die.

My cell rings just as I'm lighting a joint.

"Hi, Beez!"

Mom. Buzzkill.

"What's up, Ma?"

"You sick? Your voice sounds hoarse."

"Change of seasons," I say, coughing for effect.

It's February.

"So I went to that meeting," she says.

"What meeting?" I reply, combing my memory for a hint of what she's talking about. Nothing turns up. I can't be that burned out, can I?

"The one you sent me to?"

Now I remember. A couple of weeks ago, I recruited Mom to help me with my screenplay about the Weight Loss industry. (I figure, if I write a smart exposé that proves all those diets are bunk, no one will blame me for being fat anymore.) During my research, I heard about groups of fat people who get together to talk about food at meetings all over the country. It isn't a diet club, exactly. I have no idea what it is, but like a detective with a good tip, I begged Mom, down in New Jersey, to snoop for me: "Just go to one of their meetings and tell me what they say so I can put it in my screenplay."

And my mother, the good little codependent soldier, agreed.

"Oh, right," I say. "How'd it go?"

"Well, it was different."

"Different how?"

"I can't really describe it," she says.

"O-kay. Did you get anything for me?"

"You're not supposed to talk about what you heard there."

"What the hell? Did you go to Fight Club?"

"Maybe you should go and listen for yourself."

"Me?" *I say, horrified, like she's accused me of pedophilia.*
"I think you'll find it pretty interesting."
There's an odd shrillness to her voice. She's up to something.
"I don't get it. Why can't you just tell me what they said?"
"Just go," she says. "And call me after."

I go online to find a list of their meetings, and wouldn't you know it, there's one beginning within the hour, right down the block from my dorm. For some reason, this fills me with dread. I look out at the gray fog enveloping the trees. Ugh. If I didn't already want to kill myself, this day would do the trick. My warm bed beckons invitingly, as does the pint of Ben and Jerry's waiting in the freezer. But, dammit, my whackadoo mother has piqued my curiosity. I suppose I can wait until later to get stoned and contemplate suicide. With a resigned sigh, I pull on my boots and jacket.

I trudge up Tremont Street in the freezing cold, my boots splashing in the slush puddles, cursing my decision to go to college in Boston. Phoenix would have been a much better move. Finally, I arrive at a tall, stately stone church and stop at the door.

Experience has proven that I will not become a pillar of salt if I walk into this place. But who knows what else could happen?

You've come this far, *I think.* And it's freaking cold out here.

I push the door open.

Inside, a sign indicates that the meeting is at the top of a marble staircase. As I climb, the squeak of my boots echoes off the high ceilings. I'm good and winded by the time I reach the meeting room, so I steal a minute to collect myself and peek in through the door's small window. A group of a dozen men and women sit around a folding table. Only two of them are actually fat; the rest, I assume, are spies. I scan the room for the requisite scale and the piles of packaged food and supplements I'm going to have to buy, but there are neither; only a few pamphlets and a neat stack of books sit on the middle of the table. Save a giant hanging poster with what looks like some kind of wordy declaration, the room is spare.

This can't be the right place.
I check the door again: It is.

Just when I'm about to lose my nerve, one of the men at the table locks eyes with me through the window. He tips his chin back gently, inviting me in.

Damn. No escaping now.

The door is one of those deceptively light ones that swing and slam into the wall behind you, announcing your entrance to the entire building. I head for one of the empty chairs, my face burning with embarrassment, loud as a symphony with my slurping boots and swishy down jacket. I get a few sympathetic smiles, but for the most part, all attention is on the woman speaking. She's thin and angular, a brown bob cutting a razor-sharp line against her cheekbone. There is absolutely no reason, as far as I can tell, that she should be here.

"It wasn't as bad as I thought it would be," she says, twisting a diamond ring around her knobbly finger. "I was able to just tell my husband that I was disappointed that he'd forgotten Valentine's Day, and it didn't have to be this huge fight. I didn't use it as an excuse for bad behavior or to eat something I shouldn't. I could just express my feelings and have that be okay, you know?"

Around me, people are nodding like truer words have never been spoken. I, meanwhile, understood no more than "Valentine's Day."

The woman goes on for another fifteen minutes, saying things like, "accepting my powerlessness," "turning it over," and "rigorous honesty." At one point, she gestures to the poster, which I see now is a list of "Twelve Steps", and calls it a "guide for living." I swear she's speaking English, but it's a cryptic, coded English that everyone in the room understands but me.

What is going on? Why isn't she talking about food?

When the woman finishes, a small blue basket materializes and everyone goes digging for their wallets.

Here we go. This must be when they hit you up for membership.

But when the basket reaches the scruffy man beside me, he holds onto it.

"You're new, right?" he whispers to me.

"Um, yeah?"

"Newbies don't pay. Just stick around and listen." The man winks at me and passes the basket over my head.

After a few announcements, the woman asks if anyone would like to "share." A couple of hands go up.

"Go ahead, Chris," the woman says, pointing to the man next to me.

"Hi," he says. "My name is Chris and I'm a compulsive overeater."

As the rest of the group choruses, "Hi, Chris!", those last two words make me vibrate like a gong. I have no idea what a compulsive overeater is, but I know instantly that I am one. I go light with relief and elation, like a balloon filling with air. This thing has a name. And if it has a name, that means it's an actual thing, that other people have. I'm not the only one.

I'm not a freak.

Chris also speaks in this cryptic English, as do the other people who share, but I don't care. I know with more confidence than I've ever had about anything that if I said to these people, "I can't not eat it," they would know exactly what I meant.

On my way out of the meeting, Chris takes my arm.

"Keep coming back," he says.

So I do, for the next two years, vainly trying to translate their "recovery" speak into a language I can understand. They suggest that if I'm like them, I'm powerless over food. So what's the point, then? If I'm powerless, I'm beyond hope; I might as well eat myself to death. Yet all around me are people who have emerged from the living death of compulsive eating, Anorexia, and Bulimia to become happy, useful human beings. How do they do it? The secret is elusive, though I sense it has something to do with hard work, something to which I am profoundly allergic. I wait for one of them to step in and fix it for me, but no one does.

Things get worse. I ignore suggestions from the people in the meetings, convinced that without the anesthetic of food, I will die. One woman invites me to call her each day to talk about what I'm eating, but it feels like she's asking me to show her my underwear. Another suggests I read the steps in the program's basic text, but I stick with the "happily ever after" stories in the back. Someone else tells me to "ask your higher power for help," and I back away like she's invited me to a Manson family reunion. Meanwhile, I wrestle myself into periods of what they call "abstinence" like I'm trying to get a foothold in an avalanche. The inevitable fall takes me to darker and darker places. I thought I was sick before, but now I see the twisted things I can do with food, and just how much of my life it steals away. I'm offered a chance to work at Disney World, a lifelong dream, and I destroy it by skipping my shifts to binge. One morning, I call in sick and walk to the convenience store across the street to buy a tub of ice cream and a dozen doughnuts. I bring it home and eat until my stomach is close to bursting. I run straight to the bathroom, free to puke out loud since all my roommates are working. Afterward, I lay on the couch while the room spins around me.

I am never doing this again, *I tell myself.*

Ten minutes later, I go back to the convenience store.

That Spring, I intern at a Hollywood film studio, the beginning of a potentially promising career, but I can't focus on anything but the cornucopia of junk food they have in the bungalow. I stare down the piles of shiny packages and technicolor treats, willing myself not to touch them. I've realized that taking even one bite is like setting a herd of buffalo on the run; the stampede doesn't stop until they say it does. But sitting in my office, so close yet so far, is torture. The day comes when I can't take anymore, and I rip open a box of ring dings (my old friends) and polish them all off. It feels so good I could cry, then so terrible I could cry harder.

These stupid meetings have killed eating for me. It's not fun anymore, because now I know too much. It's like I'm in the mob.

By the time I graduate college, I feel like I've been through a war. My skin is pasty and spattered with pimples. My eyes are dead. With no real plan, I move home, take a job as a classroom aide for autistic children, and fall into a graduate program in education. Mom and Dad are downsizing as kids move out; they swap the big house for a townhome a mile away. Packing up my childhood bedroom, Mom and I pull my headboard away from the wall, revealing a two-by-five-foot block of wrappers I've stuffed behind my bed over the last 15 years. Mom gapes at it, then looks to me for an explanation.

"How'd that get there?" I ask weakly.

In the new house, I'm given my own space in the basement, where I hide away to eat, watch movies, and rot.

Meanwhile, my mother has been attending her own meetings and transformed herself into a poster child for the program. Fifty pounds lighter, she's demented with joy, her high energy now super-charged. She bounces between work and meetings and spinning classes, buzzing on the phone with friends from her meetings. She still pours her life story out for everyone, though, like a puppy running infinities around people's legs. When I go to meetings with her, I'm "Debbi's daughter," which I both resent and play into. We have a "Best Friends" routine with tandem jokes and inflated stories that we perform to attract the attention we both crave.

"I need you to drive Dena to school in the mornings," she says, cleaning up after dinner. I sit at the island and watch her as I work through a bag of dried mango. "I can't get her there and make it to work on time."

"Do I have a choice?"

"You're living here rent-free. I think you can help out a little."

I bristle. "I help."

"Dropping your laundry in front of the washing machine doesn't count as helping. Pick up your elbows." I comply, and she sprays the granite with Fantastik. "It's not like you're driving an hour away. The school is down the block, it'll take you two minutes, and that'll be the end of it."

I roll my eyes. "Whatever."

"What is with you?" she says, ripping off a paper towel with unnecessary force. "Ever since you came home, you're just...miserable."

"I'm fine."

"You don't like your job?"

"The job's fine, Mom."

She wipes wide circles on the countertop, leaving dots of condensation that shrink, then disappear. "You're lonely? You miss your friends from school?"

"That's not it."

The truth is, there's not one answer to this question. Everything makes me miserable, from my now-empty mango bag to the fact that I woke up today. Misery is my default setting and my dark pleasure. Mom's insistence on nudging me out of it is maddening, like when she used to wake me in the morning by popping my lock open with a scissor and booming, "GOOD MORNING, REEZIE!" I would throw my pillow and scream at her to get out.

"What is it, then?" Mom says. "Talk to me!"

"Oh my God, Mom! Really? Can't I just reserve the right to be miserable?"

"Sure, if you could be miserable alone. But you have to make everyone around you miserable, too." She states this as fact, which stings more than if she'd meant it as an insult.

"Wow, Mom. I feel so much better now."

Her face softens. "You'll never know, until you're a mother, how painful it is to watch your child suffer. All I want is for you to be happy. I would give you my abstinence if I could. Anything to fix it."

I don't actually think the words before they leave my mouth; they just come out, like someone is speaking through me: "Maybe it's not your job to fix me."

We're both stunned into silence, because what I just said has never occurred to either of us. Mom stares at me, sadness reflected in her drawn eyebrows and gathered lips. But then the brows move gently apart, relaxing, and her eyes fill with hope. It's like she lost something, then remembered where she left it.

My body crackles with terror and exhilaration, like I've impulsively quit my job. Only I didn't quit anything; I just fired my mother as CEO of my life. I have no idea what's going to happen next, but I sense that I've set something in motion.

A few nights later, I chat with a guy on a dating site. We've been talking for three weeks and our chemistry (online, anyway) is perfect. He's smart and funny, he has a good job, and he's not bad looking in his picture. I haven't posted mine, hoping to evade the inevitable question. But tonight, he asks it: What do you look like?

I sink inside, debating whether or not I should tell him the truth. Maybe lie to buy some time? No, better to vet him now.

I'm fat, *I write.* But I'm going to lose the weight.

He doesn't reply. Ever.

Over the next thirty minutes, waiting for him to respond, I stew in shame so familiar it's almost comforting, the way my fat is comforting because it keeps my life contained to this basement. But something has cut its potency like water: I know, in a place beyond intellect, that this

248

is the last time I will ever apologize for myself. My shame container has topped off. I will accept no more.

I am done.

I drive a long way to a meeting my mother doesn't go to. The people there are smiling, attractive, and well-dressed. For months, I've listened to them say they've lost 100, even 200 pounds, and kept it off for 20 years. If they didn't have pictures to prove it, I would never believe them. Tonight, a black-haired woman named Gemma with toned arms and a sleek wardrobe speaks about how she binged her way past 200 pounds, and the hard work she did to get better. Some of the other women speak, too. For the first time, I really listen, and an unexpected thought comes to me:

Maybe if I do what they do, I'll have what they have.

The cartoon lightbulb above my head illuminates.

We reach the point in the meeting where the leader asks those who have recovery to stand. Every week before this, I've stood up, presenting myself as one of them. This time, I stay in my seat. I have never felt more vulnerable, but I force myself to sit still and look at this group of people who are living the life I want. I can choose to rot away in my parents' basement, keeping my world small and my body big as armor against terrible things that could happen to me. But to do so might be the worst thing that could ever happen to me.

When the meeting ends, I corner Gemma and beg her to sponsor me. "Please. Tell me what to do and I'll do it."

Gemma eyes me to gauge if I'm serious, then says, "If you mean it, I'm game."

For maybe the first time ever, I do what I'm told. I stop eating sugar and flour, which Gemma explains react in my body like alcohol does in an alcoholic. I have an allergy, not a weak will, that makes me unable to stop once I start. For three days, I walk around with hands shaking like I'm coming off of crystal meth. I cut out alcohol and drugs, because, as Gemma says, "You're eligible." I weigh every morsel of food I eat on a scale, and report it to Gemma every day. ("It's not about what you're eating," she says, "but about being accountable after years of breaking your word.") No longer inundated with chemicals, my taste buds can discern the surprising sweetness of a pepper, the distinct texture of an egg. My meals begin to have beginnings, middles, and ends, instead of spanning my waking hours.

The space between them, however, is interminable. I have been self-medicating since I was eight years old, and now, as my friend Melissa says, "I am a woman without a drug." Just being alive hurts. Years of compressed feelings, stuffed on top of each other like a trash compactor, are emerging, sometimes a handful at a time. I'm weepy and laughing by turns, processing memories decades old. The sweep of my rage terrifies me, my loneliness a well with no bottom. I feel naked before the entire world. After a month, I'm edging toward straightjacket territory. Desperate for escape, I wake up before the sun and drive to the Cape House, calling Gemma on the road.

"This is horrible," I say accusingly. "I've never been in so much pain. When am I going to be happy?"

"We're not shooting for happiness here," Gemma replies. "We're shooting for peace."

"What's the difference?"

"Happiness is a feeling, like any other feeling. It comes and goes. Peace is a state of being that doesn't change, no matter how you feel."

I let that one sink in for a minute.

"You need to pray," Gemma says.

I nearly spill my coffee. "Pray? To Whom?"

"To the God of your understanding."

Whizzing up the Merritt Parkway, I picture salt pillars, human sacrifices, Nazis, and terror attacks. "No, thanks. The God of my understanding scares the crap out of me."

"So, fire that God and hire another one."

"You can do that?" I say, surprisingly shocked at what sounds like sacrilege.

"Why not?"

Suddenly, I remember a story I read in one of Dad's Jewish books, which I happened to thumb through when I was helping Mom pack up the library. It was about an atheist who lived in the town of Berditchev, Russia, who proclaimed to everyone his disbelief in a God who was cruel, remote, and cold. When he met the Chassidic Rabbi Levi Yitzchak, the man again declared why he didn't believe in God. The great rabbi listened, then said, "You know, the God you don't believe in, I don't believe in, either."

"God can be anything you need," Gemma says. "A parent, a mentor, a friend. It's all accurate, because God is everything. Pick whatever God you want, as long as it's not you."

As if he's right beside me, I hear Dad's voice from that night in Israel, urging me to trust the Creator of good things. At the time, I refused to even consider the prospect. Now, I've been forced open through desperation - though I'm not quite ready to wave the white flag.

"Do I really need a God? I mean, I'm not stupid. I should be able to find peace by myself."

"Really?" says Gemma. "How's that working for you?"

This is an excellent point.

"So how do I pray? What do I say?"

"Say anything. Say everything. Just tell the truth."

When I get to the Cape, I don't even bother taking my things into the house. I walk straight to the beach, ignoring the rocks poking the bottoms my thin flip-flops. Emerging through a tunnel of trees, the calm, gray-blue bay comes into view. I kick off my shoes and descend the wooden steps to the sand, perfectly smooth from the outgoing tide. Sitting on an enormous rock, I look up at the cloudless, aquamarine sky.

"I don't know if You're there," I say. "But I was told that if I want to get better, I have to talk to You. So I'm talking to You. If You're there, I need You to help me. Please."

Almost every day of my childhood, I recited Hebrew prayers I only half-understood, but this is the first time I've ever really prayed. It feels foreign, unnatural, but not uncomfortable. I swing my head around to see if anyone is watching, but the place is empty. It's just me.

And God, apparently.

"I did it," I tell Gemma later. "I don't feel any better, though."

"That's okay," she says. "You've made a beginning."

At night, the Sinai Desert is an ocean of silver sand. As I trod through the shifting landscape, the only sound is the ragged inhales and exhales of my fellow tourists, young professionals like me whose sedentary bodies are unadapted to late-night hikes. My calves burn and my feet hurt, but I keep going, raining sweat, too prideful and too curious to give up.

"We're almost there," comes the South-African-accented whisper of our tour guide, Matan, a man of forty with a short, stocky build, wire-rimmed glasses, and a rotating wardrobe of polos and khakis.

I liked Matan from the very first day of our trip, when he pointed to the knitted yarmulke on his head and said, "Don't be intimidated by this. I'm not here to convert you; I just want to show you around a bit." He called himself a "Kippah Sruga" ("knitted yarmulke"), a member of Israel's "Dati", Modern Orthodox, set, an observant Jew rooted in tradition, yet fully engaged with the modern world. At eighteen, Matan became religious and moved to Israel, fought in the IDF, and has been showing tourists around the country ever since. Matan is the first Orthodox man I've met, besides my father, to wear anything other than the black and white costume de rigueur of the Ultra-Orthodox. He talks about literature, technology, and film, including a winning reference to "Bill and Ted's Excellent Adventure." I had no idea that there were Orthodox people like him.

"Oh, yes," Matan said when I mentioned it to him. "And you'll find plenty more around here."

From that moment, I was Matan's devoted student, drinking from his well of history as we toured the ruins of Caesarea, roamed through the galleries and synagogues of Tzfat, and climbed once again to the top of Masada, where we screamed, "Am Yisrael Chai!" ("The Nation of Israel Lives!") at the ghosts of enemies that have risen against us and faded to dust over three millennia.

The Israel I saw at 14 is not the same one before me now, at 22. The shadowy, claustrophobic country I ran from has been razed and built over into a land that is expansive, bright, and beautiful. Some things are still the same: the purple-gray Kinneret Sea, Masada's crumbling ramparts, the dirty, slick stone of Dizengoff Square. But I take them all in with the wonder moviegoers must have felt in the 1930's as they watched Dorothy step from black-and-white Kansas into the dazzling color of Oz.

Tonight, after dinner and tea in a Bedouin tent, Matan asked a handful of us to join him on a walk. I surprised myself by agreeing, the same surprise I felt a few months ago when I signed up for this tour of

Israel. At the time, I told myself that I was only doing it because the trip was free, but deep down, I knew it had something to do with the strange impulse to search for a trip to Israel in the first place.

In the months since I begged Gemma to sponsor me, I've been slowly coming to, the world around me shifting into focus. Each morning, per Gemma's instruction, I sit in meditation. It was torture in the beginning; I could barely manage two minutes of quiet. But eventually, I learned to settle myself, and my meditations got a little longer each day. My mind still chatters at me much of the time, my thoughts whizzing past each other like birds in an aviary. But sometimes, I can reach a place of stillness. Once or twice, I've even found my lacuna, where the feeling of both inner completion and outer connection is sweeter than any food I've ever tasted. I'm starting to think that feeling is what the sages meant by "dwelling with God."

I have a lot more to say to God now. It's not as awkward as it was in the beginning, when I felt like I was talking to myself. Now I get a vague sense that my words are directed at Something - what, exactly, I don't know, but knowing seems to be irrelevant. I once thought that certainty was the foundation stone of spirituality, which is perhaps why I could never find my footing. Turns out, the opposite is true. Action has eased me into belief, like an amateur tightrope walker whose tentative first steps grow more confident at the sight of a net beneath them. I can never be sure of what God is or isn't, but I do stand convinced that whatever God I'm working with is working for me. An unknown writer I came across had a similar experience: "I have recently been feeling myself moved by God...At first, as in the past, the scientist in me thought, 'This isn't real; God is just functional in some way.' Then I realized that a leaf grows toward the sun because it feels good, and finally, I will do the same." My friend Danielle described it more succinctly: "I've believed, and I've not believed. Believing is better."

Every day, I repeat my request to God for help, not knowing what form it will take or where it will take me, but anywhere is better than where I've been. And now, it seems, it's taken me to Israel. I still don't quite understand what I'm doing here, rediscovering a country I swore I'd never return to. It's like someone has tossed an invisible line across the ocean, hooked me with it, and reeled me in.

"We're almost there," Matan says, urging us up a steep slope. At the top, he stops us. "Look down."

I gasp. The sand drops off just inches from my sneakers into a deep, perfectly circular valley of sand, like a crater left by a giant ice cream scooper. I try to see the bottom, but it's too dark.

Matan tells each of us to grab a partner. "You'll need help getting down."

"We're going down there?" I ask, pointing into the valley.

"Not to worry," he says, teeth flashing white in the darkness. "I haven't lost anyone yet."

I turn to the girl next to me, a grad student named Julia who looks just as shaky as I feel. We grab each other's forearms and start our unsteady descent. The sand moves under our shoes, and our fingers tighten on each other's skin to keep from slipping. I focus on the red bandana tied around her hair, and the thick, dark curls springing out from the bottom. Her hair reminds me of Alisa, whom I think of everywhere on this trip. But thinking of her now doesn't paralyze me the way it once did. There's no more fear, only sadness, and a growing feeling I will later identify as purpose.

We all reach the bottom of the valley in one piece, though most of us have sand to wipe from our knees after slipping. After the last of us makes it, Matan whispers, "Look up."

As our heads tip to the sky, I hear a collective gasp at the thousands of stars above us, each one bright as daylight, framed by a ring of moonlight meeting the earth.

"See those stars?" says Matan. "Those are the same stars your ancestors looked at three thousand years ago."

The hair on my arms stands up. They're not just stories, *I think, with the feeling of recalling something long forgotten.*

The next day we go to the Kotel, the Holy Temple wall where years ago, I wrote to the God I didn't believe in to make me thin. The Kotel looks exactly the same, but it feels as if I've never seen it, nor felt the charged energy around it, before. My approach to the wall is uncertain, like it's an animal I'm feeling out for friendliness.

The second I touch the stones, I am overwhelmed by a sense of homecoming that is somehow inseparable from all my years of anguish, as if they are two halves of the same circle. I somehow understand that without dancing so close to death, I could never know the heartbreaking beauty of coming alive. The awe and gratitude are so profound I am too small to contain them, and I break open inside.

This is God's side of the tapestry.

It takes me a long time to collect myself, even after we've left the Kotel courtyard and our group winds through the streets of Jerusalem's Old City. Matan appears at my side with a tissue.

"I don't know why I can't stop crying..." I say, wiping my eyes.

He gives me an understanding smile. "Have you ever heard the word, 'orlah'?"

"No."

"The Torah uses it to describe a covering. On men, it's a physical covering that we cut off as a circumcision, but it represents something deeper. Each person, man and woman, has an orlah *on their heart which separates them from life. We're called to remove the* orlah, *to open ourselves up, and live."*

He smiles at me again.

"It looks, to me, like you have removed yours."

Chapter Sixteen

Mom has been asleep for over 36 hours, moving not a millimeter from her original position: legs strained against the bed rails, arms curled into her chest, and face turned to the side, nose-deep in Ralph fur. The coughing has stopped, and there is a deep stillness to her sleep that suggests she is beyond waking.

"Maybe we should lower the Ativan so she won't be so drowsy," Dad says.

"Dad, I don't think it's the Ativan."

Journey's End defines a coma as "a state of deep unconsciousness that lasts for a prolonged or indefinite period." I am certain, regarding my mother, that this is what a coma looks like.

Della confirms it when she arrives.

"Morphine?" I ask, recalling something about the drug's capacity to speed up the dying process.

"I doubt it. Her dose is too small." While some patients take anywhere from five to sixty milligrams of Morphine toward the end of life, Mom's dosage has never gone higher than three. Her low threshold is a source of melancholy amusement for Dad and the nurses. "Probably, she's just getting close."

"So what do we do now?"

"Same thing you've been doing. Wait."

I exhale through my teeth. "The waiting is killing me."

"So forget waiting," Della says. "Go play with your baby. He'll keep you entertained."

I follow her instructions and get down on the floor with Ezra, who is on his belly, reaching desperately for a block that is just beyond his grasp.

"Sorry, Dude," I say. "You want it, you gotta get it."

"You want an omelette?" Gabe asks from the kitchen. He has a whole production going with peppers, onions, mushrooms, cheese, and his prized Sriracha. Erin sits nearby, his lazy sous chef, eating grapes from an Edible Arrangement.

"I'm good," I say.

Noah appears, sleepy-eyed, in his pajamas. "EGGS!" he bellows, caveman-style. "Plain cheese, please."

Gabe, slicing an avocado, shakes his head. "Boring."

"I don't need your artisan California crap. I stick with the classics."

Erin perks up, pointing at Ezra. "Look! He's.."

Ezra has pulled himself up to hands and knees and is rocking back and forth like a car revving up at the starting line.

"Aaaaand he looks like he's ready to make the move…." Gabe says, like a sports commentator. "But will he do it?"

Ezra lifts his tush into the air in downward-dog position, then plants his knees back on the ground, eyes fixed on the bright yellow block just a foot away.

"A false start, but he's determined…" Gabe says.

"Come on, Ez!" calls Erin.

"He lifts a knee…"

Ezra brings one knee tentatively forward. The other one follows.

"SUCCESS!" Gabe cries, and the room erupts in cheers.

"Well played," says Noah.

I sweep Ezra up and cover him with kisses. "Good job, Buddy! I'm so proud of you!"

Ezra strains against me, looking down at the floor.

"The block, idiot!" Noah says.

"Right…" I hand the block to Ezra to another round of cheering, and my son's eyes twinkle with what looks like triumph.

I'm high on Ezra's crawl for the rest of the day, caught between the thrill of my son's milestone and the mourning of his babyhood. These are the moments when I need a handle on time's insidious speed, the simultaneous slogging and sprinting that breaks my heart. Ezra's newborn days moved in slow motion, yet nine months have passed in a blink. My whole life, in fact, has been a cycle of leisurely seasons that race by, leaving me longing for the happiness I didn't know I felt at the time. As for these last six weeks with Mom, they have been both the longest and the shortest of my life, harrowing and tender, unbearable and priceless. While the end has hurtled toward us, my family has stolen a second season together under one roof, holding each other in heartbreak, closer than we will ever be again. And though I wish for the end to come, for all our sakes, I wish just as much to live here forever.

I slide a pan of chicken into the oven and press "Bake", but it doesn't turn on.

I jab at the button again, then again. The oven stays dark.

"Dammit," I mutter, and head to my parents' room, where Dad is working.

When Mom first got here, she said to Ben and me, "You mark my words: I'm going to lay here dying and Dad'll be sitting there working." We laughed at the time, but her prediction was spot-on: my father deeply concentrates on his computer screen, talking on a headset to someone in New York, while his wife lays comatose three feet away. It's not callousness, but necessity: bills are impervious to death.

"Hold on a sec," he says into the headset, then looks up at me. "What's up?"

"Oven's not working."

He nods wearily. "Alright. I'll call someone."

Dad returns to his phone call while I grab my laptop and pull a chair next to Mom. As I write, I keep one eye on Dad as he moves from computer to fax to Mom's morphine drip.

Through the headset, a muffled voice asks, "How's she doing?"

"It's not good," he says, with no hopeful addendum.

In the last week, my father's last drops of optimism have drained away. He makes no suggestions that things could turn around, no expression, even, of the desire that they will. On the blog, he writes, "We pray for her complete recovery but realize that the power to effect that prayer is not in human hands." No declaration of surrender could be clearer. Dad tells his readers, in a sadly self-deprecating tone, of his struggles to care for Mom while sleep-deprived, his fumbling in changing her diapers, keeping her comfortable in the hospital bed and administering oral medication while she sleeps. Between the lines are the cries of a drowning man.

Meanwhile, Dad continues to report the minutiae of Mom's care. On the surface, these facts and figures illustrate the minutiae of caring for a dying woman, but on a deeper level, they are the only stable anchor to which my father can cling:

Della told me to go in the Hospice Pharmacia ComfortPak we keep in the refrigerator and identify a small container with a red cap. The medicine inside is Atropine in a 1% concentration. The instructions read, "Place 2 drops under the tongue every four hours as needed for excess secretions…" Atropine is extracted from a deadly nightshade whose scientific name is atropa belladonna…Atropa is from the Greek atropos*, which is one of the three fates. Its meaning is to "cut the thread of life." In contrast, belladonna comes from the Italian for "beautiful lady", because Italian women used the deadly nightshade to dilate their pupils, a look that they felt made them more beautiful to their male suitors.*

My eye is drawn to movement on the computer screen, rows of characters in green type moving upward. These are my father's thoughts in numerical form, the product of a mind more complex than most, and I don't understand any of it. Since the night Dad told us his story, he has gone quiet, retreating into himself, moving through us, not with us, with a manic energy. When I woke him from a nap yesterday, he jumped out of bed like a warrior called to combat, so quick and fierce it startled me.

I wish he would speak to us again, not just to his invisible audience, if only to give himself some relief.

But as distracted as Dad is, he is tuned in at high frequency to his wife. Mom's lips just begin to show a crust of white before he's swabbing them or wiping them moist with a washcloth. Every few minutes he monitors the morphine drip to ensure she's out of pain. And he's the first one to notice the tear.

"Look," he says, beckoning me over. A single tear has formed at the corner of Mom's right eye and slowly moves down her face. "Didn't *Journey's End* say something about this?"

"*Lacrima Mortis*, it's called," I say. "The Tear of Death." According to the pamphlet, this one, last tear is part of the body's release of stored toxins. But seeing the long, glossy trail the tear leaves on my mother's cheek, it's impossible to see it as anything but weeping.

"Is this it?" I ask.

"I don't know."

"Maybe we should open the door. I heard Della say that's a thing for dying people."

Dad rushes across the room and slides the door open, filling the room with the smell of Spring.

Mom's eyes flutter. Dad and I gasp.

"They're open!" he exclaims.

Open they are, though unfocused and heavy-lidded. I stare into them, willing them to see me. "Hi, Mom. It's Rea. I'm so happy to see you." I'm talking too loudly, but I don't care.

"You had a big *schluff*," Dad says.

"You did. You slept for a long time. I love you, Mom," I say, loading each word with the intention to keep her lucid just a little longer. "We opened the door for you. Do you feel the breeze? It's a beautiful day. It's Springtime."

Dad tries to give her water but it drips out of her mouth. She moans softly and her eyes close again.

"It's getting close," I tell Erin. "We need to get this place together."

We spend hours scrubbing the kitchen and dining room, then stripping the sofa to wash the slipcovers. There will be lots of company soon, and Mom would be horrified to think this place wasn't pristine. There's a comfort in the work, a place to put the energy, and my mind shuts off to everything but the task at hand. I barely notice the two repairmen who come to poke at the oven, except to slip by them when I need something from the kitchen. It doesn't occur to me, even, to shut Mom's door, to quiet the sound of the oxygenator, to hide the presence of death in this house. It's so familiar now, I don't even see it.

At some point, the repairmen call Dad in and explain the problem. At first they speak in laymen's terms, but Dad's response shows them they can talk shop with him. They fall into an easy, masculine rapport, batting around technical jargon and discussing various parts. The repairmen instruct Dad on how to fix the problem himself, should it come up again. In their eyes, he's capable.

On the way out, one of the men gives Dad a gruff pat on the shoulder. "Hang in there," he says.

Dad's eyes turn downward. "Thanks."

Chapter Seventeen

Gabe wakes me in the middle of the night.

"I'm scared," he whispers, taking my hand. "I'm scared of death. I feel it."

A few hours later, I bring Ezra downstairs to say good morning to Mom. Her breathing is quick and short, and she gurgles as if her lungs are full of water. The rosy pink flush on her cheeks pulls my hand to her head: she's burning with fever. There's nothing to do, though; *Journey's End* says this fever isn't an indication of illness.

Dad has given up on work now. He sits at Mom's side, reciting Psalms. Ben, Gabe, Dena and I go about our morning business in a state of tightly-strung expectancy (Sammy and Noah are in Boston, taking an exam), until a cry from my parent's room makes us jump.

"She opened her eyes!" Dad says.

We rush into the room and surround Mom, whose eyes are halfway open, staring straight up at the ceiling.

Dad leans close to her, whispering. "I love you, Willie. You were so good, Willie, a good wife and a good mother. I'm sorry for everything I did or said that hurt your feelings. I didn't mean it."

She moans to him. I can almost hear her saying, *Forget it, Willie. It's fine.*

Dad shifts to the end of the bed to make room for us. Dena puts her lips close to Mom's forehead. "I won't ever give up, Mom. You taught me that. I'll never give up because of you."

A relationship, in essence, is an exchange of words. The nature of the relationship rides on the backs of those words, their meanings, and the meanings behind their meanings. Our words carry love, anger, expectation, gratitude. Sometimes we toss them at each other without thinking. But never once, in the course of any relationship, do we consider the last words we will ever say to each other. We are baffled when the end comes, even when it's expected, because after a lifetime of words, we are limited to only a few to express what the whole exchange has meant to us. Words are like time that way; we think there will always be more.

I do the best I can with the ones I have left. "Thank you, Mommy. Thank you for everything. Thank you for teaching me how to be a good mother, a good wife. Thank you for showing me how to take care of everyone. Thank you for fighting for me. I'm alive today because of you."

Tears roll down Mom's cheeks. At the end of the bed, Dad breaks down.

Ben rushes in with the baby.

"Mom, Ezra's here," I say, taking Ezra in my arms. "Say, 'Hi, Bubbles.'" I give him the signs, then lean him against her cheek: "Give Bubbles a kiss." He rubs his face against her. When I pull him away, he leans down for her again. I let him have another snuggle, then hand him back to Ben.

Gabe moves in and kisses her on the cheek. She moans, a single sound containing all her her pain, her love, her gratitude. *How I will miss you.*

Her thoughts are so clear, they make me laugh and cry at the same time. *"Ha...Ha..."*

Goodbye.

We stand around her, crying, until she drifts off again.

The waiting gets to be too much for Dena and Gabe, and they go out on a made-up errand. Half-dazed, I play with Ezra in the living room and fold laundry. Right after I finish lunch, I hear Dad call my name. "I think she's taking her last breath…"

My parent's room is silent, save for the hum of the oxygenator. Mom is completely still, her mouth open, a film on her teeth and tongue. Her color is strange: gray Elizabeth Arden skin, white lips, blue fingertips. Ben follows me in and takes my hand.

Dad leans close to her face and holds his fingers to her neck. "I think I feel a faint pulse…"

Ben squeezes my hand, and I look at him. He shakes his head.

Dad leans in closer, presses his fingers deeper. "I thought I heard one…"

I feel another squeeze. Ben shakes his head again.

Gabe and Dena appear at the door. The minute he sees my face, Gabe's eyes go wide.

"I think she's gone," I tell him, even though I don't think. I know.

Dena takes Mom's pulse and leans down to see if she's breathing.

"Nothing," she says decisively. "She's gone."

I've been anticipating this moment for six weeks, considering every possible reaction I might have to the sight of my mother dead. But now that the time is here, I simply stare at her face, the glassy orbs of her eyes, and her chest, still and hollow as a drum. I'm surprised to feel no fear, only keen awareness of my smallness before the sacred, of bearing witness to a passage as right and elemental as a birth.

Suddenly, I feel a need to do something: make a phone call, flip the laundry, drive across the country. "Should I call the rabbi?" I ask.

"Not yet," Dad replies, sinking onto the bench at the foot of the bed. "I need a minute."

"Did anyone call Noah?"

Dena and Gabe look at each other, then at me.

"I'll do it," Gabe says, pulling out his phone.

"Call Della, too," I say.

As Gabe murmurs into the phone, Dena and I stand beside Mom.

"We should cover her face," Dena says. "It's freaking me out a little."

"Okay."

Together, we pull the sheet over her head. A wail behind us makes us start.

"I can't believe this," Dad gasps. "This is terrible…"

His grief is too thick around him for us to get close. I graze his shoulder with my hand, then let him be. Wrapping myself in one of the fleece blankets Mom got from the hospital, I walk out the sliding doors and into a gray, blustery afternoon. It is strangely silent, as it was inside. Despite the roiling clouds, there is no wind, like the world is holding its breath. Time moves slowly, still attached to the event that just occurred. *Mom died nine minutes ago… ten minutes ago…*It's the same bubble of time I sat in after giving birth to Ezra, when everything was suspended around the moment I delivered my child.

Della arrives to pronounce Mom dead, then packs away some of the equipment and Mom's old prescriptions. She has me fill Ziploc bags with coffee grounds so she can dispose of all the pills. Coffee makes it unappetizing, she explains, to any human or animal that might go digging through the trash. I doubt the effectiveness of this method, considering the number of times I wiped dirt and other questionable substances off of food and ate it. If a drug addict is already waist-deep in trash, I doubt a few coffee ground will deter them.

Two gentlemen arrive in a van with the name of a funeral home on it, one a light-haired twentysomething, the other a stocky, swarthy man in his forties with a Greek last name. They both wear black wind jackets with logos that match the one on the truck.

"The plan at this point," the older one tells Dad, "is to bring her to our place, local, until someone from the Jewish funeral home can come pick her up."

Even before he's done speaking, Dad is already pushing a thumb against his lips in protest. Jewish law requires that a body be accompanied at all times, from the moment of death to burial, and at a non-Jewish funeral home, the risks that this law might get overlooked are high.

"She needs to be in Canton overnight," he argues. "She needs someone with her all the time."

The two men look at each other, nonplussed.

"Take a seat in the living room," Dad says, with no mind for courtesy. "I'll take care of this."

Though clearly uninitiated in Jewish mourning rites, these men are savvy enough to know not to argue with the bereaved. They file out obediently behind me, nervously clearing their throats and pulling at their collars. We point them to the stools at the island and hand them glasses of water they don't touch, discomfort coming off of them like steam. We have nothing to say to them, nor the energy to try. Instead, Erin and I busy ourselves with putting the freshly washed slipcovers back on the sofa. A few feathers from the cushions escape and float gently around us, like snow in a globe, batted about by the breezes our bodies make when we move.

Abruptly, the door to my parents' room swings open and Dad strides out. "Everything is resolved," he says. "A representative will meet you at the funeral home in one hour to pick her up."

"Very good, sir," the younger man says, like a butler.

I follow the men into Mom's room where the older man slips his arms under Mom's back. On a stretcher beside the bed, the younger opens a burlap body bag the color of burgundy - funny, I expected white - then pushes Mom's legs straight up into the air, grunting slightly with exertion. I know immediately that I should not be watching her handled this way, like a body instead of a person, but I stay still. As they move her over on the bed, the fitted sheet pulls up and curls over her face. She looks tiny, like a little girl.

"You promise you won't leave her alone?" Dad asks them.

"Of course, sir."

On three, they shift Mom's body into the bag, zip her up from foot to head, and roll her to the door. Before they leave, the older man stops and looks at Dad.

"We're sorry for your loss, sir."

Dad, Dena and I follow them, trance-like, out the front door, where they roll the body toward the van. Dena stays on the stoop, but I keep going until I'm halfway across the yard, giving Dad the last stretch alone. As the men open the back, Dad leans down and kisses the bag where her face would be. Deftly, they kick the legs up under the stretcher, roll it into the truck and shut the doors.

With the sound of the ignition, Dad howls. "They're taking her away..." he says, like they've tricked him. The van backs up slowly and he steps away, tears streaming down his face. "They're taking her away..."

He takes small, tripping steps backward toward the front steps, where he sinks down, drops his head in his hands, and keens. His grief is immense, reducing him to the motherless child who has now lost his best friend. The weight of it has him doubled over. It terrifies me, so I turn back to the van, just disappearing behind the trees.

And it hits me: that was the last time I will ever see her.

Everyone wanders through the house like zombies, including Noah and Sammy, who arrive from Boston wearing our same stunned expressions. As soon as I see Sammy, I remember that it's her birthday.

God, You did not go easy on this woman.

When Dad is calm again, he sits us down to discuss the logistics of the funeral, who will speak, where donations should be sent. It will take place tomorrow, as Jewish custom dictates that bodies be buried as soon as possible. In some cases, a family can lose a loved one in the early morning and bury them that afternoon. I only half-hear him, because while he asks our opinions, the decisions are ultimately his. As Della says, "Your father runs a benevolent dictatorship."

I print out a list of things we're prohibited to do for the week of shiva and tape it on the fridge, going through the motions of being a mourner while feeling like a bystander. Like everything, from learning my mother's diagnosis to seeing her zipped up and carted away in a bag, has happened to someone else.

In the late afternoon, Noah, Dena and Gabe find me. Noah holds a large plastic bag.

"Come for a walk," he says.

The air is warmer than I thought it would be, the wind kinder on my skin, but I pull my sweater closed out of habit. Dena puts her arm around me and I slip mine around her waist. We walk quietly down the to the beach, the four of us in a row, coming upon an empty stretch of sand and a far receded tide.

There are no words exchanged as we head down the stairs and walk the shore for shells. As we drop them in Noah's bag, they hit each other with a *clack*. Noah stops us when the bag is half-full and fills the rest with sand.

"She was supposed to get better," I say to no one in particular.

"No," says Gabe. "She just wasn't supposed to die."

Then we walk home, four children alone, and not another soul in sight.

Chapter Eighteen

Today is my mother's funeral.
Today is my mother's funeral.
Today is my mother's funeral.
No matter how many times I tell myself, it doesn't register.

I dress Ezra with a strange detachment, as if we're in a dream. He burbles at me while I slide one chubby thigh, then another, into his pants. I should smile at him, so I do, but the shift in facial muscles is purely mechanical. I put on the gray jacket I bought for the funeral, the skirt, the tights, both distant from and hyperaware of every sensation: the feel of nylon against my shaved legs, the skirt clasp pressing against my back, the pinch of high heels after a year in flats and sneakers. I color my washed-out face with makeup, thinking what a waste it will be when I cry.

Ben and I fasten the baby into the back of Dena's car and buckle up next to him. Alex takes the wheel, Dena beside him, while Dad, Noah, and Sammy get into their car with Gabe and Erin. As a drizzle of rain patters the windows, our small procession pulls out of the driveway for the hour-long trip to Millis. The closer we get, the bigger my dread becomes. I dread seeing the casket. I dread watching it sink into the ground. I dread seeing other people's grief.

The green, tranquil cemetery is much more beautiful than I remembered. The sky has cleared, and sunshine pours over the tall, swaying trees, the rolling fields, and the aged headstones. I look for Mom's gravesite on the hilltop, among the rest of our deceased, but it isn't there. It stands alone in a grassy alcove far removed from everyone, the first of ten plots reserved for our immediate family.

As Alex stops the car to the sound of crunching rocks, I eye the hearse that's parked by the grave with apprehension. The trunk is open, and I can see the casket inside. The slam of the car door rings loudly in my ears. Ben unbuckles Ezra, but I stay glued to my seat.

"I can't do this," I say.

My husband gently takes my arm. "You can."

I let him guide me out of the car, up the hill, and into the cemetery. Someone takes Ezra, and I let them, struck by the number of people who have come. After six weeks of seeing almost no one but my own family, the parade of faces is overwhelming and surreal. There are characters from the many chapters of our family's life, friends from our old synagogue, a multitude of cousins, childhood neighbors, and my parents' New York people, all mingled together like an out-of-sequence photo album. A few try to talk to me, but I can't focus.

There's Jane, one of my mother's best friends, a comedienne who lived down the street for twenty years. For a moment, I'm excited to see her, anticipating the fun we'll have when Mom gets here.

That's when I fall apart.

I grip onto the person next to me - Ben? Dena? - half-crying, half-talking, with no idea what I'm saying. People nearby watch me with wet eyes, shaking their heads in pity. Someone says it's time for the burial, and everyone heads down the hill. My family lines up obediently behind the casket, a simple box of polished pine, but my feet won't move.

"I can't do this..." I say. "I can't do this..."

Dena takes one of my elbows, Ben takes the other, and they steer me forward. I have no strength in my body to fight them; I can only protest with words.

"I can't do this," I say over and over, though it's not what I mean. I'm trying to tell them to stop now, before she's in the ground, when she and I are still in the same world. I don't care if she's dead and I'm alive; I can't live in a world where she isn't. Don't they know this isn't right? It's not supposed to happen this way!

"Daddy!" I cry. "I can't do this!"

My father, who is walking in front of me, turns back to look at me with wretched eyes. I'm making it worse for him.

"I'm sorry," I whisper to Dena, who squeezes my hand. "I'm sorry..."

My tears stop suddenly when we reach the grave, where the casket is laid on top of a harness. I'm a spectator again, removed from everything. Reb Zalman, a family friend and rabbi of a Jewish outreach center on the Cape, speaks of his last visit with Mom, just a few weeks ago. She told him of her newfound spiritual life, of her connection to Torah learning and Shabbos.

"As I was leaving," he says, "She cried to me, 'Please, please, take care of my children!' What can be more powerful than the cry of a mother for her children?"

He concludes with a verse from Devorah, the ancient prophetess of Israel, whose name my mother shared:

"Uri, Uri, Devorah, Uri, Uri, Dabri Shir...
Rise up, Devorah,
Rise up, Debbi,
Rise up, Rise up
Ascend to the heavenly throne and sing your song
Continue to pour your heart out before Hashem
Plead to Hashem in a melody no one knows but you
Pray that your children follow that which you have taught them
Pray for the wellbeing of your children and your dear husband
Sing to them the song of strength and courage amidst challenge."

Dena speaks, then Noah, then Gabe. I speak. Then Dad. People wipe tears from behind their sunglasses, smile at funny memories, while others fan themselves in the unexpected heat. My Aunt Suzie paces the top of the hill with my son in her arms.

Then they lower the casket into the grave. People line up to shovel dirt over it, the final respect you can pay the dead. Dad works hard, sweat glistening on his face, grunting quietly as he lifts each shovelful. Even after the casket is covered, when it's customary to stop, he pushes on, until the grave is completely filled. When Dad finally walks away, clapping dirt off his hands, Dena and I are the only ones left.

I want to lay on my belly atop of the mound of dirt and sand and shells covering Mom, like a newborn on its mother's chest. Instead, I sit on the ground beside the grave. Dena sits down next to me. A breeze sets the trees swaying, sunlight playing peek-a-boo through the branches. We are silent for a while, looking up the hill at the other family graves. There is Dad with his two brothers, standing in a mournful row over their mother.

"This sucks," Dena says.

"Yup."

"We're going to have to take care of each other now."

I rest my head on her shoulder and look down at the fresh dirt, where my hand rests next to my sister's. Mine are tanned and small as a child's, while hers are white and strong and womanly, identical to Mom's.

"I found out what Mom said to Alex," she says.

"You did? How?"

"It was one of those days when she was hopped up on all the drugs. She wanted to know how long the nurses said she had to live. I wouldn't tell her, in case it messed with her morale. She got *really* mad at me."

"Oh, man..."

"She asked me again, so I said I would tell her, but only if she told me what she said to Alex first."

"You're so bad!" I say.

"She thought about it for a minute, then came out with it. She told Alex, 'This is going to be the hardest time of Dena's life. I know you two have only been together for six months, but if you're not in this for the long haul, you should go now.'"

I gasp. "She didn't!"

"She did. I think she just needed to know how the story would play out for me. That all of her kids were set. Alex reassured her that he was in it, and that was it. So she said to me, 'Now, tell me what the nurse said.' I said, 'No,' and walked out."

We both laugh, good and long.

Dena's gaze wanders over to the parking lot. "They're all leaving. We should go."

Neither of us move.

After a minute, she says, "We can't stay here forever."

"Just a little bit more. They won't leave without us."

We sit, listening to the wind in the grass, feeling the sun on our backs, until Ben starts walking up the hill toward us.

"It's time," Dena says with finality, pulling herself up. She holds her hand out to me. "Come on."

I'm tempted to refuse and sit here indefinitely. I could set up camp, like a peaceful protester, with my food scale and my books, build a little yurt under the trees, and live out my days in silent companionship with my dead mother. But then I see Ben coming closer, with Ezra in his arms.

The world keeps turning.

I use my sister's strong grasp to pull myself to my feet, then brush the dust from my skirt.   "Bye, Mommy," I say, and leave her.

The Cape House is busy when we get back, with Aunt Suzie, Sammy and Erin cooking Shabbos for everyone.

I'd forgotten today was Friday.

"We've got a full house tonight," Erin says. "Suzie and Arthur are staying for dinner, and I think your Dad asked Charlie and Karen, too."

"I thought it was just us for dinner," I say, trying not to sound annoyed.

"Me, too. Change of plans, I guess."

As a mourner, I'm not allowed to prepare food for anyone, even myself, so I sit back as the three of them chop and spice and stir. I'm not sure what to do with myself; after weeks of constant activity, my momentum has yet to slow. It's like when I used to spin in circles for fun, falling to the ground with dizziness while the room continued whirling around me.

Mom's absence at Shabbos dinner is so palpable, you could offer it a seat. We repeat our usual routine, but this time, there's only one pair of hands to bless us. Dad's "Woman of Valor" sounds like a torch song. We have the same wine, the same food, even the same challah recipe, but without Mom's showmanship, the magic is missing.

As we sit down to dinner, a crew of Dena's friends arrive to offer support. They surround her, giggling and talking, and suddenly our family dinner has turned into a party.

"Add more water to the soup," Dad jokes to Suzie.

The crowd flows from the dining room out to the living room, filling every available seat, including the floor. It reminds me of my senior prom night, when Mom invited all my friends to stay, collected their keys, and told them to find a place to sleep. There were teenagers draped on couches and chairs, and one curled like a cat on the same glass table I'm eating at now.

People chat happily, balancing plates across their knees. A boom of laughter echoes off the ceiling.

"They better not wake the baby," I grumble to Ben.

"You know," he says, putting his arm around me, "this is exactly how she would have wanted it."

"What do you mean?"

"A house full of people, everyone having a good time. This was her *thing*."

He's right, of course, I realize with amusement.

Did we really think she would leave without a party?

In a dressing room at The Gap on Broadway, I unbutton a pair of red corduroy jeans whose siren song from the window pulled me in off the street. I nabbed the last pair hanging from the rack: size 2. As I pray silently, the soft material grazes my ankles and calves, rises past my knees, up my thighs, and settles around my waist. The button closes easily, with no need to suck in my stomach. I admire them on my reflection, slung just right on my hips, perfectly hugging my butt.

They fit.

I fit into a size 2.

This shouldn't be a surprise, considering that I've been eating abstinently and going to meetings for the last year and a half. The flesh has melted off my bones. I've been cold for months, and my skin is spotted with bruises from the lack of cushion. I keep miscalculating how much space I take up; sitting in a chair (with my legs crossed!) I'm shocked by the ample space left on the seat. The scale says I've lost 120 pounds, but it's not until this very moment, wearing a pair of size 2 Gap jeans, that I get it.

I'm thin.

I. Am. Thin.

I want to run out of this dressing room and shout it to the world: "I'm Thin! I'm Thin!" An extravagant musical number would follow, with cashiers doing backflips and waving chinos like flags. Out on the sidewalk, balletic meter maids would leap and twirl, quarters flying like confetti, as a street musician with a didgeridoo led a grand parade to Lincoln Center. Flanked by the cast of Rigoletto, the courtyard fountain would shoot into the air in time with our harmonic crescendo: "She's THIIIIIIINNNN!"

Instead, I quietly purchase the jeans by handing them the tag - they can bury me in these babies - and ogle myself in every store window on the way back to my parents' apartment.

I'm the first one home, which means it's my job to walk Jazz, who sticks her nose in my crotch and jumps on her hind legs with pure canine joy.

Just the sight of her pisses me off.

"Don't ruin my JEANS!" I growl, headlocking her to get the leash on. "Let's go."

The second we're out of the building, Jazz drops her hips and pees on the sidewalk. I smile awkwardly at the doorman, then lead her down toward the pier. As usual, she darts forward and pulls me along, then stops unexpectedly so that I trip over her.

"Just do it, okay?"

Jazz finds a patch of grass and does her business as a flock of pigeons lands nearby. Oh, no.

The dog proceeds to lose her mind, running in all directions at once. The pigeons, fearless little bastards, sashay up to her, then retreat at the last second, saucily fluttering their wings ("SIKE!"). Jazz goes into something like a seizure.

"JAZZ! HEEL!" I yell, but it's pointless. With all my strength, I drag her off the grass and back toward the building, intermittently tripping, while the anger that started bubbling at the sight of her reaches a boiling point. A pigeon alights not ten feet in front of us, I swear, just to screw with the dog, and Jazz almost rips my shoulder out of its socket.

"JAZZY! NO!"

Fueled by a sudden, inexplicable rage, I pull hard on the leash, harder than I need to, and she flies back toward me, paws rising from the ground, and hits her head against the fender of a parked car.

"Ooh!" I say, feeling both terrible and gratified.

Jazzy, unhurt, gives her head a cheerful shake. She looks back to the spot where the pigeon landed, and, finding it empty, trots onward. Looks like there's no need to mention the incident to my mother.

Mom's home when we get back, staring into the open fridge and eating balls of fresh mozzarella with her fingers. Her phone is cradled between her ear and shoulder, and two empty pudding cups and an open bag of Tostitos rest on the counter beside her.

"You can be upset," she says in preschool singsong. "But what does program teach us?"

I have to will my eyes not to roll. It's all I can take listening to Mom cast herself as the omnipotent sponsor when she's clearly in relapse. I couldn't tell you exactly when it started, but somewhere between the day I got abstinent and my parents' move to New York, foods I haven't seen in awhile, which come in shiny bags and colorful boxes, reappeared in the cabinets and on Mom's nightstand. Bereft of her friends, her meetings, and the only community she'd known for twenty years, Mom has resumed her old hobby of foraging in the kitchen for the company of food, and drifting from room to room like a plane waiting for clearance to land. Mom's Manhattan extends little further than this apartment; she commutes out to New Jersey for work, buys everything she needs there, and pulls right back into the lot under our building. I took her to a meeting with me on 86th street, where she kept her jacket on and her arms crossed, holding her elbows. When she spoke, it was fluff, Debbi playing "DEBBI!", but it meant nothing to a crowd that didn't know her. Mom seems so small in this sprawling city full of people and titanic buildings, even as her body grows bigger. I, on the other hand, have never been smaller in my life, but I feel as if I tower over her.

As Mom chats with her sponsee, I work around her in the narrow kitchen, packing my lunch for tomorrow, dicing carrots and peppers, frying tofu, and measuring it all to the exact tenth of an ounce on my scale. I could do this later, after dinner, but I want her to see me do it, partly in hopes of helping her, and partly to fan my secret flame of superiority. Grazing her heel, I mumble an apology, and she gives me a civil nod. This is how it is for us now, dancing around each other in tight quarters, exchanging courtesies while quietly simmering, occasionally exploding, and counting down the weeks until I finish my degree and move out.

As I pack my lunch away, Mom migrates to the living room and drops onto a stuffed burgundy chair. Through the window behind her, twilight sets in, and the maze of apartment buildings begins to coalesce into a hazy mass of gray. It's my favorite time of day in the city, watching hundreds of windows illuminate like tiny, winking eyes. It makes me feel like God, looking down on an infinity of storylines playing out parallel to each other.

It's also time for my dinner.

I prepare my meal, soothed by the rituals I've created around food: the cutting, the spicing, the cooking, the rigid measurement, and finally, the eating, always at the same seat at the table, with a book, in deep communion with my food. Just as you wouldn't tap someone on the shoulder while they're making love, speaking to me while I'm eating is unacceptable. Once, to tease me, my father took a piece of zucchini from my plate and ate it, and I practically sprang across the table at him like a wildcat. I huddle around my program like Gollum with his precious ring, maintaining a tight circle that only Gemma and my recovery fellows can penetrate. To stick, it needs to be mine alone, safe from any outside influence - especially my mother's. I communicate my shut-door policy to her in everything I do, from my haughty farewells ("I'm off to a meeting!"), to the solo mealtimes, to the CIA-agent intensity with which I answer the phone and retreat to my room (top-secret recovery business, you know). I'm dimly aware that my self-importance borders on nauseating, and that my family tiptoes around me like a highly sensitive bomb. But I fear that even the slightest deviation will send the whole structure tumbling down. Anyway, they should just be happy for me, because I'm thin and pretty now. And when you're thin and pretty, you can behave however you want.

Which is a good thing, because I've never been angrier in my life.

I thought that when I got thin, all would be sunshine and rainbows. But I feel more manic now than I ever did at 250. Gemma says this is normal.

"Everything is rosy when you first get abstinent, like you're falling in love," she says. "But everyone falls off the pink cloud eventually. Then you rage for a couple of years."

She isn't kidding. My rage is a black poison running with my blood, filling every molecule, and activating with the slightest provocation, be it a Fairway cashier moving in slow-motion or a flock of pigeons taunting my mother's dog. When one of the kids in my class wouldn't stay in his seat, it took every ounce of self-control not to cold-cock him. But nothing infuriates me more than watching my mother walk the solitary island of this apartment, need on her like an open wound, as she waits for my father to come home. When he does, she transforms into a 50's housewife, offering dinner and company with a side of desperation. On friendlier evenings, Dad half-acknowledges her presence with a grunt, then escapes into the television. Many times, though, Mom will float around him, her kisses and conversation unnoticed, like she's a ghost he can't see.

After dinner, reading on my bed, I hear Mom moving about the kitchen, cooking for her and Dad, though fifty bucks says he won't be home for hours. Eventually, the cooking sounds quiet, and Mom's heavy footfalls round the parquet floors. Her door closes, then opens again. Her steps, ambling and slow, increase in volume as she gets closer and closer to my room. She rounds the corner and leans against the doorway, waiting for me to acknowledge her.

"What's up?" I say in half-welcome, peering over the rim of my book.

"What are you up to?"

I tap the book's cover.

"No plans tonight?"

"Nope."

"Carly's not around?"

"Don't know. I didn't ask her."

"You're so young," she says, looking at me in her awestruck Mom way, like she can't believe I exist. "Why don't you go out and meet people? They have a million Jewish singles things around here."

"I don't want to."

"Why not?"

Not long ago, I would have made up some deflective excuse or snapped at Mom to mind her own business. But I've learned that telling the truth, even if it hurts, is a lot less painful than excavating for it later. Rip the band aid, as it were, instead of peeling it off, centimeter by tortured centimeter.

I put my book down. "I'm afraid, I guess. Rooms full of strangers intimidate me. New York strangers, especially. I have no threshold for small talk, and I never know what to do with my hands since I don't drink. Usually, I just end up feeling lonely and leave early. I'd rather save myself the hassle and stay here."

Mom's eyes widen in surprise, and then she says, almost whispering, "I feel that way, too."

I remember her the night of Mishket's wedding, fidgeting in her "sheitel", white suit, and full makeup, with one protective arm across her chest.

"You do?" I say expectantly, leaning toward the door.

She nods, confirming her own discovery. "Yeah. I do."

For a moment, the hilly landscape from which I have peered both up and down at my mother levels out, setting us eye-to-eye. And we can, perhaps for the first time, see each other.

Then she ruins it by saying, "Gemma has done an amazing job with you."

I'm instantly furious. Again. Mom has totally missed the point, locked as she is in her old ways of thinking. She assumes that if I'm better, Gemma must have done it. Like Mrs. Garcy, who couldn't believe I wrote my haiku by myself.

I laugh darkly. "Yeah. I had absolutely nothing to do with it."

"That's not what I meant."

"Whatever, Mom." I pick up my book and place it in front of my face, effectively dismissing her. I feel her standing there, bewildered by how quickly things turned, and frustrated as hell with her mercurial, selfish, profoundly ungrateful daughter. Then I hear her footsteps again, moving away from my doorway and stopping in the kitchen, where the refrigerator opens.

The next few months whizz past, with Mom and I saying little to each other. As I wrap up my degree, I travel up to Boston to interview for a job and find a place to live. I discover a tiny one-bedroom on a hilly street in Allston that's nowhere near as fancy as my parents' (okay, it's not fancy at all) but when I sign for it, it's mine. My own place. Back in New York, I fit my belongings into only a few suitcases and a couple of boxes. My parents and Gabe travel with me to the Cape House for New Year's weekend, to help me move in on the first of January. With the voices of Eddie Murphy and Dan Aykroyd in "Trading Places" coming from the television downstairs, I walk through the house, tagging a few pieces of furniture to take with us in the U-haul: a bed frame, a queen mattress, a chaise lounge, a stuffed bench. There's a comfort in knowing that these familiar things will be with me in my new home, like tethers on a hot air balloon that keep it from drifting too far. Mom takes me to Job Lot for a wooden dining set so small and delicate it looks like it belongs in a doll house.

We pull up to my apartment at 9 a.m. on New Year's Day. The street is desolate, silent, and covered by a thin layer of snow. Dad and Gabe unload my things and carry them up one flight, while Mom helps me set up the living room and kitchen. Within two hours, the place transforms from a few empty rooms into a home. As my excitement grows, so does the fear of the big aloneness I will feel when they leave. For all the confines of living at home, the squall beneath every word my mother and

I exchanged, I was safe there, taken care of. Now I will have to take care of me.

Dad and Gabe wrap me in hugs, wish me luck, and head back down to the truck. Mom stays for a minute, looking around.

"You like it?" I ask.

"I do. Do you?"

"I love it."

"That's all that matters. Enjoy it in good health." She wraps me in a hug and murmurs into my hair, "I'm proud of you."

When she pulls back, I see her tears.

"I'll see you, Mom," I say, my voice wavering.

"Call me when you're settled in."

"I will."

Then she's gone, and the aloneness hits, full-force. I rush to my bedroom window and look down at the street, where Dad and Gabe are waiting in the U-Haul with the engine running, their empty Dunkin' cups angling against the windshield. Mom alights my building's front steps, her coat a bright pink spot against the snowy street. The headlights on the Jeep, parked behind the U-Haul, flicker as she clicks her keys.

I'm suddenly desperate to say something to her, something important, though I'm not sure what. I knock on the window and call to her, but she doesn't hear me. The frame, frozen shut, won't budge when I try to push it open. I yell for Mom, louder and louder, waving my arms, pounding on the glass, praying I don't wake my new neighbors. Heedless of my calls, Mom gets into the Jeep and the small caravan pulls away. As the taillights of the U-Haul disappear onto Kelton Street, I defeatedly rest my forehead against the cold window pane, and realize what it was I'd wanted to say:

Thank You.

One Spring Sunday at a hardware store on Harvard Avenue, I survey a dizzying wall of color swatches for the perfect shade to paint my room. Like reading Braille, I use my fingers to "feel out" dozens of pink panels: Pink Pearl, Pink Parfait, Tickled Pink, Pink Lady - all variations on the same cloying theme. Repelled, I wander down the wall, past the cheery yellows, the minty greens, the uncommitted "greiges." At the display of blues, I stop, drawn to a swatch just above my eye level: Kona Waves. A touch deeper than Sky, it's clear and clean and calming, like the water in the Bahamas.

I catch myself smiling.

This is my color.

But pink is your favorite, *my head argues, presenting the walls of my childhood bedroom as evidence.*

But is it?

I rewind to the day I saw my renovated room for the first time. Mom sweeps the door open and gestures me in like an usher at Radio City. I walk past her, holding a duffel from camp. I slow down the tape, expanding the seconds I look around the room, take in the peach-colored walls, and gape at the sea green ceiling.

It's a pastel nightmare.

I'm beyond disappointed; It's like she stole my room. Why didn't she ask me what I wanted?

I turn back clockwise, seeing the hint of a scowl around my mouth in the mirrored doors of my closet. Then I face Mom, her eager expression reflecting the months of work she put into this room, just to make me happy.

"It's pink! Your favorite color!"

Agreeing is easier than admitting I don't like what she's done. It takes only a millisecond to shove my disappointment down, down, down, until it disappears.

"It's awesome!" I say, so convincingly that even I believe it.

Fifteen years later, I realize that the last color I want my bedroom to be is pink.

I hate pink.

My favorite color is blue.

I almost laugh out loud: such a simple thing I never knew.

I wonder what else I don't know.

Hugging the swatch to me, I step over to the counter and wait with anticipation while they mix the paint.

"Nice color," the cashier says, handing me the can.

"I know!" I exclaim. "Isn't it gorgeous?"

I spend the next year peeling myself like an onion. I chop my hair short, no longer needing a long, black curtain to hide behind. I weed out my tailored, Mom-inspired clothing and swap it for bolder prints, brighter colors, and cuts that accent, rather than camouflage. I'm not a fat girl with only women's clothes to choose from anymore; I'm a petite twentysomething with a TJ Maxx at the end of my block. I take myself on dates around the city: movies at the Coolidge Corner Theater, sunrise walks through Brookline, services at an historic synagogue in Back Bay. In the summer, I walk with Gabe and Erin through the North End during the parade of Santa Maria di Anzano, where black-robed priests carry an effigy of Mary and her baby, draped with dollar bills, on their shoulders. Two neat rows of children follow holding lit candles, the Catholic version of "Madeline." I observe myself in each new place, no longer contained in the four safe walls of my parents' basement, and watch my reactions: Excitement? Discomfort? Curiosity? I use these clues to discern my own preferences and aversions, gradually disentangling them from my mother's or anyone else's I'm compelled to please. At work, I notice that I am frustrated 98 percent of the day, and that I long for the last bell even more than my students do. Teaching is not my passion like it is Mom's. I want to be a writer. This knowledge scares me, so I set it aside for the time being. I see it, though, and it sees me.

New people come into my life who have no idea what I used to be. They treat me like a regular person, clueless that the human doings they take for granted, like fitting on on an amusement park ride or eating vegetables, are triumphs to me. Experiences they assume we share are blank pages in my history. I play a hurried game of catch-up, gathering knowledge my peers have had for a decade. It's like that Samuel Butler quote, "Life is like playing a violin solo in public and learning the instrument as one goes on," only I am the instrument, and the concert started twenty years before I came in.

In the beginning, I mention my mother often in conversation, falling back on the old "Debbi's daughter" routine. But over time, she takes less and less real estate. I polish a solo routine, then chuck it, discovering I don't need a routine at all. To Mom herself I can speak no more than twice a week; I'm still bristly and supersensitive, and one innocuous comment can leave me fuming for days. Once, I indulged in a third conversation - my defenses were down; I'd had a miserable day at work - and I needed a full week off before I could call again. I have to carefully measure what I tell her, because she will take whatever information I give her, sprinkle it with pizzazz, and broadcast it to the world like Fox News. So I stick with the basics: work, weather, shopping, my siblings. My love life is not off-limits, exactly, but reports are given on a need-to-know basis. Once in awhile, just to get high, I'll throw her a bone:

"So I went on a date the other day..."

"Oh yeah?" she'll say with affected nonchalance, while inside, she serenades the skies like Maria Von Trapp.

I always end up regretting it a few weeks later, when, unable to contain herself, she asks after a relationship that has fizzled out like a faulty sparkler. I'm not a superstitious gal, but I suspect that once I've mentioned even the most promising romance to my mother, it is irreversibly condemned to die.

It's also possible that it's me. I've been watching myself in relationships, both romantic and platonic, and it's like watching a hurricane overturn the neighborhood. I burn through people like cigarettes, discarding them when they're no longer of use. I lead on eager, available men to feed my ego and shatter myself against dangerous ones. Only when I'm broken enough do I slink away, whimpering like a kicked puppy, until my bloodhound nose detects another, irresistible candidate.

One night, I go to a Purim party dressed as Carmen Sandiego, where the only one who gets my costume is a cantorial student from Argentina. He's tall and geeky and sings like a Latin James Taylor. I swoon, he catches me, and for a while, we dance a one-armed tango. I beg him to encircle me, but he resists. I go so far as to introduce him to Mom, a shameless ploy she sees right through.

"He likes you," she warns, "but he likes himself better."

I ignore her and try bulldozing him. The cantor finds someone else to sing to.

Mangled, I call Gemma, repeating verbatim my plea from two years before: "Tell me what to do and I'll do it. I can't stop hurting people. I can't stop hurting myself."

"Ah," she says. "Now the real work begins."

I descend into the dark mines of my past and write my way out. It's a desperate errand, executed with the focus and intensity of someone trying to save her own life. Gemma tells me to ignore what others have done to me and look only at how I've hurt them. The damage I've caused is breathtaking. I've lied to, and stolen from, almost everyone I've ever met. I've bled my parents and cut off my siblings like a gluttonous baby bird, swiping every worm the mama bird brought back to the nest. I've placed myself at the center of the universe, first demanding rescue from the illness I myself fed, then expecting everyone to drop to their knees and praise me because I'd recovered. I wanted a gold medal for becoming a functional human being. I see over and over the little, brutal ways those attitudes have affected my life and the lives of those around me, how I used people and hid from them at the same time, until I'm so sick I want to divorce myself. It reminds me of when I got 60 stitches in my shin after an open heating duct sliced it down to the bone. For a long time, the wound was red and oozy, with scabby flakes around the edges. The new flesh, as it formed, was a milky mucous, like the gunk on a newborn calf. Looking at the mess, it was hard to imagine that my leg was actually healing.

"Why are you torturing me like this?" I cry to Gemma. "I get the point already!"

She laughs and says, "Think of it like a clothesline, from the days people dried their laundry outside. You hang something in the sun enough times, the patterns start to fade. Patterns fade in the sunlight."

"I'm the worst person on the planet."

"I could think of a few worse people. Rasputin wasn't a doll."

"So, Rasputin, then me."

"What if you were just a flawed human being like everyone else?"

I consider this. "I don't actually like you."

"Good. If I wasn't on your resentment list, I wouldn't be doing my job. Keep writing."

The truth begins to dilute my rage. My perspective widens, and I can see events as they played out for the others involved. Often, they hurt me because I'd hurt them first. As for the ones who had acted unprovoked, I could no longer say that what they'd done was unforgivable, because if they couldn't be forgiven, then I, who had done the very same things, couldn't be, either.

The misfortunes of my life flip to reveal their gleaming undersides. Until it turned on me, addiction kept me alive. Food numbed out pain too great for a child to survive, buying me time until adulthood to face it. Obesity protected me from doing even more damage, because I couldn't be trusted with a "civilian" body until now. A lifetime of pain taught me compassion, while my disease enabled me to recover more whole than I was before I got sick. I begin to see myself like the Japanese potters who fill the cracks in their vessels with gold. Instead of hiding the flaws, the gold calls attention to them, the beauty of the piece enhanced by its brokenness. Being broken means I'm broken open, *transformed from a self-contained vessel to a channel, able to give and receive. Like Leonard Cohen says, "There's a crack in everything. That's how the light gets in."*

A friend once told me that a miracle is a shift in perception. If this is true, then a miracle is happening to me.

A similar shift is happening to Mom, who is up at the Cape House for the summer, scribbling away with the same drive I am. She has crawled back to recovery, though it will never be as it was for her in the beginning. She will wrestle with food for the rest of her life, but she will also search deeply for herself and her God. Back in New York, she's started going to synagogue and Shabbat meals with my father, finding friends among the wives of the Upper West Side. She rides on the back of his motorcycle to Brooklyn, he with his yarmulke and tzitzit, she in her jeans and leather jacket, and buys him a black Borsalino hat for his birthday. She even studies Torah with a partner over the phone. While not observant like Dad, Mom is connected to her Judaism and to a God who loves her, no matter how many questions she asks.

"I was up until four in the morning last night," she tells me. "I was writing about my mother, just sobbing and sobbing."

"How come?"

"It was just so sad. She should never have had children, but that's what you did then. She had nothing to give me. Nothing. I was so angry at her for that."

"And now?"

"It's still sad. I'm sad for me as a little girl. But my mother was just doing the best she could with what she had."

So did you, *I think.*

A few weeks later, Mom reports that she's made amends to my father, listing the many mistakes she's made as his wife. Dad's forgiveness was instant, she says. "He told me, 'I just wanted you to be happy, and to have what you wanted.'"

So did you, *I think.*

Months later, I sit in Gemma's living room and read her everything I've written. When I get to what I've written about Mom, I cry. "All I did was hurt her, and all she did was try to help me."

"Yes."

"Neither of us knew that she couldn't."

"Well, you both didn't understand that part of love yet. It isn't saving the other person, or being saved. It's letting the ones we love save themselves."

"Right..." I say with a sigh.

"Listen," says Gemma, "she got plenty out of it, too. Your mother needed to feel needed, and you did that for her. But don't think for a second that she didn't save your life. Because she did, more times than you probably realize."

"Can you ever really make that up to someone?"

"Never. But you still have to try. Tell her the truth, about everything. Clean up the past. Then spend the rest of your life being the daughter she deserves."

"What if she still bugs me? She has a way of pushing my buttons..."

"What do you expect? She installed them. It's part of the territory with mothers and daughters. They are the models against which we measure ourselves, for better or worse. It's why we seek their approval and resent ourselves for it at the same time."

I glance at her sideways. "You sound like you have some experience with this."

"Just a little," Gemma says with a wink. "Just pray for her, and be kind."

I drive to the Cape House on a weeknight in August, when Mom is there alone. I find her reading in the living room, one leg draped across the arm of a white leather chair.

Mom looks up when I come in, but doesn't seem surprised to see me. She holds up her book and begins as if we're in mid-conversation. "I got halfway through this thing and realized I already read it."

"Was it as good the second time?"

She shrugs and tosses the book on an end table. "Same old shit. What's going on, Reez?"

"I want to talk to you."

Mom sits up. "Okay. Let's talk."

So I start talking. I don't stop for a long time. She listens, her face unreadable.

"There's something else I have to tell you."

Her eyes flash with expectation.

"Do you remember what I told you years ago? About that thing that happened to me?"

She hitches her elbow onto the armrest and rests a finger across her top lip. "I do."

"It wasn't true. It was a lie."

She doesn't say anything.

"I'm sorry, Mom. I'm so, so sorry."

She smiles slightly. "You think I didn't know?"

The wind rushes out of me.

"You knew? How could you know?"

"I'm your mother," she says. "I know everything."

"And you never said anything? How did you not hate me? Didn't you want to punish me forever?"

"I think you've punished yourself enough."

I sink against the back of the couch, mind blown.

My dark secret was never a secret at all.

"Come here," she says.

"What?"

"Come," she says, tapping her lap.

I laugh. "Come on, Ma."

"You're never too old," she insists, beckoning to me.

I rise from the couch and curl in her lap like a child. Her strong arms enwrap me, and I give into the warmth of her body, her familiar smell, and the sound of her breath, submerging into them like a tub of warm water.

I am held, enveloped, and washed anew.

And it is a blessed, blessed relief.

Chapter Nineteen

The phone rings and Erin grabs it. "Oh, hey!" she says.

It's probably Mom, I think, scanning the room. *She's the only one not here.*

Then I remember.

It's another condolence call, one of dozens we've received since Shiva began. Erin brings the phone to Dad, who sits in the living room with my siblings and me on beach chairs, low to the ground, according to the laws of mourning.

"Jacques!" Dad booms into the phone. "It's so good to hear your voice!"

Sitting shiva is strange. Waves of people flow in and out, ostensibly to comfort us, but the atmosphere here is like a happy reunion. We clap with joy at the sight of old friends, standing up to hug them and begging them to eat. The spread of food on the island is enormous: a gorgeous fish platter sent in by Dad's company, a Zabar's box from a cousin in New York containing thirty babkas, at least 100 bagels with spreads, and, you guessed it, more Edible Arrangements. Sometimes, the reality of what we're doing here will sideswipe me like a rude non-sequitur and the tears will start. But mostly, between the good conversation, the funny stories, and not having to cook for anyone, our week of mourning has been a gentle cushion between what we've just been through and its aftermath.

A number of Dad's friends from New York make the four-hour drive to see him, arriving at the beach house in their black hats and suits. Dad is thrilled and talks with them for hours, dropping Jewish slang that leave Gabe, Dena, and Noah mystified. I understand most of it but stay quiet, as I am not invited into the conversation - except at the end, when the visitors stand and recite the traditional words when departing a shiva house: *May the Omnipresent comfort you among the mourners of Zion and Jerusalem.*

Dad doesn't speak to us much, preoccupied as he is with the correct observance of mourning and ensuring there will be a minyan for all three daily prayer services. As Shiva goes on, my siblings spend less and less time in the living room.

At night, after the evening prayers, everyone leaves and the house gets quiet. I stand in front of Mom's picture with Ezra and stare at it for long minutes, our faces reflected in the glass. Ezra says his usual goodnight to her. After he's asleep, I call the house line just to hear Mom on the voicemail message. It hurts more after, but I call again, unable to stop myself.

I lay in bed with Ben and cry.

"I'm angry at God," I declare.

"That's okay. He can take it."

"This isn't fair! She wasn't done yet!"

"Maybe she was," Ben says thoughtfully. "I've been thinking about her, and you. You gave her the ultimate gift, you know. She got to see you take care of her, take care of the baby, take care of the family, take care of *yourself.* And she gave you a gift, because you got to see it, too."

"I didn't know if I could do it."

"She knew. And she knew it was one of the most important things you'll ever do. More than any worldly thing you'll ever accomplish. You could win every award on the planet and none of it will matter more than this. She wanted you to know that family is everything. Family is life."

"She had to die for me to figure that out?"

"No, you knew it already. Or else you would never have done what you did for her."

I wake early in the morning, as usual, and sit in the quiet kitchen with a cup of tea. I don't expect to see anyone for a couple of hours, so I'm surprised when Gabe appears.

"I didn't sleep very much," he says. "Thinking."

"About?"

"The house feels weird without her. It's like she's here, but she isn't."

"Come sit."

He makes himself a coffee, then slides into the seat next to me.

"What do you do after something like this?" he says. "After you're hit with this incredible amount of pain? It's a crossroads: you either deal with it and move forward, or just…"

"Check out," I say, voicing my own temptation at the cemetery.

"Right. I'm gonna be okay. I thought I would fall apart, but I feel free. Like I could do anything."

"I feel like that," I confide, "but different. I'm a Mom, so I can't do everything I want. At least, not right now. But there are things I can still do, that I need to do, that I've put off too long."

"What about Dad?"

"What about him?"

"I'm afraid he's going to go down a path that will take him farther and farther away from us. It won't even occur to him that we need him closer. I think there's just going to be a big void left in our family."

"Mom connected us to him," I say. "Now we have to do it ourselves. We can tell him we need him, show him how to be with us. Mom taught us how; now we can teach him."

"Don't you think she already tried?" Gabe takes a long, thoughtful sip of his coffee, then says, "Is it true, what Reb Zalman said about

Mom? Was the Jewish thing, the spirituality, really that important to her?"

"Yes," I say, right on the heels of the question. "By the end, especially, it was more important to her than anything."

He accepts my reply in silence.

"When do you go to Boston?"

"Day after shiva ends."

"You looking forward to it?"

"It'll be good to get back to my life."

I feel a pang, anticipating the emptiness of this house after everyone leaves, how much wider the distance will be after all this time spent together.

"It's been good," I say, "to be with you."

His smile is warm and sad. "Yeah."

Shiva ends, and we walk to the beach to mark our departure from the state of mourning and the resumption of public life. Some people from the minyan come along with us for a view of the ocean. Dad walks with them, leaving Gabe, Dena and I, carrying Ezra, to follow. Noah stays behind, opting out of the ceremony.

"I was hoping this would be a family thing," says Dena.

"I can tell Dad," I offer.

"Nah, forget it."

The day is windy, and we don't stay out long. Dena and I head back up while Dad stands on the sand with his friends. Toward the top, I miss a step and fall forward in slow motion, my arms and torso curving instinctively around the baby. My shin smacks against the wood, and a purple bump quickly begins to form. By some miracle, Ezra comes away without a scratch.

Mourning laws have prohibited me from bathing during Shiva week, and I am so dirty it's making me itch. As soon as we get back from the beach, I run to the shower, anxious to wash away a week's worth of oil, grease, dirt, and body odor. I shampoo my hair twice, shave, and treat myself to thick coconut skin cream. The entire time, I feel vaguely guilty, like I'm washing her away.

For some reason there's only one tube of toothpaste in the house, and it's in my parents' bathroom. Mom was good at pre-stocking necessities, buying in bulk from the big box stores. Someone else will have to do it now. I enter their room with some trepidation, thrown by how large it looks now without the hospital bed, the humming oxygenator, and my mother's presence. Flotsam covers the rice bed: Mom's Amex card, her leave of absence papers, some plastic tubing, the death certificate. Her makeup bag, a bottle of foundation, and nail polish remover all sit on the bathroom counter, waiting for her to come back and use them. I put some toothpaste on my brush, clean my teeth, then wander out slowly, stopping at her nightstand. I touch her red-framed glasses, which sit open, angled toward the bed like she's just taken them off. Her Burt's Bees lip balm, some loose change, and the calendar in which she wrote her entire life are still in the top drawer. I flip the calendar open, looking back on appointments that took place just two months ago, written in her confident, color-coded hand. Back further, there's Ezra's due date and Noah's wedding. And now forward again, to just a month ago, when her handwriting began to falter. After that, the appointments come fewer and farther between, until today, which stands empty, as does every day on the rest of the calendar - except one day next week, when she's supposed to see her therapist in New York. I think it's safe to cancel the appointment.

In the next drawer down are a couple of twelve-step books and yellow lined paper filled with Mom's notes from her Torah classes. Across the top, it reads, *May the Lord answer you on the day of distress; may the Name of the God of Jacob fortify you.* It's from Psalm 20, which we were encouraged to recite seven times each day as an appeal for my mother's recovery. Below the passage is a list of biblical women, Sarah, Rebecca, Rachel, and Hannah, with an arrow pointing from it. *No children*, Mom writes. *God wanted their prayers.* The word "prayers" is underlined three times.

Beneath the list are examples of other biblical figures who struggled for their heart's desires or who suffered great loss: Aaron, whose sons were killed, and Moses, who after forty years of leading his stiff-necked flock through the desert, never got to enter the land of Israel. Beside their names, it says, *Prayers not always answered* - another arrow - *NOT THE POINT! Trust in God is comfort and strength. He gives us EXACTLY what we need.*

Then, on the line below: *Be GRATEFUL!*

I run my fingers over the words, so absorbed that the pad slips out of my hands, flutters to the floor, and slides beneath the nightstand. I drop to my knees and peer into its underside, where the pad rests in silhouette. From the corner behind it, a glimmering strip of cellophane catches my eye, its lettering obscured by sunlight. Curious, I reach past the notepad for the cellophane, which, out of the glare, I see is the tail end of a Twizzler wrapper. Sitting back on my knees, I stare at it as two separate memories collide:

I would give my abstinence to you if I could. Anything to fix it.

Don't think for a second she didn't save your life. Because she did, more times than you probably realize.

And for a moment, I calculate the deal my mother made with the devil, offering up her recovery, maybe even her life, in order to save mine.

Then I brush the thought away, embarrassed by its self-centeredness. It's too neat, too formulaic, not to mention impossible.

But as I tuck the notepad back in the drawer and leave the room, I wonder.

I wonder.

The house begins to empty. Noah and Sammy go home to Waltham. Gabe and Erin leave for Boston. Dena and Ben go to the gym. And Dad, after a trip to Home Depot, loads up the Jeep for the drive back to New York.

"Bye, Ezra B," he says in his Yiddish intonation, rubbing his thumb along the baby's cheek. "I'll see you soon, Beez."

He pulls me in for a long hug, from which I am loath to let go. Borne out of the crisis of Mom's illness, my father and I forged a partnership which has evolved into friendship. I don't want that to end, now that the crisis is over.

"You're the only parent now, Dad. We're going to need you."

"I have a lot to learn," he says. "You're going to have to help me."

"We can do that."

"I'm probably going to make mistakes. People may get hurt."

"Everyone makes mistakes, Dad. It's what people do."

"Well, just be patient with me. I'll be there as best I can."

Neither of us really knows what that means, or how that will look in the future. But I believe that where there's willingness, there's always reason to hope.

Ezra and I stand in the driveway, waving, as Dad's car disappears up the road.

We are alone in the house for the first time in weeks, the hours before us dauntingly open. After six weeks of frantic activity, we have nothing to do. I wrap some toys in a beach blanket and the two of us sit on the front lawn, the sun warm on our skin. Ezra's hair shines gold as he looks this way and that, taking in at the trees, the grass, the sound of the breeze. When I say his name, he smiles at me, and I can't resist scooping him up. Swaying to our own silent rhythm, I sing:

"Hit the Road Jack, and don't you come back no more, no more, no more, no more..."

Made in the USA
Middletown, DE
17 February 2017